Kickoff
Praxisnahes Englisch für Schule und Beruf

von
David Christie

Ernst Klett Verlag
Stuttgart · Leipzig

Kickoff – Praxisnahes Englisch für Schule und Beruf

Autor: David Christie, Oxford

Berater: Ilse Halbeck, Hannover; Katrin von Gartzen, Hannover; Melanie Rechmann, Hannover; Martina Ullrich, Düsseldorf; Bernd Deininghaus, Dortmund; Petra Schuster, Bad Dürkheim; Kerstin Streiff, Gießen

Werkübersicht:

Kickoff Schülerbuch	978-3-12-808236-3
Kickoff Lehrerhandbuch mit Audio-CDs (2) und Lehrer-Service-CD	978-3-12-808237-0
Kickoff Workbook – Wirtschaft	978-3-12-808238-7
Kickoff Workbook – Technik	978-3-12-808239-4
Kickoff Workbook – Sozialpädagogik, Hauswirtschaft, Gesundheit	978-3-12-808240-0
Kickoff Lehrer-Workbook für alle Ausrichtungen	978-3-12-808241-7
Kickoff - Vokabeltraining	http://www.klett-kickoff.de
Kickoff - MP3-Audios zum Runterladen	http://www.klett.de/online

1. Auflage 1 5 4 3 2 1 | 2012 2011 2010 2009 2008

Alle Drucke dieser Auflage sind unverändert und können im Unterricht nebeneinander verwendet werden. Die letzte Zahl bezeichnet das Jahr des Druckes.

Das Werk und seine Teile sind urheberrechtlich geschützt. Jede Nutzung in anderen als den gesetzlich zugelassenen Fällen bedarf der vorherigen schriftlichen Einwilligung des Verlages. Hinweis zu §52a UrhG: Weder das Werk noch seine Teile dürfen ohne eine solche Einwilligung eingescannt und in ein Netzwerk eingestellt werden. Dies gilt auch für Intranets von Schulen und sonstigen Bildungseinrichtungen. Fotomechanische oder andere Wiedergabeverfahren nur mit Genehmigung des Verlages.

© Ernst Klett Verlag GmbH, Stuttgart 2008.
Alle Rechte vorbehalten.

Internetadresse: www.klett.de

Abbildungsnachweis Titelseite: Getty Images, Digital Vision; Image Source

Projektleitung: Matthias Rupp
Redaktion: Chris Caridia, Publishing Services, Berlin
Gestaltung: B2 Büro für Gestaltung, Andreas Staiger, Stuttgart
Illustrationen: Tanja Kischel, München; Jeonsook Lee, Köln; Andreas Staiger, Stuttgart
Druck: Offizin Andersen Nexö, Leipzig
Printed in Germany.

ISBN 978-3-12-808236-3

Vorwort

Kickoff motiviert Schülerinnen und Schüler mit praxisnahem Englisch und verdeutlicht ihnen: Warum muss ich Englisch können? Dadurch übernehmen sie Verantwortung für den eigenen Lernprozess, werden sie bestens auf Klassenarbeiten und Prüfungen auf dem Weg zum Mittleren Bildungsabschluss vorbereitet und erhalten die nützlichen Sprachkompetenzen für die anstehenden beruflichen Herausforderungen.

Kickoff zeichnet sich durch eine leicht zu bewältigende Progression, Klarheit und Benutzerfreundlichkeit sowie der Zielgruppe angepasste praxisnahe Themen und Texte aus. Neben dem Schülerbuch, das auf die beruflichen Handlungssituationen vorbereitet, ist das Workbook die berufsspezifische Ergänzung: Es bietet parallel zum Schülerbuch weitere vertiefende Übungen sowie zusätzlich branchentypische berufliche Seiten, die gezielt Wortschatz, Sprachmaterial und Fertigkeiten der einzelnen Berufsfelder (Wirtschaft, Technik, Hauswirtschaft, Soziales und Gesundheit) trainieren. Das Lehrwerk kombiniert somit in einzigartiger Weise berufsfeldübergreifendes und -spezifisches Englischlernen.

Kickoff holt die Schüler mit einer grundlegenden Vertiefung der zentralen Kompetenzen ab und führt sie dann zielsicher zum Mittleren Bildungsabschluss:
- **Foundation** besteht aus einem 12-seitigen Vorkurs *Entry* sowie den *Units* 1–8,
- **Upgrade** aus den *Units* 9–14.

Jede *Unit* besteht aus vier oder fünf Doppelseiten:
- **Check-in** (Doppelseite) stimmt auf die Themen und die Grammatik der *Unit* sowie auf die *Activities* im letzten Teil der *Unit* (= **Check-out**) ein. Der Kasten **Am Ende dieser Unit kann ich …** macht die Lernziele der *Unit* bereits zu Beginn für die Schülerinnen und Schüler transparent.
- **Training** stellt die Grammatik, den Wortschatz und die Redemittel bereit, die die Schülerinnen und Schüler brauchen, um die Aufgaben im weiteren Verlauf der *Unit* erfolgreich zu meistern. Auf den beiden Doppelseiten finden sich Lesetexte unterschiedlicher Länge, Aufgaben zum Hörverstehen sowie ein abwechslungsreiches Angebot an Übungen, das die Lernenden systematisch auf Klassenarbeiten und Prüfungen vorbereitet. Blaue, kurze Grammatikkästen erläutern die neue Grammatik und fordern die Schülerinnen und Schüler immer wieder auf, eigenständig Bildung und Gebrauch abzuleiten (Entdeckendes Lernen).
- **Language** (eine Seite) fasst zunächst die Grammatikregeln der *Unit* auf Deutsch zusammen, festigt sie dann in Übungen und schließt mit einer *Words*-Aufgabe zur Wortschatzfestigung.
- **Check-out** ist in den *Units* 1–8 einseitig und fordert die Schüler zu text- und sprachproduktiven *Activities* auf. Die Seite endet jeweils mit einer *Revision*-Aufgabe, die eine Grammatikregel der vorhergehenden *Units* wiederholt, und eignet sich für die Erarbeitung im Unterricht und/oder zu Hause. In den *Units* 9–14 endet die *Activities*-Seite mit einem *Project*; es schließt sich die Doppelseite *Go For It! The magazine for college students in Germany*, an.

Das Lehrwerk ist gekennzeichnet durch viele Lernhilfen:

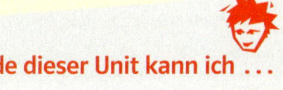

= Zusammenfassung der Lernziele

Tips and tricks

= Sprachtipps und Hinweise auf typische Fehler deutschsprachiger Lerner

So läuft's besser

= Fertigkeitstraining (skills)

Hier und dort

= Tipps zur interkulturellen Kompetenz

= Entdeckendes Lernen

808236-0001

= MP3-Audios zum Runterladen, einfach die jeweilige Nummer unter www.klett.de/online eingeben.

= Begleit-CD mit Tracknummer

*
= Anspruchsvollere Übung

R / P / I / M
= Kompetenztraining mit Übungen zur Sprach[R]ezeption / Sprach[P]roduktion / [I]nteraktion / [M]ediation (Sprachmittlung)

Foundation (year 1)

Unit	Topic	Language	Check-out activities	Page
Entry	English, English, everywhere	to be; pronouns; possessive adjectives; genitive 's; there is/are; to have; the time; simple present statements	test	6
1	At college	simple present: statements, questions, negatives	• writing an email • making a school brochure	18
2	People and jobs	present continuous / simple present	• filling in a questionnaire • making a jobs file	26
3	Free time	likes and dislikes; comparison of adjectives	• writing a blog • doing a class survey about free time activities	34
4	Products then and now	simple past	• giving important information in German (mediation) • giving information in English (information gap)	42
5	Do's and don'ts	must, have to	• explaining college rules to visitors • describing life in Germany (chat room)	50
6	Success stories	present perfect with *for*, *since*	• writing about yourself • writing a biography of a successful person	58
7	Looking ahead	future: will, going to	• writing an email about future plans • doing a class survey about lives in 10 years	66
8	A month in New Zealand	polite language (would/could)	• comparing countries • introductions and polite conversations	74
	Test			82

Upgrade (year 2)

Unit	Topic	Language	Check-out activities	*Go for it!* magazine	Page
9	Travel	relative sentences; more about the present continuous / simple present	• writing a holiday postcard • doing role-plays with travel situations • doing Internet research	Where do people speak English?	86
10	A visit to a company	adjective/adverbs; more about the present continuous	• writing an email about a visit to England • writing a report about a company visit • making a poster about a company	How hard should you work?	96
11	Future technology	*If*-sentences type 1	• writing a diary • writing ideas about the future • making a radio programme	Movies about the future	106
12	Job hunting	*If*-sentences type 2	• writing about a cartoon • answering interview questions • writing a CV	Job interview tips	116
13	Global business	passive	• doing a class survey on where things come from • giving the main ideas of an article in German • making a poster about global business	Other countries, other customs	126
14	Job satisfaction	past perfect; *If*-sentences type 3	• writing a short personal biography • role-play: finding out about another person • doing a radio interview about jobs	Get the best grades in your exam	136

Anhang

Grammar summary	146	Alphabetisches Vocabulary	183	▶ Die Hörtexte befinden sich sowohl im Lehrerhandbuch als auch Online als Download.
Partner files	155	Country factfiles	190	
Grundwortschatz und Zahlen	159	Abbildungsnachweis	192	
Unitbegleitendes Vocabulary	162			

Entry
English, English, everywhere

Am Ende von Entry habe ich ...
→ die Basis-Grammatik und den Grundwortschatz des Englischen wiederholt,
→ Englisch als Weltsprache kennengelernt.

1 Hi. Can you speak English?

R A Read about Silke and Robbie. Where are they?

This weekend, there's a music festival near Cologne. There are bands from Europe and the USA. Lots of young people are at the festival. Silke and Robbie are there too.

R/P B Listen. Then read their dialogue with a partner.

Robbie Hi. Can you speak English?
Silke   A bit!
Robbie My name's Robbie.
Silke   Hi. I'm Silke.
Robbie Where are you from?
Silke   I'm from Dusseldorf in Germany. What about you?
Robbie I'm from London in England.

▶ Cologne   ▶ lots of   ▶ what about you?

Check-in | Revision | Check-out

I'm Brooke. I'm from Chicago, Illinois, in the USA.

P **C** **You're at the festival too. You meet Brooke. Make a dialogue with your partner. Take it in turns to be Brooke.**

Brooke Hi. Can you speak English?
You …

P **D** **Say 'hi' to your class.**

Hi. I'm …
Hello. My name's …

P **E** **Finish the sentences.**

1 Silke and Robbie … at a music festival.
2 Where … the festival? – It … near Cologne.
3 Robbie … English. He … from London.
4 Where … you from? – I … from Germany.

▸ to meet ▸ to take it in turns ▸ dialogue

Das Verb *to be*	
I am (I'm)	I'm not
he is (he's) she is (she's) it is (it's)	he isn't she isn't it isn't
we are (we're) you (you're) they are (they're)	we aren't you aren't they aren't

Fragen:
Where **is** she from?
Where **are** you/they from?

Entry 7

> Check-in   > **Revision**   > Check-out

2 What are their names?

R/P **A** Lots of people in the world speak English. Where are these native speakers from? How old are they? What are their jobs?

Marianne is from … She's … (years old). She's a …
Phil, Adam and Lilly are … They're … They're …

Hi. My name's Marianne. I'm 18 and I'm from Canada. I'm a secretary.

Hello. Our names are Phil, Adam and Lilly. We're from Britain and we're all 17. We're students.

My name's Gordon. Hi. I'm 21 and I'm a computer technician. I'm from New Zealand.

Hi. I'm Brandon and I'm from the USA. I'm 22 and I'm a construction worker.

G'day. We're Akio and Georgina. We're nurses and we're from Australia. We're 19.

P/I **B** What are their names? Ask another student.

He's 21 and he's a computer technician.
– His name's Gordon.
She's from Canada.
– Her name's …

▶ secretary ▶ nurse ▶ technician

8 Entry

> Check-in   **Revision**   Check-out

P **C Read about Hannah and finish the sentences with the words in the box.**

Hannah is Gordon's girlfriend. Gordon is the guy from New Zealand on the last page. This is Hannah's family.

dad's • Hannah's • sister's • brother's • mum's

dad: Patrick

brother: Jack, 14

Hannah, 19

mum: Emma

sister: Sophie, 19

1 Hannah's … name is Jack. Jack is 14.
2 Her … name is Sophie. Hannah and Sophie are twins.
3 Her … name is Patrick. He's a painter and decorator.
4 Her … name is Emma. … mum is a doctor's receptionist.

I **D Ask a partner.**

> What's your mum's/dad's name?

> Do you have a brother or a sister? What are their names?

R/P **E What's right: a or b?**

1 This is Marianne. a) He's b) She's from Canada.
2 He's from the USA. a) His b) Her name's Brandon.
3 These two people are from Australia. a) Her b) Their names are Akio and Georgina.
4 a) Hannahs b) Hannah's dad is called Patrick.
5 a) Her b) His mum is called Emma.
6 Hannah and Sophie are a) Jacks b) Jack's sisters.

▸ sentence   ▸ (in the) box   ▸ receptionist

Genitiv 's

Gordon 's girlfriend
(Gordons Freundin)
My girlfriend 's dad
(Der Vater meiner Freundin)

Entry **9**

> Check-in   > **Revision**   > Check-out

3 A holiday in Montana

R **A** Read about Jan.

1 Where's he from?
2 Where does he want to go this summer?

Jan Wisniewski is from Frankfurt in Germany. Jan likes all sports – walking, cycling, canoeing, football, … This summer, he wants to go on holiday to Montana.

P/R/I **B** Jan wants to go to a hostel in Montana. You can see the hostel brochure on the next page. Jan is on the phone to Matt, the hostel warden.

1 Complete the sentences below with *there's* or *there are*.
2 Listen and check your answers.
3 Read the dialogue with a partner.

Matt High Mountain Hostel. Matt speaking.
Jan   Hi. My name's Jan. I'm from Germany. I have some questions about the hostel. Is that OK?
Matt Sure, Jan. What do you want to know?
Jan   How many rooms are there?
Matt OK. **(1)** *There's* one room for eight people. **(2)** … two rooms for four people, six rooms for two people and **(3)** … also four rooms for one person.
Jan   What about facilities?
Matt Well, **(4)** … a dining room, **(5)** … four washing machines, and **(6)** … two computers. **(7)** … a TV room – oh, yes, and **(8)** … a small shop.
Jan   Thanks very much, Matt. That's great.
Matt You're welcome. Bye.

▶ next   ▶ (youth) hostel   ▶ to go on holiday (to)

10   Entry

> Check-in   > **Revision**   > Check-out

Welcome to the High Mountain Hostel

Rooms
* 1 room for 8 people
* 2 rooms for 4 people
* 6 rooms for 2 people
* 4 rooms for 1 person

Facilities
* Dining room (breakfast 7.30, lunch 1.00, evening meal 7.00)
* 4 washing machines
* 2 computers with Internet access
* TV room
* Shop (open 8.00 – 4.00 for snacks, drinks, maps etc.)

Contact us
* Phone 271-389 24465
* Website www.highmountainhostel.com

1 **C** It's summer and Jan is at the hostel. He has some questions for Matt about the town. Take it in turns to be Matt and Jan.

Is there a swimming pool in the town?

Yes. There's a swimming pool here.

Is there a movie theater?

Yes. There are two. Here and here.

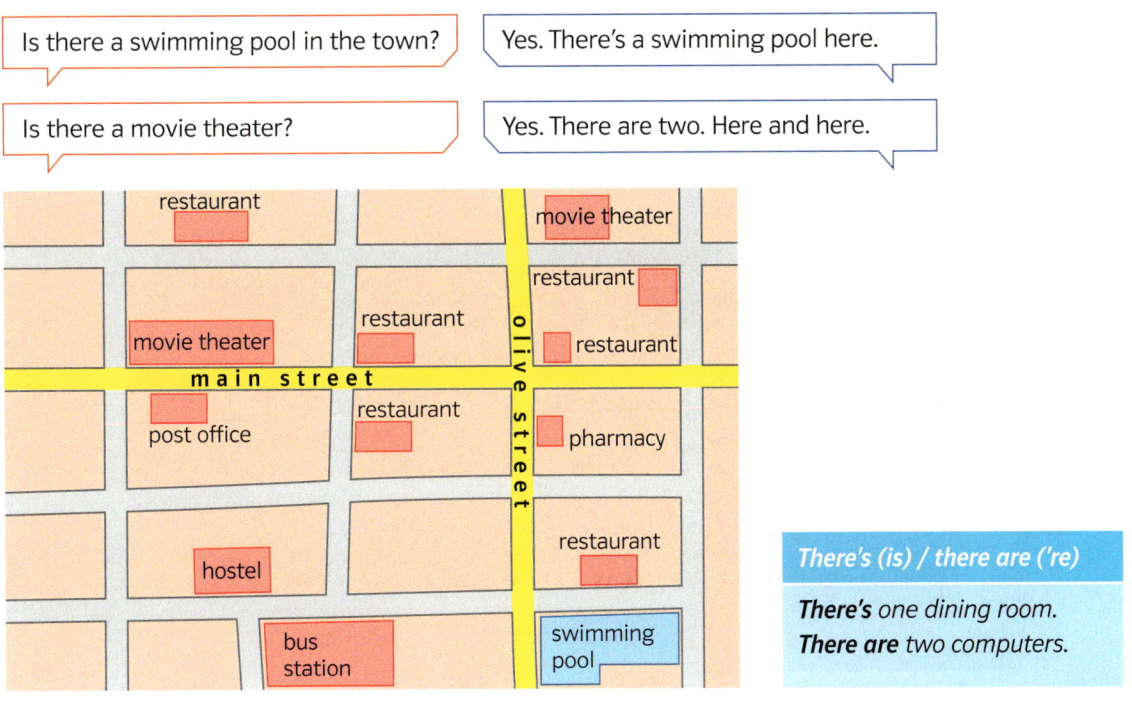

▶ map   ▶ movie theater (US)   ▶ main street

There's (is) / there are ('re)

There's one dining room.
There are two computers.

Entry 11

> Check-in   > **Revision**   > Check-out

4 Rich and famous

R **A** Lots of rich and famous people are from English-speaking countries. They're film stars, sports stars, singers and musicians, and their names and faces are on posters, on TV and in films. But what do you know about them? Try the quiz!

JOHN TRAVOLTA
True or false? Note down 'T' or 'F'.

1. John Travolta is from the USA.
2. He's a pilot and he has three private planes. One is a Boeing 707.
3. His house in Florida is at an airport and his planes are in his garden.
4. He has two children, a daughter and a son. His daughter's name is Ella and his son's name is Jett!

VICTORIA AND DAVID BECKHAM ('POSH AND BECKS')
Which is right? Note down a, b or c.

5. Posh and Becks are from
   a the USA.   b Australia.   c England.
6. They have … children.
   a one   b two   c three
7. They have a $22 million house in
   a Hollywood.   b New York.   c London.
8. David Beckham has 10
   a brothers.   b tattoos.   c Rolls Royces.

MADONNA
True or false? Note down 'T' or 'F' again.

9. Madonna's real name is Maria Ciccone.
10. She's from Italy.
11. She has 3 sisters and 4 brothers.
12. She has a British husband called Guy Ritchie.
13. They have a house in England.
14. They don't have a house in America.

▶ on TV   ▶ true/false   ▶ child/children   ▶ airport

12 Entry

> Check-in | **Revision** | > Check-out

R/P/I **B** Ask a student in your class to read out the answers on page 155. How many right answers do you have? Tell the class.

I have … right answers.

P/I **C** What do you have? Work with a partner.

1 First copy and fill in the questionnaire for YOU.
2 Ask your partner the questions and fill in your partner's answers.

> Do you have brothers and sisters?

> Yes, I have …

> Do you have a …?

> No, I don't have …

3 Tell the class about your partner.
  Linda/Benjamin has …
  (S)he doesn't have …

	Which things do you have?	YOU	YOUR PARTNER
1	brothers and/or sisters		
2	a bike / a car / a motor bike / a scooter / a skateboard / inline skates		
3	a mobile phone / a computer / an MP3 player		
4	a tattoo		
5	a Madonna album		
6	a poster of a famous person		
7	a musical instrument (a guitar etc.)		

P **D** Finish the sentences with the correct forms of *to have*.

1 I … a mobile phone but I … (not) a private plane!
2 … your friend … an MP3 player?
3 He … an MP3 player, but he … (not) have a computer.
4 Lots of American film stars … big houses in LA.
5 … you … a Madonna album?
  – No! I think Madonna is terrible!

Das Verb *to have*

I have	I don't have
he has she has it has	he doesn't have she doesn't have it doesn't have
we have you have they have	we don't have you don't have they don't have

Fragen:
Do I/we/you/they **have**?
Does he/she/it **have**?

▶ to fill in (a questionnaire) ▶ private ▶ mobile phone

Entry **13**

5 A blog

A Match the clocks and the times.

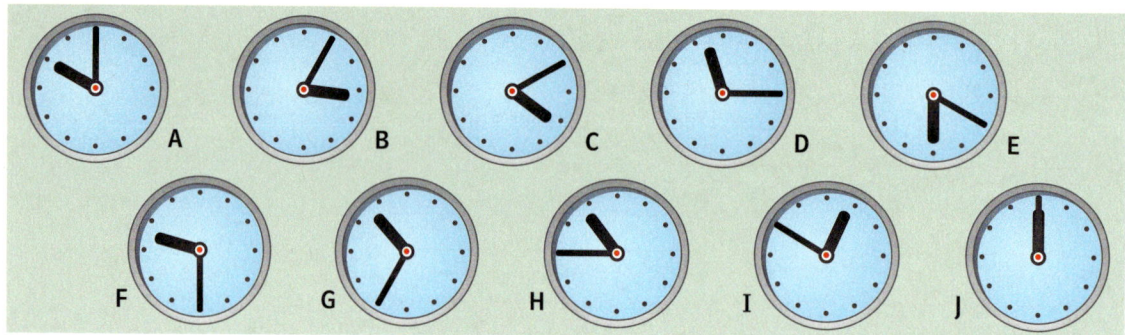

1. ten past four
2. ten to one
3. five past three
4. ten o'clock
5. twenty past six
6. twenty-five to eleven
7. half past nine
8. (a) quarter to eleven
9. (a) quarter past eleven
10. 12 o'clock/midday/midnight

B Work with a partner. Point to a clock and ask the time.

What time is it?
– It's …

C Listen to Julie's blog. Note down the missing times.

WELCOME TO MY BLOG

About me
I'm Julie Chang. I'm from New York in the USA. I'm 20 years old and I work for a fashion company.

My day
I work from Monday to Friday. I get up at **(1)** … Then I jog in the park. At **(2)** … I travel to work on the subway. I start work at **(3)** … I eat my lunch at **(4)** … I go home at **(5)** … I say 'hello' to my friends in my apartment, then I cook my supper.

▶ to match ▶ to point to ▶ missing

> Check-in   > **Revision**   > Check-out

P **D Finish the sentences about Julie.**

1 Julie *is* from New York in the USA.
2 She ... 20 years old.
3 She ... for a fashion company.
4 From Monday to Friday, she ... up at 6 o'clock, then she ... in the park.
5 She ... to work on the subway. She ... work at 8.30.
6 She ... home at 5 o'clock, she ... 'hello' to her friends, then she ... her supper.

Tips and tricks

Times and days:
- **on** Monday, Tuesday, Wednesday, …
- **in** the morning, the afternoon, the evening
- **at** 6 o'clock/the weekend

R/P **E Read Florian's blog. Make sentences about Florian.**

He's from …   He's a …   At the weekend he …

Willkommen! Welcome!

About me
My name's Florian Becker. I'm from Duisburg in Germany. I'm 17 and I'm a student at a vocational college.

My weekend
I'm a student from Monday to Friday but at the weekend I'm me! On Saturday, I get up at midday. In the afternoon, I read magazines, I listen to music, or I surf the Internet. In the evening I meet my friends and we go to town. On Sunday morning I always go to the swimming pool, then I work out at a fitness club. In the afternoon I meet my friends again. In the evening, we often go to the cinema.

P **F Now write a blog about YOU.**

– What's your name?
– How old are you?
– Where are you from?
– Are you a student at a vocational college too?
– Write about your weekend.

Das *simple present*			
Denk daran: *he/she/it* – das **s** muss mit!			
he	work	get	go
he/she/it	work**s**	get**s**	go**es**
we	work	get	go
you	work	get	go
they	work	get	go

▸ subway (US)   ▸ vocational college   ▸ fashion   ▸ company

Entry **15**

> Check-in   > **Revision**   > Check-out

6 What can you understand?

R/P **A** Look at the pictures. Find …

> a waiter • a bus driver • a girl in a shoe shop •
> a hotel receptionist • a shop assistant •
> a mechanic • a man in a restaurant •
> a backpacker • a woman with a car

A

B

C

D

E

R **B** Listen to these five short conversations. Match the pictures and the conversations.

Conversation 1: *That's picture …*

R/P **C** Listen again. What can you understand? Make sentences.

1	The man in the restaurant wants	a	to go to the youth hostel.
2	The backpacker on the bus wants	b	to know her shoe size in Germany.
3	The woman with the mechanic has	c	to know about 'Gemüse'.
4	The man on the phone to the hotel wants	d	a problem with her car.
5	The girl in the shoe shop wants	e	to book a room.

Hier und dort

Can you speak English?
Englisch hat sich zu einer echten Weltsprache entwickelt. Man begegnet ihr überall: in Liedern, mit *native speakers* auf einem Musikfest, auf Reisen, im Internet oder in der Arbeit mit ausländischen Kunden.
- In *Entry* hast du verschiedene Personen kennengelernt, die Englisch sprechen. Kennst du weitere Personen oder Situationen? Gib Beispiele.
- „Wenn Engländer oder Amerikaner in Deutschland Urlaub machen, sollten sie Deutsch können!" Findest du das auch?

▶ conversation   ▶ to want to (go)   ▶ on the phone

Check-out

P **What can you do now? Find out! Choose the correct answer a, b or c.**

Question		a	b	c
1	My name's Charlotte. What's … name? – I'm Christoph.	my	her	your
2	Where … you from? – I'm from Germany.	are	is	am
3	This is my friend. … name's Anja.	Their	Her	Our
4	My … name is John.	brothers'	brothers	brother's
5	… three rooms at the hostel for two people.	There's	There are	Is there
6	How many computers are there? – … one.	There's	There are	Is there
7	… a mobile phone? – Yes, and an MP3 player.	Have you	Does you have	Do you have
8	Mike has a mobile phone but he … an MP3 player.	don't have	doesn't have	has not
9	Lots of people in my class … a mobile.	have	are have	is have
10	What time is it? – It's 3.30.	= half past four	= half past three	= half to four
11	What time is it now? – It's 6.45.	= a quarter past six	= a quarter before six	= a quarter to seven
12	Hi. My name's Mary-Lou and I … in New York.	works	am work	work
13	At the weekend, Oliver … up at midday.	is get	get	gets
14	Jack and his two friends often … to the cinema at the weekend.	go	goes	are go
15	I'm from England. … about you?	Where	What	From
16	Greg is from …	australia.	Australien.	Australia.
17	Tony eats his lunch … 1 o'clock.	on	at	in
18	I watch TV … the evening.	on	at	in
19	White Horse Hotel. Nicole …	speak.	speaking.	speaks.
20	Thanks very much. – You're …	OK.	welcome.	goodbye.

Entry 17

Unit 1
At college

Am Ende dieser Unit kann ich …
→ über meinen Kurs reden,
→ einige Berufe nennen,
→ etwas von meinem Alltag erzählen,
→ eine persönliche E-Mail schreiben.

1 An email from California

R/P **A Look at the picture above.**

1 How many people are there in the picture?
There are …
2 How many boys are there and how many girls?
3 Where are they? At home? At college? In town?
4 What do you think? What country are they from?
I think …

Tips and tricks

What can you see  the picture?
There are seven people  this photo.

▶ at college   ▶ at home   ▶ in town

18 At college

> **Check-in** > Training > Language > Check-out   **1**

Posteingang

Von:	email@occ.edu
Betreff:	Hi from us to you

Hi!

We're students at the Ocean Community College in San Diego, California in the USA. Our names are Laura, Luis, Marcie, Mitch, Nat, Beth and Sue. We're all on a business course at our college.

5 You don't know us, but we'd like to write to some students in Germany. Wir kann ein Bisschen Deutsch aber nicht sehr gut – so PLEASE could you write to us in English!!?? Perhaps we can send emails about us and our colleges – we can write to you and you can write to us. What do you think?

10 It would be really cool to know about your college in Germany, your course, what you want to do when you finish … and about the place where you live. You can contact us at the address above.

Hoping to hear from you soon,

The guys from OCC

R **B Read the email above.**

1 Find the names of the people in the photo on page 18.
2 What's the name of their college? Where is it?
3 What do they want to do with you?
4 What do they have questions about?

R **C Look at the email again. What are these phrases in English?**

- Wir hoffen bald von euch zu hören!
- Was meint ihr dazu?
- Es wäre echt cool!

▶ perhaps   ▶ really   ▶ address

At college **19**

1 > Check-in > **Training** > Language > Check-out

2 Meet Luis and Beth

R/P **A** Read what Luis says and then finish the sentences about him below.

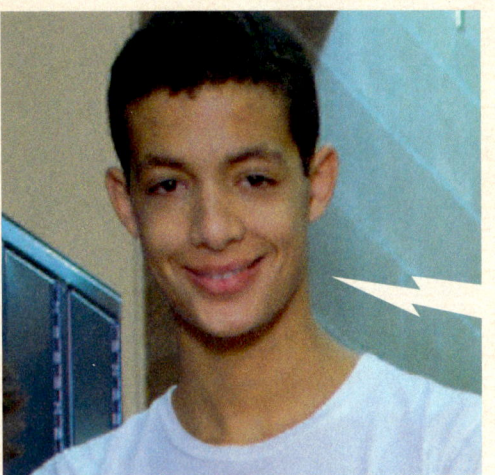

1 Hi again. I'm Luis. I'm 18 years old and I live in San Diego, California. I'm a student at OCC, the Ocean Community College. I'm on a business course and when I finish the course, I want to
5 work in a marketing company, maybe in LA.

I go to college five days a week, Monday to Friday. Most days the lessons start at 7.30 in the morning and finish at 2.30 in the afternoon. We get a lunch break from twelve to one. There's a cafeteria in the
10 college and I usually eat there.

There are 20 people in my class. They're all great guys and I often hang out with them at the weekend.

1 Luis … in San Diego, California.
2 He's on a business course. When he … the course, he … maybe to work in a firm in LA.
3 Luis … to college five days a week.
4 Most days his lessons … at 7.30 and … at 2.30 and he … a lunch break from twelve to one.
5 He thinks the people in his class are OK. He often … them at the weekend.

Hier und dort

In der Alltagssprache in GB und den USA wird immer die '12-hour clock' benutzt.:
*My lessons start at **half past seven** and finish at **half past two in the afternoon**.*

P **B** What about YOU?

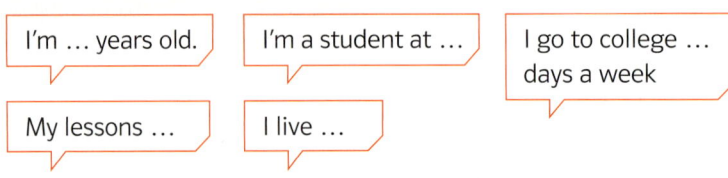

I'm … years old.   I'm a student at …   I go to college … days a week
My lessons …   I live …

The simple present				
	want	live	go	finish
I	?	live	go	finish
he/she/it	wants	?	goes	finishes
we	want	live	?	finish
you	want	live	go	?
they	want	live	go	finish

Can you give the missing forms?

▸ on a course ▸ maybe ▸ most days ▸ (to get) a lunch break

20 At college

R **C** Now listen to Beth. Which is right? Note down a) or b).

1 Beth a) is b) isn't 18 years old.
2 She a) is b) isn't on the business course at OCC with Luis.
3 Beth a) likes b) doesn't like small towns.
4 San Diego a) has b) doesn't have about a million people.
5 San Diego a) is b) isn't in the north of California.
6 When Beth finishes college she a) wants b) doesn't want to work in a marketing company.
7 She a) wants b) doesn't want to get a job straight away after college.

R/P **D** What's the same and what's different for YOU? Copy and fill in the table below. Then make sentences with *and … too* or *but*:

Beth is 18 and I'm 18 too.
Beth is 18 but I'm not 18. I'm 16.

	Beth	Me
age	18	?
course	?	?
small towns	?	?
after college	?	?

Das simple present: Verneinung		
I	?	
he/she/it	?	live in California.
we/you/they	don't	

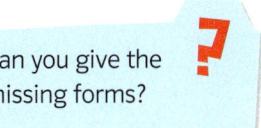
Can you give the missing forms?

▸ to get a job   ▸ straight away   ▸ north/south/east/west

At college

1 > Check-in > **Training** > Language > Check-out

3 A brochure

R A Read about Amber and find out … 808236-0002

1 Amber Johnson is a student at
   La Jolla High School near San
   Diego. Almost all American
   teenagers go to high school
5 and they leave when they're
   18 years old. Amber is 18 now,
   so it's her last year at school.
   Next year she wants to go to
   OCC. She wants to be a
10 computer technician. Today,
   she has a brochure about the
   college. You can see a page
   from the brochure on page 23.

1 Where does she go to high school? How old is she?
2 What does she want to do next year?
3 What job does Amber want to have one day?

R B Amber has lots of questions about the college and the courses there. Look at the brochure and find the answers for her.

1 How big is the college and how many students are there?
2 How many courses does the college offer?
3 Can I train to be a computer technician?
4 How long do the courses last?
5 How much do the courses cost?
6 How can I contact the college?

P C What about YOU?

1 What course are you on? Can you find an English name for the course?
2 How long does your course last?
3 How much does your course cost?

Hier und dort

Sowohl in den USA als auch in Großbritannien findet die Berufsbildung auf einem *college* statt, und die Lernenden sind *students*. In *Kickoff* benutzen wir durchgehend diese Wörter für dich und und deine Schule.

Das simple present: Fragen			
	do	I	
Where	?	he/she/it	live?
	?	we/you/they	

Can you give the missing forms?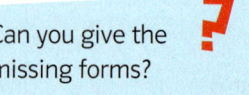

▶ to want to (do something)   ▶ a brochure   ▶ to last (one year / two years)   ▶ to cost

22 At college

> Check-in   > **Training**   > Language   > Check-out   **1**

OCEAN COMMUNITY COLLEGE

Who do you want to be?

COURSES AT OCC

We offer courses in all these subject areas ...
- Art and Design
- Automotive Mechanics
- Business and Business Administration
- Computers and Information Technology
- Construction
- Health and Beauty
- Music and Media
- Retail Services
- Social Work and Child Care
- Sport
- Electronics

With over 25,000 students, OCC is one of California's biggest community colleges. Most students come to us after high school at 18, but the college is for everyone. Our oldest student at the moment is 68!

5 Because we are so big, we offer over 200 different courses. So whether you want to be a hairdresser or a secretary, a computer technician or a dancer, we can help you.

Courses at OCC don't last 'a year' or 'two years'. You get 'credits' when you come to classes. When you have enough 10 credits, you finish the course. So you can finish your course in one year, two years, or even longer if you want.

Courses cost between $1,000 and $5,000 dollars but you can get help with money if you need it. We have all the details – just come and talk to us.

15 **How to contact us:**
Visit our website: www.occ.edu
Email us at: info@occ.edu
Call us on: 619 318-4005 (toll free)

▶ at the moment   ▶ enough   ▶ it costs ($1,000 dollars)

4 Language practice

Das simple present → Grammar summary 1

Das *simple present* wird verwendet:
– für Tatsachen, die für eine längere Zeit gültig sind
– um auszudrücken, was jemand oft oder regelmäßig tut.

	work	like	go	finish
I	work	like	go	finish
he/she/it	works	likes	goes	finishes
we you they	work work work	like like like	go go go	finish finish finish

Fragen werden mit *do/does*, **Verneinungen** mit *don't/doesn't* gebildet:
Where **do** you **live**?
Where **does** he **live**?
I **don't live** in the USA.
He **doesn't live** there.

P **A** Finish the sentences. Use the *simple present*.

1 Where … Beth live? – She … in California.
2 Where … Luis live? – He … in California too.
3 Where … Beth and Luis go to college?
   – They … to college in San Diego.
4 Where … you live? – I … in Germany.
5 Where … you go to college? – I … to college in … (where?).
6 When Luis … his course he … to work in LA.
7 Where … you want to work when you … your course?
   – When I … my course, I … to work in … (where?).
8 Luis … in the USA. – He … live in Germany.
9 I … live in the USA. – I … in Germany.

R/P **B WORDS** What are the missing words?

job • lessons • last • student • class • course • cost • cities • high school

1 Luis is a … at Ocean Community College in California.
2 He's on a business …
3 Most days, his … start at 7.30 a.m. and finish at 2.30 p.m.
4 There are 20 people in his …
5 Beth doesn't like small towns. She loves big … like San Diego.
6 Amber goes to … in San Diego.
7 What … does she want to have one day? She wants to be a computer technician.
8 In the USA, college courses don't … '1 year' or '2 years'. You get credits when you go to lessons.
9 And in the USA, you pay for your courses. A course can … $5,000.

She wants to be a computer technician

24 At college

5 Activities

P **A** Look again at the email on page 19. Write an email back to 'the guys from OCC'.

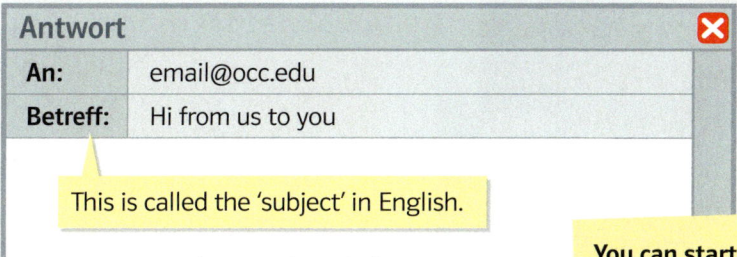

This is called the 'subject' in English.

Dear Laura, Luis, Marcie, Mitch, Nat, Beth and Sue,

Thanks for your email. I think it's a great idea to send emails.

In letters and emails in English the first word always has a CAPITAL letter!

You can start an email like this:
- Dear *(name),*   – Hi *(name),*
- Thanks (very much) for your email.
- I got your email yesterday. Thanks!

You can finish like this:
- Looking forward to hearing from you (soon).
- Please write back / write again soon.
- Yours, • Best wishes, • All the best,

✱ P/I **B** Make a brochure.

Work in a small group (2–4 students). Make a brochure in English about your college. Look at the brochure about the San Diego college on page 23 for ideas. You can give information about:

the name of your college • where it is •
how many students there are • the courses at the college •
how long the courses last • a 'typical' day at your college • …

P **C** REVISION Finish the sentences with *there is* or *there are*.

1 … seven people in this picture.
2 How many students … in your class?
   – … usually 20.
3 … a big community college in San Diego, California. … over 25,000 students at the college.
4 … a website address on their brochure?
   – Yes, … an address at the bottom of the page. And … a phone number to contact them.

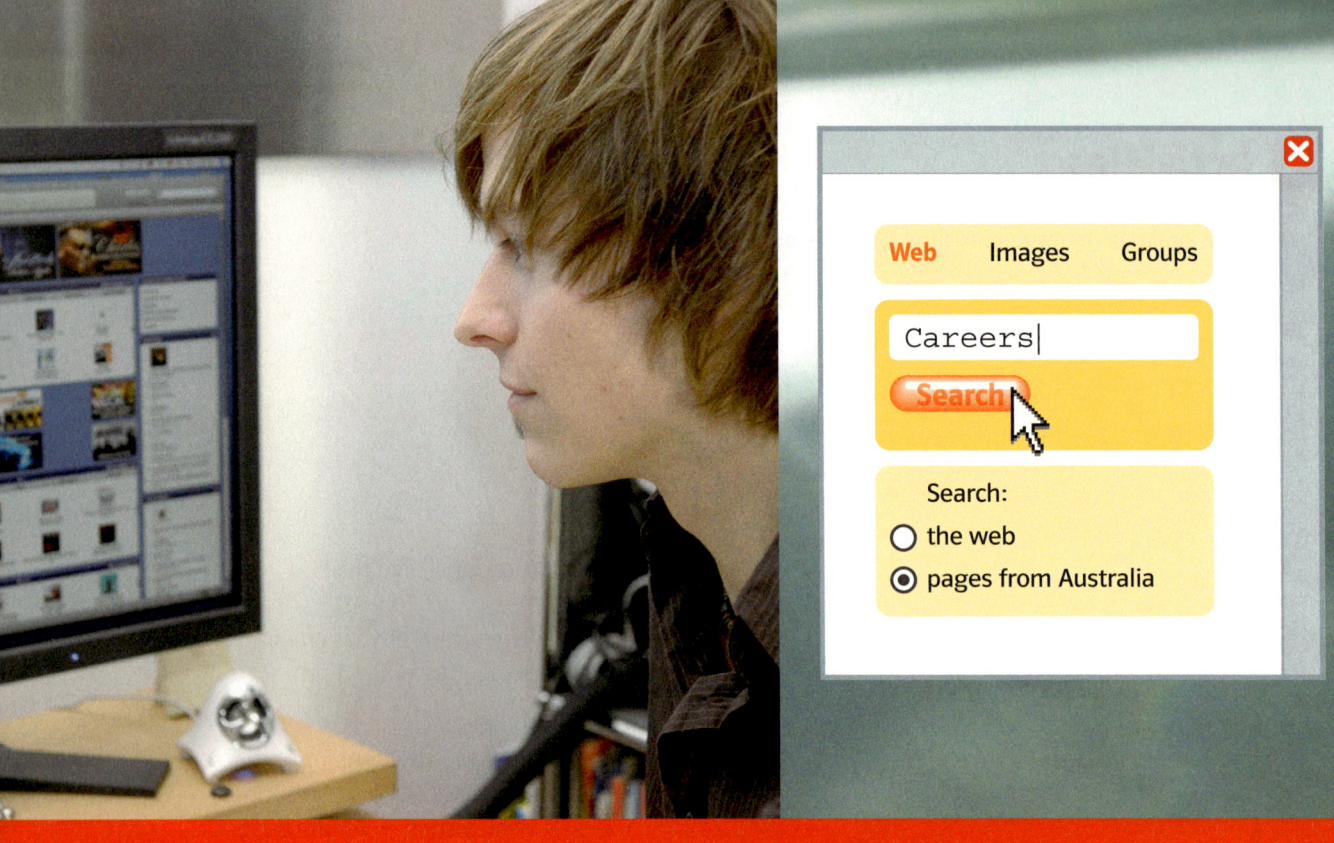

Unit 2
People and jobs

Am Ende dieser Unit kann ich ...

→ mehrere Berufe nennen und beschreiben,
→ sagen, was ich nach der Schule machen will, und meine Arbeit beschreiben,
→ sagen, was Leute oft oder gewöhnlich machen und was sie gerade im Moment machen.

1 A careers website

R/P **A** Look at the picture above. The student in the picture is called Jack.

1 Where do you think he's from? Why?
2 What's he doing right now? Is he ...
  – reading a magazine?
  – using a laptop?
  – listening to music?
3 What information is he searching for?

P **B** And you? What are you doing at the moment? Are you ...

  – looking at a website?
  – reading a magazine?
  – ...?

▸ career ▸ information ▸ to search for ▸ to look at

26 People and jobs

| Check-in | Training | Language | Check-out | 2 |

JOB PROFILE
FITNESS TRAINER

What does a fitness trainer do?
A fitness trainer (or personal trainer) helps people with exercises and exercise machines. (S)he also often talks to people about their diets and a healthy lifestyle.

Where does a fitness trainer work?
A fitness trainer usually works inside in a fitness club or a sports centre.

When does a fitness trainer work?
The hours of work for a fitness trainer can be long. Fitness clubs are often open in the evenings and at weekends.

Fitness trainers usually like …
sport, keeping fit, helping people, working with people.

808236-0003

R **C** Look at the job profile above from a careers website. True or false?

1 A fitness trainer usually works outside – for example, at a sports stadium.
2 A fitness trainer doesn't usually like sport.
3 A fitness trainer often works with people.
4 A fitness trainer often works on Saturday and Sunday.
5 A fitness trainer often talks to people about what they eat and how they live.

Tips and tricks

She's **a** fitness trainer.
I'm **a** student.
After college, I want to be **a** …

P/I **D** Talk in class

1 Where do you want to work one day? Do you want to work inside (for example, in an office) or outside?
2 Are you a friendly person? Do you want to work with people or to help people?

▶ hours of work   ▶ usually   ▶ often

People and jobs **27**

2 > Check-in > Training > Language > Check-out

2 Which job?

R/P **A** Read what these four people say and the job profiles below and on page 29. What do you think? Which job is best for each person? Why?

I think the right job for person A is to be a …
Person A wants to work outside / work with his hands / meet people …
and a … (job) works …

A: I want to work with my hands. I think mechanical things are cool – I like bikes, cars and motor bikes.

B: I don't want to work inside. I hate offices! I like flowers and plants.

C: I love fashion and beauty. I want to work with my hands. And I'm a really friendly person. I want to meet lots of people in my job.

D: I have five small brothers and sisters. I want to work in a team and to help kids.

JOB PROFILE
GARDENER

What does a gardener do?
A gardener looks after flowers and plants, cuts grass etc.

Where does a gardener work?
Gardeners usually work outside in gardens or parks. They sometimes also work in garden centres.

When does a gardener work?
A gardener normally works five days a week but the hours can be longer in the summer.

Gardeners usually like:
nature, being outside.

JOB PROFILE
MECHANIC

What does a mechanic do?
A mechanic repairs and services cars and other vehicles.

Where does a mechanic work?
Mechanics usually work in a workshop.

When does a mechanic work?
Workshops are normally open five days a week from around 7.30 a.m. to around 6 p.m.

Mechanics usually like:
mechanical things, working with their hands, working in a team.

▶ each ▶ inside ▶ normally

28 People and jobs

> Check-in   > **Training**   > Language   > Check-out   **2**

JOB PROFILE
NURSERY ASSISTANT

What does a nursery assistant do?
A nursery assistant looks after young children 2–5 years old. (S)he plays with children, reads stories, helps the smaller children etc.

Where does a nursery assistant work?
Nursery assistants work in private or state nurseries.

When does a nursery assistant work?
Nurseries are usually open 5 or 6 days a week from around 8 a.m. to around 4 p.m.

Nursery assistants usually like:
children, working in a team, meeting and helping people.

JOB PROFILE
HAIRDRESSER

What does a hairdresser do?
A hairdresser cuts men's and women's hair.

Where does a hairdresser work?
A hairdresser usually works in a salon with other hairdressers.

When does a hairdresser work?
Salons are usually open five or six days a week from around 9 a.m. to around 5 p.m.

Hairdressers usually like:
fashion and beauty, meeting people, working in a team, working with their hands.

P **B** Look at the four pictures. What are the people's jobs? What are they doing at the moment in the pictures? Use the verbs in the box.

work • play • cut • talk • dance • wash • repair

Person A is a … Right now (s)he's …

A

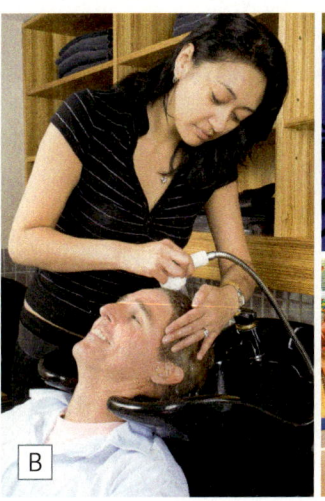
B

C

D

Das present continuous		
I	am	work**ing**.
he/she/it	?	sit**ting**.
we/you/they	?	play**ing**.

Can you give the missing forms?

▶ to look after   ▶ around (6 p.m.)   ▶ open from … to …

People and jobs **29**

3 An interview in Australia

THE MAN WITH SIX JOBS

R A A reporter from ABC Radio in Australia is in the small town of Turkey Creek today. She's interviewing Pete Collins. Pete has six jobs. What are they? Listen and put the pictures 1–6 below in the right order.

▶ hunter ▶ to hunt ▶ customer

> Check-in   > **Training**   > Language   > Check-out   **2**

B Make sentences about Pete and his jobs. Use the phrases below. You can listen to the interview again if you need to.

In the mornings Pete/he …

When?	What?	Where?
In the mornings In the afternoons In the evenings Sometimes	he cuts hair he works as a barman he delivers letters and packages he repairs cars he hunts crocodiles he serves customers	in his workshop. everywhere in Turkey Creek. in his bar. in the river. in his shop. in his hairdressing 'salon'.

P/I **C** Make questions about Pete's day. Ask another student in your class.

What does Pete do in the mornings?
– In the mornings he … Then he …
When does he cut hair? – He cuts hair …
Where does he serve customers? – He serves customers …

R **D** Listen to these six short conversations. Which job is Pete doing at the moment? What's he doing in each conversation?

Pete is a … at the moment. He's …

P/I **E** Work with a partner. Ask questions about the pictures on page 30.

What's Pete doing in this picture?
– He's delivering letters and packages.

P/I **F** Talk about Turkey Creek and Pete.

1 Where is Turkey Creek? In northern / southern / eastern / western Australia? Is it a big or a small town?
2 What do you think? Does Pete have a nice life? Why (not)?

Hier und dort

Einige Unterschiede zwischen Deutschland und Australien:
– **Größe:** Deutschland 357 000 km², Australien 7,7 Millionen km².
– **Bevölkerung:** Deutschland 82 Millionen, Australien 20 Millionen.
– **Temperatur im Dezember:** Deutschland 5 °C, Australien 30 °C.

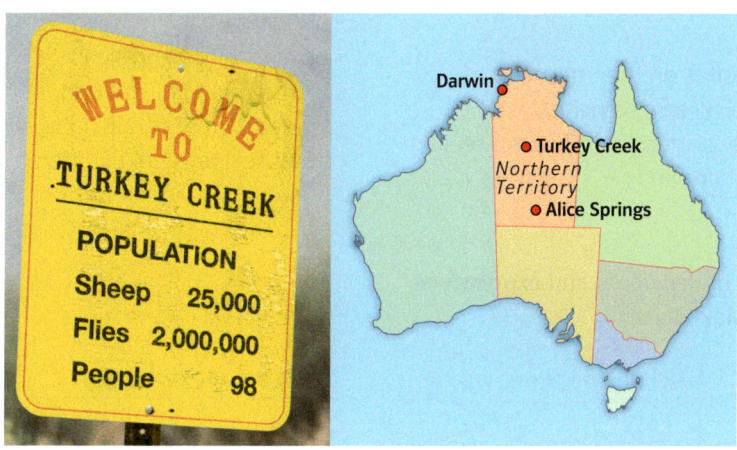

▶ northern   ▶ southern   ▶ eastern   ▶ western

People and jobs   **31**

4 Language practice

Das simple present und das present continuous → Grammar summary 2

Das simple present:
für Aussagen, die für längere Zeit gültig sind, sowie für Dinge, die wir oft oder regelmäßig tun:
*Jack **lives** in Australia.*
*A mechanic **usually works** in a workshop.*

Das present continuous:
für Aktivitäten, die gerade im Augenblick des Sprechens stattfinden. Es wird häufig mit Zeitangaben wie *at the moment* und *right now* verwendet:
*What **are** you **doing** at the moment?*
***I'm learning** English right now.*

Bildung:
Das present continuous wird mit *to be* und Verb + *-ing* gebildet.

I **am** ('m)	
he/she/it **is** ('s)	work**ing**
we/you/they **are** ('re)	

Fragen und **Verneinungen** werden mit den Frage- und Verneinungsformen von *to be* gebildet:
***Are** you working?*
***I'm not** working.*

P A Finish the sentences with the *present continuous* forms of the verbs.

1. At the moment, Jack … **(look at)** a careers website.
2. The children in the picture … **(play)**.
3. I … **(not/play)** at the moment. I … **(learn)** English.
4. What … Pete … **(do)** right now? He … **(repair)** a car.
5. She … **(not/cut)** his hair, she … **(wash)** it first.

P B In sentences a and b, one verb is in the *simple present* and one is in the *present continuous*. Finish the sentences with the right forms.

1. (to cut) a Hairdressers … people's hair.
   b Kelly is a hairdresser. She … a man's hair right now.
2. (to work) a It's 8.00 p.m. and Harry … in his fitness club at the moment.
   b He's a fitness trainer and he often … in the evenings.
3. (to look at) a Jack often … websites on the Internet.
   b Right now he … a careers website.
4. (to deliver) a In this picture, Pete … letters in Turkey Creek.
   b He's the postman there and he … letters every day.

So läuft's besser

Vokabellernen ist immer etwas schmerzhaft – aber das muss sein, um in der Sprache weiterzukommen. Zwei Tipps:
- Schreibe neue Vokabeln immer in ein Vokabelheft und wiederhole sie regelmäßig.
- Neue Vokabeln prägen sich besser ein, wenn sie in Kategorien gelistet und gelernt werden, z. B. Jobs, Städte, Freizeitaktivitäten usw.

R/P C WORDS Look back at the unit. How many words and expressions can you find for these categories? Make lists.

Jobs	Where people work	What people do
fitness trainer	a kitchen	cut hair
postman …	…	…

> Check-in   > Training   > Language   > **Check-out**   **2**

5 Activities

P **A** Write about YOU and jobs. You find this questionnaire on an international website. It's for college students and it asks about your ideas about jobs. Write your answers. Use full sentences.

QUESTIONNAIRE

Hello all college students! We'd like to have your ideas about jobs! Please write to us and give us your answers to these questions.

1 What's your name and where do you live?
2 What course are you on at your college?
3 What things do you want in a job? (Do you want to work with your hands, to meet lots of people, … ?)
4 What do you want to do after college? What job do you want to have?
5 Describe the job. (What does a person with that job do? Where does (s)he work? When?)

*P/I **B** A jobs file. Work in a small group (2–4 students) and make a jobs file.

- Choose about five jobs which you find interesting.
- Find pictures of people with the jobs. (You can look in magazines or on the Internet.)
- Write four or five sentences about each job. Say what a person in this job does, where (s)he works.
- Describe your pictures. What's the person in the picture doing at the moment?

P **C** REVISION Can you give the plurals of the words?

1 One photo, two **photos**.
2 One hairdresser, two …
3 One man, two …
4 One woman, two …
5 One child, two …
6 One country, two …
7 One sheep, two …
8 One person, two …

People and jobs **33**

Unit 3
Free time

Am Ende dieser Unit kann ich …
→ über meine Freizeit sprechen,
→ sagen, was ich gerne (und nicht so gerne) mache,
→ meine Vorstellungen über Teilzeitjobs ausdrücken,
→ einen Blog über mich schreiben.

1 Cat's blog

R/P **A** The girl in the pictures above is Catherine – her friends call her 'Cat'. Look at the pictures and read what Cat says.

1 Where do you think Cat lives?
   I think …
2 Why is Covent Garden her favourite place there?
   Because …
3 What does she love doing there?
4 What are Cat and her friends doing at the moment in the picture above?

P **B** What about YOU? Do you have a favourite place in your town? What is it? Why?

My favourite place is Covent Garden. It's an old market and it has the best shops, the nicest cafés – and the craziest people in London. I love going there with my friends.

▶ free time ▶ to call (her Cat) ▶ favourite (place)

Cat's blog

Hi! I'm Catherine –
My nickname is Cat.
Welcome to my blog.

Quick Facts

I'm 17 and I live in London, England. I love living in London. I think it's the coolest city in the world. I'm a student at a further education college or FE college. That's where people train for jobs. I'm on a full-time, 2-year graphic design course.

Free time

I go to college five days a week from 9 a.m. to around 5 p.m. and on Monday, Wednesday and Thursday evenings I have a part-time job. But my life isn't all work, work, work. I get plenty of free time too. I like reading, shopping, going to the cinema – and blogging, of course. But the most important thing for me is friends. I have some great college friends. In the week, we often go for a coffee after lessons, and we always hang out together on Saturdays.

R C Read Cat's blog above.

1 What's an 'FE college'?
2 What course is Cat on at college, how long does it last, and when does she go to college?
3 When does she have free time?
4 What things does she like doing in her free time?
5 Which activity is the most important for her?

P D And YOU?

1 When do you have free time?
2 Do you have a part-time job?
3 What do you like doing in your free time?

▸ nickname   ▸ FE (further education) college   ▸ plenty of

Tips and tricks

Wenn du im Unterricht etwas nicht verstehst, kannst du fragen:
– *Excuse me. What does … mean?*
– *How do you say … in English?*

3 > Check-in > Training > Language > Check-out

2 Activities in and out of college

R **A** Look at the notices below. Cat and her friends are students at Hatton FE College in London. There are lots of clubs and activities at the college for the students. There's always information about these on the college noticeboard.

1 You like team sports. What team sports are there for students at the college?
2 You like exciting and 'extreme' sports. How can you do these at the college?
3 You like theatre, singing and dancing. Which person at the college can help you?
4 After lessons today you want to keep fit for half an hour, have a sauna, then go to a hairdresser. Where can you do these things at college? How much does it cost?
5 You don't like sports, you don't like drama and your hair is fine. What other activity is there for you?

DRAMA CLUB
Interested in drama? Want to be in our summer musical? See *Jill Townsend* room 2B at lunchtime today!

Adventure weekends
CAMPING – ROCK CLIMBING – KAYAKING – CYCLING – MOUNTAIN BOARDING **AND LOTS MORE!**

Interested? There are regular weekends all year – and they aren't expensive! Contact Sally Driver (on the Sport and Leisure course) for more details.

Sport For All
There's plenty of sport at Hatton College! To find out more, look on the college intranet for the times of our training sessions.
- Football club
- Rugby club
- Basketball club
- Netball club

FITNESS CENTRE
The Fitness Centre is open Mon – Fri 7 a.m. – 8 p.m. It is **FREE** for all students – so come and keep fit!
We have a sauna too!!

Do you like writing?
THE HAT is Hatton College's college magazine. Want to know more? Come to ROOM 21 today at 17:00

Do you need a little help with your hair? Visit the *HAIRDRESSING SALON!*

▶ activity(-ies) ▶ notice ▶ noticeboard

36 Free time

> Check-in   > **Training**   > Language   > Check-out   **3**

R B Cat's friends are talking about the things they *like* and *don't like* doing. Copy the table below, then listen and complete your table with the letters from the box.

a listening to music	g shopping
b surfing the Internet	h writing
	i watching TV
c mountain boarding	j reading
	k sports
d keeping fit	l working on her/his car
e football	
f going to the cinema	m painting (pictures)

Justin
Malik
Craig
Hayley

name	(really) likes/loves	doesn't like (so much) / isn't keen on / hates
Justin	k, e, d	
Hayley		
Craig		
Malik		

P C Make sentences about Cat's friends.

Justin really likes …, but he doesn't like … so much / isn't keen on …

I D Interview a partner.

1 First write two lists: a) things you like doing and b) things you don't like doing. There are lots of ideas above and in the box below.
2 Make a conversation with a partner.
3 Write a short text about your partner.

> skateboarding • inline skating • jogging • playing hockey • playing video games • watching DVDs • cooking • hanging out with friends • swimming • chatting online • taking photos • chilling out (= doing nothing)

I (really) like …

I'm not so keen on …
I think it's boring/stupid/crazy.

What about you?
What do you like doing?

Likes and dislikes

I like shopping.
I love **?** TV.
I'm not **?** on painting.
I **?** like **?** the cinema.
I hate **?** music.

Can you give the missing words?

▶ really (like doing)   ▶ to be keen on   ▶ boring/stupid/crazy

Free time **37**

3 A part-time job

A Here's another page from Cat's blog. True, false, or 'not in the text'?

1. Cat has a part-time job three evenings a week.
2. She works in a fish and chip shop near her house.
3. Cat likes the customers in her fish and chip shop.
4. One of the old customers who is often in Cat's shop is 103 years old.
5. One of Cat's friends has a part-time job at the weekends in a supermarket.
6. People always say that a part-time job isn't a good idea.
7. Cat (and her dad) think that a part-time job is a bad idea too.

Cat's blog

My part-time job

On Monday, Wednesday and Thursday evenings I have a part-time job. I work in a fish and chip shop from 6 until about 10.30. Mr Kent, the owner, says we sell the best fish and chips in London.
5 The most important thing for me is that I earn money, but I love doing the job too. We have lots of really nice customers. I think the nicest customers are the old people. They always tell jokes and we laugh a lot with them. Lots of my friends also have part-time jobs. One works in a supermarket. He works on Saturdays
10 and Sundays – all day. I think my job is better because I'm free at the weekends. People sometimes say that a part-time job is bad. They say it's more important to do college work. I think I can work and do my college work, so it's OK. And now that I'm 17 it's good to have my money. (My dad thinks that too!)

Hier und dort

Neben den heutigen *burgers* und *pizza* sind *fish and chips* das ursprüngliche britische *fast food*. *Fish and chip shops* sind überall anzutreffen. Traditionell werden *fish and chips* mit Salz, Pfeffer und Essig *(vinegar)* gegessen. Vorsicht bei dem Begriff *chips*, der in Deutschland, GB und den USA verschiedene Bedeutungen hat:

Deutschland	Pommes	Chips
USA	fries	chips
GB	chips	crisps

▶ fish and chip shop   ▶ to earn money   ▶ to tell jokes/a joke

Free time

| Check-in | Training | Language | Check-out | **3** |

R/P **B** Look at Cat's blog again. First give the missing words in the sentences below, then copy and complete the table.

1. Cat thinks that now she's 17 it's … to have *her* money.
2. Cat thinks her job is … than her friend's job in the supermarket.
3. The owner of Cat's fish and chip shop says his fish and chips are … … in London.
4. Cat likes the customers in the shop. She thinks that … … customers are the old people.
5. People sometimes say that college work is … … than a part-time job.
6. For Cat … … … thing is that she earns money.

good	…	the …
important	…	the …
nice	…	the …

P **C** Look at the three pictures and make sentences. Use the *comparatives* and *superlatives* of the adjectives.

1. The fish and chips cost £3.50 and the burger costs £2.10. So the burger is … (cheap) than the fish and chips and the fish and chips are … (expensive) than the burger.
2. The pizza costs £4.50. It's the … (expensive) of the three meals. And the burger is the … (cheap).
3. Which meal do you like? Well, I think burgers are … (nice) than pizzas, but the … (nice) meal of all is fish and chips.
4. Are fish and chips healthy? Mmm, not really. But they're … (healthy) than burgers. The … (healthy) meal of all is the pizza.
5. There are three fish and chips shops in my street. I think Mr Kent's shop is the … (good) shop of the three. It's … (good) than the *Corner Fish Bar* and that's … (good) than *Mike's Fish*. In fact, *Mike's Fish* is the … (bad) chip shop in London!

£3.50

£2.10

£4.50

I **D** Talk in class.

1. Do you have a part-time job? What is it? When do you work?
2. What are the *best* and the *worst* things about a part-time job?
3. "A part-time job is bad. It's more important to do college work." What do you think?

Comparatives and superlatives		
cheap	cheaper	the cheapest
old	?	?
nice	?	?
healthy	?	?
important	?	?
expensive	?	?
good	?	?
bad	?	?

Can you give the missing forms?

▸ healthy ▸ in fact ▸ the best/worst thing about

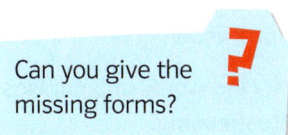

Free time **39**

4 Language practice

1 Sagen, was man gern oder ungern macht

Mit *I like, I love, I don't like, I'm not keen on* und *I hate*, kann man sagen, was man gern oder ungern macht. Auf diese Verben folgt ein Substantiv oder ein zweites Verb + *-ing*.
*I like **computer games**.*
*I love **watching** DVDs.*

2 Steigerung des Adjektivs

Kurze einsilbige Adjektive und Adjektive auf *-y* enden gesteigert auf *-er/-est*:
*I think burgers are **nicer** than pizzas.*
*Yes, but pizzas are **healthier** than burgers.*

Für mehrsilbige Adjektive wird *more/most* verwendet:
*The **most important** thing for me is that I earn money.*

Good (better/best) und *bad (worse/worst)* sind unregelmäßig:
*These fish and chips are good, but those are **better**.*

Merke: Wenn man über Steigerungen spricht wie „besser als", heißt „als" *than*.

P A Make sentences that are true for YOU.

I	love hate like don't like	doing homework. phoning my friends. sport. reading newspapers. computer games. eating pizza.

P B Finish the sentences with the adjectives in the correct form.

1. London is … **(big)** than Paris or Berlin. It's the … **(big)** city in Europe.
2. Cat says the … **(nice)** people in her fish and chip shop are the old people.
3. Justin likes playing football but he doesn't like watching TV. He thinks playing football is … **(interesting)** than watching TV.
4. Cat thinks friends are very important. In fact, she thinks they're the … **(important)** thing in her life.
5. Which is … **(good)** – going to the cinema or watching DVDs? – I don't know!

P C WORDS Find words and phrases in the unit which have the opposite meaning.

1. cheap   *(expensive)*
2. good
3. interesting
4. part-time
5. young
6. to love
7. last
8. not many

5 Activities

P A Write a blog for YOU. Use full sentences and write about 100 words. Here are some things you can write about:

- Do your friends have a nickname for you?
- When do you have free time?
- What do you like doing in your free time?
- Where and when do you do these things? Who do you do them with?
- Do you have a part-time job? Why (not)?

✱ I/P B A class survey. Do a survey in your class about free time activities. Make a graph then write about the results.

10 people in the class like ...
2 people like ...
1 person likes ...
The most popular free time activity is ...
Next is ...
Then ...

computer games   watching TV

P C REVISION Finish the sentences with the verbs in the correct form of the *simple present*.

1 Where **(you/live)** do you live? – I ... **(live)** in Germany.
2 Where ... **(Cat/live)**? – She ... **(live)** in London.
3 What ... **(they/like)** doing in their free time?
   – They ... **(like)** football and skateboarding.
4 ... **(you/live)** in London? – No, I ... **(not/live)** in London.
5 ... **(Cat/live)** in Germany?
   – No, she ... **(not/live)** in Germany. She ... **(live)** in London in England.
6 The girls in my class ... **(love)** shopping but the boys ... **(not/like)** shopping so much. In fact, lots of the boys **(hate)** ... it.

Free time

Unit 4
Products then and now

Am Ende dieser Unit kann ich ...
→ über die Vergangenheit sprechen und schreiben,
→ über einige bekannte Produkte und Firmen sprechen und schreiben.

1 Did you know?

R/P **A** The man in the picture above is Dr Martin Cooper from the USA. In his hand, he has one of the first modern, commercial mobile phones. What do you think?

1. When were the first commercial mobile phones – in the 1960s, the 1970s or the 1980s?
   I think they were in ...
2. What company produced the first phones – Nokia, Siemens, ...?
   I think ... made the first phones.
3. Were the first mobiles bigger or smaller than mobiles today? How heavy were they – 250 grams, 500 grams, 1 kilogram, more than 1 kilogram?
4. Were they cheaper or more expensive than mobiles today?

▶ company   ▶ commercial   ▶ the 1960s

Tips and tricks
GB: a mobile (phone)
USA: a cell (phone)

| Check-in | Training | Language | Check-out | **4** |

808236-0006

The first mobile phone call

Dr Martin Cooper, an engineer at the Motorola Corporation in the USA, invented the first modern mobile phone. He tested the phone for the first time in 1973. On April 3 1973, he called a friend on his phone from a street in the centre of New York. People stopped and looked at him. A man with a phone in the street!

Ten years later, in 1983, Motorola produced the first commercial phones – phones for everyone. They were very simple. They didn't have text messages or cameras. They were also heavy – over a kilogram. And they were expensive. In today's money, the price of one of the first phones was about $4,000.

R **B** Read the web page about mobile phones above. Check your answers.

P/I **C** What about YOU?

1 When did you get your first mobile phone?
   I got my first mobile (last year / two years ago / in about 2004 / last month / …)
2 What things did it have – text messages, a camera, an MP3 player, a video camera, games, …?
   My first mobile had …
3 Who did you call *first* on your first mobile – a friend, your mum or dad …?
   (I think) I called …

▸ to invent   ▸ to produce   ▸ price

Products then and now **43**

4

> Check-in > **Training** > Language > Check-out

2 Trainers then and now

R **A Read this magazine article about the history of trainers.**

1. When did sports shoes first start?
2. What famous company started in 1924? (Where?)
3. What important thing for trainers happened in the 1950s?

808236-0007

THE HISTORY OF TRAINERS

Plimsolls and sneakers
The first sports shoes started over 100 years ago. They were called 'plimsolls'. They had a flat rubber sole and a canvas top and they were very simple – the left foot and the right foot were the same! In 1917, the U.S. Rubber Company made the first really comfortable plimsolls. They called them Keds. Soon, people called the new shoes 'sneakers'. 'To sneak' means 'to walk quietly'.

Sports shoes from Germany
In 1924, two German brothers started a sports shoe company in a small village in Germany. Their shoes had spikes and they were for athletes. The two bothers' names were Adi and Rudolf Dassler. Adi called the company, yes, Adidas. Athletes used Adidas shoes in lots of Olympic Games and they were soon famous. They were the best sports shoes in the world.

Trainers and fashion
In the 1930s and 40s people wore trainers for sports like athletics and basketball. Then in the 1950s a famous, young American actor, James Dean, wore trainers, jeans and a T-shirt in a movie. Trainers were now fashionable – and cheap. Soon, young people everywhere wore trainers (and jeans) too.

Hi-tech trainers
In the 1960s and 70s, companies started making hi-tech trainers. The Nike company started in the USA in 1968. Nike, Adidas and other companies made trainers with air in the soles of their shoes. These shoes were very comfortable – but sometimes also very expensive. Today, the price of a pair of trainers can be over $100.

spikes

▶ history   ▶ to happen   ▶ fashion/fashionable

44 Products then and now

> Check-in | > Training | > Language | > Check-out | **4**

R **B** Find the missing verbs in the article.

1	The first sports shoes	started	over 100 years ago.
2	They were called 'plimsolls' and they		very simple.
3	Plimsolls		a flat rubber sole and a canvas top.
4	The U.S. Rubber Company		the first comfortable plimsolls in 1917.
5	The company		the trainers Keds.
6	But soon people everywhere		them 'sneakers'.
7	In 1924, Adi and Rudolf Dassler		Adidas.
8	Adidas trainers		spikes.
9	They		for athletes.
10	Lots of athletes		Adidas trainers in the Olympic Games.
11	Soon Adidas sports shoes		famous.
12	In the 1950s, James Dean		trainers and jeans in a movie.
13	After his movie, trainers		fashionable – and cheap!
14	Companies like Nike		making hi-tech trainers in the 60s and 70s.
15	These hi-tech trainers		air in the soles.
16	They		very comfortable – but also expensive.

P **C** Look at the verbs in exercise B. Which verbs are 'regular'? Which are 'irregular'? Make two lists.

P **D** Make questions and answers about trainers.

1. when / sports shoes / start
   When **did** the first sports shoes **start**?
   – They **started** over 100 years ago.
2. when / the U.S. Rubber Company / make the first comfortable plimsolls
3. what / people / call / Keds
4. when / Adi and Rudolf Dassler / start / Adidas
5. where / athletes / use / Adidas shoes / in the 1920s and 30s
6. why / people/ wear / trainers / in the 1930s and 40s

Tips and tricks

Adidas started in 1924.
They wore trainers in the 1930s.
The first sports shoes started 100 years ago (= vor 100 Jahren).

P/I **E** Ask the class more questions with *when, where* or *why*.

Das simple past

	regular	irregular
	to start	to make
I	started	?

Fragen
When ? it start?
What ? he wear in the movie?

Can you give the missing forms?

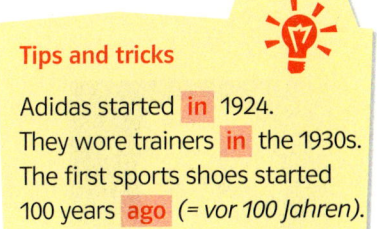

► comfortable ► ago ► example

Products then and now **45**

| 4 | Check-in | Training | Language | Check-out |

3 The history of a company

R **A** Listen to Tanja Kugler and put the pictures 1–8 below in the right order.

1 16

Tanja Kugler works for the Coca-Cola® company in Germany. She works in the Public Relations (PR) department and today she's talking to some visitors to the company. Tanja is talking about the company's history.

2 Coca-Cola in bottles

3 fanta

1 The original Coca-Cola logo designed by Frank Robinson

4 Asa Candler

5 HELLO GERMANY!

6 Coca-Cola in cans

8 Dr John S. Pemberton

7 Coca-Cola in China

▸ department (of a company) ▸ pharmacist/pharmacy ▸ assistant

46 Products then and now

| Check-in | Training | Language | Check-out | **4** |

Coca-Cola trucks from 1934 [1] and the 1980s [2]

R **B** Listen again. True or false? Note down T or F.

1 Dr John Pemberton made the first Coca-Cola in Atlanta, Georgia, in 1886.
2 His assistant invented the name Coca-Cola.
3 Dr Pemberton sold his business to a businessman in Atlanta called Frank Robinson.
4 The famous Coca-Cola bottle started in 1960.
5 The company produced the first Coca-Cola in Germany in Frankfurt.
6 The Coca-Cola company invented Fanta in Germany in 1940.
7 The first Coca-Cola in cans was in 1982.
8 Today, people drink Coca-Cola in over 20 countries around the world.

P **C** All the sentences below are wrong! Can you correct them?

1 Dr Pemberton invented the name Coca-Cola. (Frank Robinson)
 *Wrong! Dr Pemberton **didn't invent** the name. His assistant Frank Robinson **invented** the name.*
2 At first, people bought Coca-Cola in bottles. (in glasses)
3 The Coca-Cola company produced the first Coca-Cola in Germany in 1999. (1929)
4 The company invented Fanta in the USA. (Germany)
5 The company sold the first Diet Coke in 2002. (1982)

P/I **D** And YOU? Think of the time when you were six years old. Say three things you didn't do or didn't have then.

When I was six, I didn't speak English.
I didn't have …

So läuft's besser

Es gibt einige Verben, die in der Vergangenheitsform nicht auf -ed wie *I walk**ed*** enden: die unregelmäßigen Verben. Sie zu lernen ist einfach, wenn du dir jeden Tag ein Verb vornimmst und die Verben in Gruppen lernst wie z.B. *drink – dr**a**nk – dr**u**nk* und *sing – s**a**ng – s**u**ng*. Vgl. hierzu die Auflistung im Klappumschlag.

Das simple past: Verneinungen		
I he/she/it we you they	?	start make invent sell drink

Can you give the missing forms?

▸ to invent ▸ can (of a drink) ▸ at first

Products then and now

4 Language practice

Das simple past → Grammar summary 3

Das *simple past* wird verwendet, um Ereignisse in der Vergangenheit zu schildern, die jetzt abgeschlossen sind. Es wird häufig mit Zeitangaben wie *then, in 1970, last week* benutzt:
He **invented** the mobile phone in 1970.

Bildung:
Regelmäßige Verben bilden das *simple past* mit *-ed*.
Unregelmäßige Verben haben Sonderformen.
Die Verneinungen bildet man mit *didn't*, Fragen mit *did*.
Nach *did* und *didn't* steht immer die Grundform.

to be
Das Verb *to be* hat zwei Formen im *simple past*.
Es bildet Fragen und Verneinungen ohne *did/didn't*.

	regelmäßig	unregelmäßig
I he/she/it we/you/they	start**ed** didn't start	made didn't make
Did	start?	make?

I he/she/it	was	wasn't
we/you/they	were	weren't

Where **were** you last week?
When **was** your birthday?

P A Complete the sentences with the verbs.

1 Dr Martin Cooper … (invent) mobile phones in the 1970s.
2 He … (test) his new phone for the first time in 1973.
3 An American Rubber Company … (make) the first plimsolls in 1917.
4 James Dean … (wear) trainers in a movie in the 1950s.
5 After the movie, trainers … (be) fashionable.
6 Asa Candler … (be) a businessman in Atlanta.

P B Complete these sentences with *did* or *didn't*.

1 When … Motorola produce the first commercial mobile phones? – That was in 1983.
2 When … you get your first mobile?
   – I think I got my first mobile in about 2004.
3 The first sports shoes (plimsolls) were very simple. They … have air in the soles.
4 … Dr Pemberton invent the name Coca-Cola?
5 No, he … invent it. His assistant invented the name.

My first mobile

R/P C WORDS Can you find these 'business words' in this unit?

1 Produkt   *product*
2 produzieren
3 Unternehmen
4 Preis
5 Abteilung
6 Geschäftsmann
7 kaufen
8 verkaufen
9 erfinden

48 Products then and now

> Check-in > Training > Language > **Check-out** 4

5 Activities

M **A** Your friend wants to know about the history of a famous product, but (s)he doesn't speak English. Choose *one* text from this unit and give your friend the most important information in German.

✱ I **B** Find out about the history of jeans. Work with a partner. Some information in this article about the history of jeans is missing.

> When …?
>
> What …?

Partner B: Please look at page 155 now.
Partner A: Answer your partner's questions. Then ask questions to find your missing information 1–3.

A German called Levi Strauss invented today's most popular trousers – JEANS. But what do you know about him and his famous product?

rivet

Levi Strauss was born in Bavaria in Germany but in 1847 – when he was 18 years old – he went with his family to New York. In 1853, Levi went to San Francisco, California. He wanted to sell tents to the gold miners there. But the gold miners didn't want tents. They wanted strong trousers. Levi used the canvas from the tents for his new product.

The new trousers were great but they weren't very comfortable. Levi used ... (1) (a blue cloth from France). In ... (2) , Levi and a friend called Jacob Davis also started using rivets. 'Jeans' were now very strong. At first, jeans were for workers. But in ... (3) , some American movie stars wore jeans in movies and jeans became fashionable. Today, of course, millions of people around the world wear jeans.

P **C REVISION** Finish the sentences with *my, your, his, her, its, our* or *their*.

1 When did you get *your* first mobile phone?
   – I got ... first mobile two years ago.
2 Two German brothers started Adidas. ... names were Adi and Rudolf Dassler.
3 Do you like ... new car? We bought it yesterday.
4 Dr Cooper has a mobile phone. ... phone is very big.
5 That girl has a mobile too. But ... phone is very small.
6 Asa Candler started a company in 1892. ... name was Coca-Cola.

Products then and now   49

Unit 5
Do's and don'ts

Am Ende dieser Unit kann ich …
→ über Regeln in der Schule und am Arbeitsplatz reden und schreiben,
→ wichtige Schilder am Arbeitsplatz verstehen.

1 Rules

R **A** Sam is the guy on the left above. Jerry is on the right. Look at the sentences below. Who's this?

1. He's a construction worker. *That's …*
2. He's a chef.
3. He works in a kitchen.
4. He works on a construction site.
5. He must/has to wear a hard hat at work.
6. He must/has to have clean hands at work.
7. He doesn't have to wear a hard hat at work.
8. He doesn't have to have clean hands for his job.

M **B** How do you say *must/has to* and *doesn't have to* in German?

▶ rule(s)   ▶ hard hat   ▶ clean

Now wash your hands

HARD HAT AREA

50 Do's and don'ts

Check-in   Training   Language   Check-out   **5**

R/P **C** These New York community college students are in their college library. Look at the signs. What are the rules at their college?

1. Students at the college mustn't *eat or drink in the library*.
2. And they mustn't use their ... in the library.
3. Their college is a 'drug free, gun free zone'. That means they mustn't bring ... or ... to college.

M **D** How do you say "*They mustn't eat/drink/use their . . .*" in German?

P/I **E** Think about your college. Finish these sentences.

1. At my college, I must/have to …
2. I don't have to …
3. We mustn't …

▶ library ▶ sign ▶ gun ▶ drug(s)

Tips and tricks

Vorsicht!
you mustn't = du darfst nicht
you don't have to = du musst nicht

Do's and don'ts **51**

5 | Check-in | Training | Language | Check-out

2 Signs at work

R **A** There are lots of signs at work – in offices, in factories, in shops, in car parks, and on construction sites. Look at the signs on the next page. Find a sign or signs …

1 about something you wear on your ears
2 about something you wear on your eyes
3 about smoking
4 about the floor in a shop
5 about electricity
6 for car and lorry drivers
7 about a construction site
8 about your bags at an airport
9 about fire
10 about a small vehicle that transports heavy things
11 about mobile (cell) phones
12 for visitors to an office or a factory

> That's sign C (D, L, …).

R/P **B** Make two lists. Which signs say things you *must/have to do* and which signs say things you *mustn't do*?

must/have to	mustn't
sign N, …	sign A, …

P **C** Make sentences about the signs. Use the verbs and phrases below.

Sign A means you mustn't smoke.

> use • smoke • wear • leave • be careful because there is/are … • break • go • park your car • stop • drive faster than

Wear a face shield

▸ electricity   ▸ lorry   ▸ to transport   ▸ to break

52 Do's and don'ts

5

> Check-in > Training > Language > Check-out

A — This is a no smoking area
B — No mobile phones
C — No parking
D — STOP
E — 20
F — Danger 11,000 Volts
G — Caution Fork-lift trucks
H — Construction site / Keep out
I — Caution Wet floor
J — In case of fire break glass
K — Wear goggles
L — Use ear protectors
M — SECURITY DO NOT LEAVE BAGS/PROPERTY UNATTENDED
N — All visitors must report to reception

Must und have to

I			have to	don't have to
he she it	must	mustn't	?	?
we you they			have to	don't have to

Can you give the missing forms?

▸ caution   ▸ danger   ▸ in case of (fire)   ▸ Keep out!

Do's and don'ts

3 An e-zine article

R **A** Read the article and find out ...

1 What jobs does it name? Make a list. (Tip: there are nine.)
2 Which job does the article say is the most dangerous?

R **B** True or false? Note down T or F.

1 Police officers and firefighters have the most dangerous jobs in the USA.
2 Fishers in Alaska work long hours and in terrible weather.
3 The people who build skyscrapers are called steel workers.
4 Small planes are safe but big passenger planes are dangerous.
5 Cycle couriers in New York often travel in cars or trucks.
6 Per 100,000 truck drivers, around 25 die every year in accidents.

P **C** Why are the people's jobs in the article dangerous? Make sentences.

Timber cutters have a dangerous job because they sometimes have to work high in the air and ...

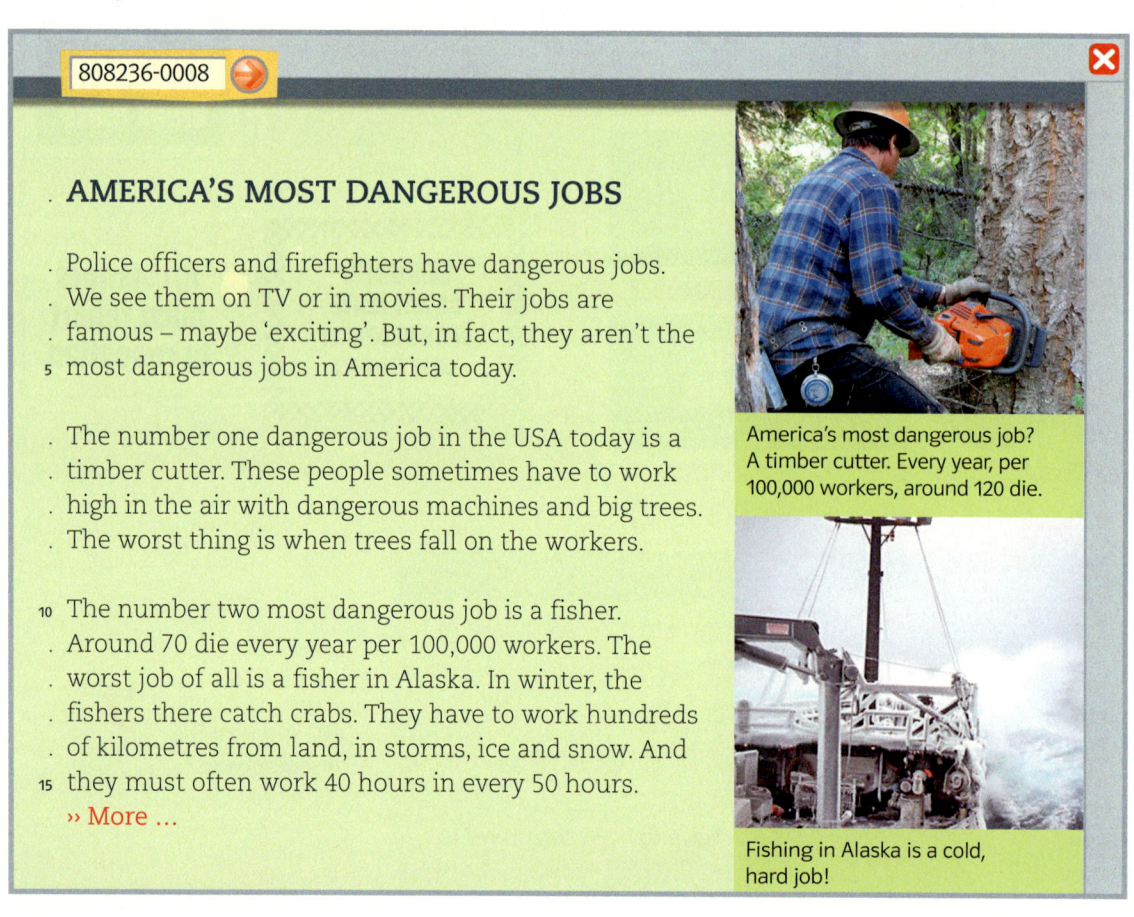

808236-0008

AMERICA'S MOST DANGEROUS JOBS

Police officers and firefighters have dangerous jobs. We see them on TV or in movies. Their jobs are famous – maybe 'exciting'. But, in fact, they aren't the most dangerous jobs in America today.

The number one dangerous job in the USA today is a timber cutter. These people sometimes have to work high in the air with dangerous machines and big trees. The worst thing is when trees fall on the workers.

The number two most dangerous job is a fisher. Around 70 die every year per 100,000 workers. The worst job of all is a fisher in Alaska. In winter, the fishers there catch crabs. They have to work hundreds of kilometres from land, in storms, ice and snow. And they must often work 40 hours in every 50 hours.
›› More ...

America's most dangerous job? A timber cutter. Every year, per 100,000 workers, around 120 die.

Fishing in Alaska is a cold, hard job!

▶ dangerous   ▶ per (100,000)   ▶ to catch

Do's and don'ts

| Check-in | Training | Language | Check-out | 5 |

There are other dangerous jobs too …

Steel workers in the States build skyscrapers and they must work very high in the air. Every year, around 60 (per 100,000) fall and die. Pilots also have a dangerous
20 job. The big passenger planes we fly in are very safe, but every year around 70 pilots die in small planes. One of the most dangerous jobs for a pilot is a crop sprayer. They must fly fast and very low. One mistake can kill them.

25 Finally, the other most dangerous jobs in America are on the roads. Traffic is always dangerous. In New York, cycle couriers deliver thousands of letters and packages every day to offices in the city. They have to work fast and they often hold cars and trucks with
30 their hands so that they can go faster. Lots of them die or have bad accidents. But the most dangerous job on the roads is to be a truck driver. Every year, around 25 per 100,000 die in an accident. The worst thing is when drivers work too long hours. Then they fall
35 asleep on the road.

Truck drivers, crop sprayers and steel workers also have dangerous jobs.

P/I D Talk about these office workers.

It's morning in New York. These office workers are in the subway. They're 'commuters' and they're travelling to work. Think about their job. What's different for an office worker? Make sentences.
Office workers don't have a dangerous job.
They don't have to work in ice and snow on a small boat.
They don't have to …

Hier und dort

Amerika ist das Land der Autos – außer in New York: Nur knapp 48 % der New Yorker besitzen ein Auto. Lieblings-Transportmittel in New York ist die U-Bahn *(subway)*. Über fünf Millionen Menschen benutzen sie täglich.

▶ high in the air   ▶ safe   ▶ low   ▶ finally   ▶ commuter

Do's and don'ts

4 Language practice

Must/have to, mustn't und don't have to → Grammar summary 8

Mit *must/have to*, *mustn't* und *don't have to* wird ausgedrückt, was man muss, nicht darf und nicht zu tun braucht. Vorsicht, denn es wird im Deutschen anders ausgedrückt!

must/have to = müssen
mustn't = nicht dürfen
don't have to = nicht brauchen

I **must/have to** come to college five days a week.
I **mustn't** smoke in the classroom.
I **don't have to** go to college on Sundays.

Bildung:
Must und *mustn't* bleiben bei allen Personen gleich.

	must	mustn't
I he/she/it we/you/they	must	mustn't

	have to	don't have to
I	have to	don't have to
he/she/it	has to	doesn't have to
we you they	have to	don't have to

P **A** *Must/has to* or *doesn't have to*? Finish the text about Ed.

Ed is an office worker in New York. From Monday to Friday he (1) … travel to work on the subway. He (2) … wear a suit and a tie and he (3) … work from 9 a.m. to 5 p.m. in his office. But Saturday and Sunday are different. Ed (4) … travel on the subway and he (5) … wear a suit or a tie. In the summer, he usually goes to the beach on Coney Island. He swims in the sea and relaxes. He (6) … work. It's great!

from Monday to Friday

at the weekend

P **B** Make true sentences about YOU with *must* or *mustn't*.

1 When I go out in the evening, my mum or dad often says: "You … come home too late!"
2 My English teacher often says: "You … speak English, please!"
3 The smokers at my college … smoke outside.
4 At lots of college in Germany, students … use their mobile phones in class.

R **C WORDS** Find words in this unit which mean the opposite.

1 dirty   *clean*
2 start
3 safe
4 low
5 best
6 slow(ly)
7 to relax
8 terrible

> Check-in   > Training   > Language   > **Check-out**   **5**

5 Activities

P A What are the rules at your college?

Two American students are visiting your college this month. They want to know the rules at the college. Write **five** important rules for them. Use *we must* and *we mustn't*. Here are some ideas:

- smoking
- mobile phones
- clothes
- tests
- food and drink
- lesson times
- classrooms
- teachers
- homework
- books/pens etc.
- MP3 players
- bikes/cars/motor bikes
- weekends

Rule 1: *We must(n't)* …
Rule 2: …

∗ P B What's different in Germany?

You're in an international chat room. Some young Americans are talking about life in the USA. Write about life in Germany. What's different for you? Write full sentences (about 70 words). Use *must/have to*, *mustn't* and *don't have to*.

bigapplegirl	In the USA you must be 21 before you can buy alcohol.
kansasguy	Smoking in the States is a real bad thing! People mustn't smoke in offices, restaurants, movie theaters or bars. Smokers have to go outside to smoke!
gonzo213	Most restaurants close early in the States. You usually have to go home at 10pm.
digitaldave	We have traffic lights here in the states with WALK or DON'T WALK – you know, to cross the street on foot. But nobody waits! Everybody just runs!
roadman	You must be 16 in the States before you can drive an automobile. And in most states, the maximum speed on highways is 65 miles per hour (about 110 kilometres per hour, I think). You mustn't drive faster. There are lots of speed cops!

P C REVISION Give the correct forms of the adjectives.

1. **(dangerous):** A truck driver's job in the States is *dangerous*, but a fisher's job is … than a truck driver's. The … job in America is to be a timber cutter.
2. **(young/old):** Greg is 16, Zack is 18 and Louise is 20. Zack is … than Greg but he's … than Louise. Louise is the … of the three, Greg is …
3. **(good):** My job is … It's … than your job! In fact, I think it's the … job in the world.

Do's and don'ts **57**

Unit 6
Success stories

Am Ende dieser Unit kann ich ...
→ mitteilen, seit wann etwas schon andauert,
→ über Erfolgsgeschichten reden und schreiben.

1 A new life

R A Read about Lukasz and answer the questions.

Lukasz Nowak was born in Poland. But in 2005, when he was 24, he moved to England. He now lives in a town in England called Danbury. Lukasz worked in Danbury first as a plumber. Then three years ago, he started his own small building firm. He now has six employees. His firm is very successful. Everybody in Danbury knows 'Lucas'.

1 Where was Lukasz born?
2 When did he move to England?
3 What town in England does he live in?
4 What was Lukasz's first job in Danbury?
5 What did he do three years ago?
6 What is Lukasz's English name?

▶ to move   ▶ (his) own (firm)   ▶ employee

Hier und dort

Großbritannien ist ein multikulturelles Land – in London werden über 300 verschiedene Sprachen gesprochen. In den 1960er Jahren wanderten viele Menschen aus Indien, Pakistan, China oder der Karibik ein. Seit 2004 gibt es auch viele Einwanderer aus Mitteleuropa – wie Lukasz.

> Check-in   > Training   > Language   > Check-out   **6**

Local success story

16 July, 2…

Do you need a plumber? What about new windows? A patio in your garden maybe? Then ring Lucas Nowak.

Lucas is from Poland – his real name is Lukasz. But he has lived in Danbury since 2005. And he has had his own building firm here for three years.

"When I first came to England," says Lucas "I wanted to stay maybe a year or two just to earn some money. But now I want to stay in Danbury. The people are very friendly and my new life here is very good."

Lucas Nowak has been in Danbury since 2005 – and he wants to stay.

R B The article above is from the local newspaper in Danbury. Look at the article and find the missing verbs for the diagram below.

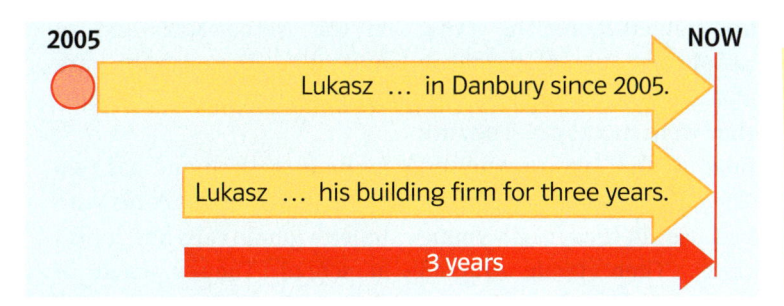

2005 → NOW

Lukasz … in Danbury since 2005.

Lukasz … his building firm for three years.

3 years

Tips and tricks

since 2005 = Zeitpunkt
for three years = Zeitraum

Vorsicht! Auf Deutsch heißen *since* und *for* beide ‚seit'!

M C Your friend wants to know about the article but (s)he doesn't speak English. Give the most important ideas in German.

▸ local   ▸ to ring (somebody)   ▸ to earn money

Success stories **59**

6

> Check-in > **Training** > Language > Check-out

2 A magazine article

A Read this magazine article about a famous British chef. Find out …

1 Why was Jamie no good at school?
2 Who are the young people with Jamie in the photo at the top?
3 Who is the woman with him in the second photo?

No good at school but great at his job

Jamie Oliver makes cooking cool. He's famous now and he's often on TV – and not just in Britain but around the world. But Jamie wasn't a good pupil at school! Here's his success story.

Jamie was born in the south-east of England in 1975. His mum and dad had a pub and Jamie started helping in the kitchen there when he was eight. School was hard for Jamie – he's dyslexic – but after school, when he was 16, he went to a college in London and trained to be a chef. Jamie was a brilliant college student. He left college in 1992. He worked in some famous restaurants in France, and then in London. In 1998, a British TV company made a film about one of the London restaurants. Everybody saw Jamie on TV and soon he was the star of the show. Jamie Oliver, the unsuccessful pupil, was famous!

Jamie opened his first restaurant in London in 2002 – but it wasn't a normal restaurant. He found 15 unemployed young people and trained them. The young people had lots of problems and it was hard work, but they were successful. They are now chefs in the restaurant. The restaurant is called *Fifteen* because there were 15 young chefs. Then Jamie trained more young people in a town in the south-west of England,

Jamie and Jools

in the Netherlands and in Australia. Now there are *Fifteen* restaurants there, too.

Jamie is married and has two children. He first met his wife Juliette (Jamie calls her 'Jools') at school. They married in 2000. Their daughters are called Daisy and Poppy.

▸ to train to be a …   ▸ chef   ▸ to leave (college)   ▸ unemployed

> Check-in   > **Training**   > Language   > Check-out   **6**

R **B Which is right? Note down a, b or c.**

1 Jamie Oliver was born
   a in the north of England.
   b in the south-west of England.
   c in the south-east of England.
2 He first worked in a kitchen
   a at school.
   b in his parents' pub.
   c at college.
3 Jamie trained to be a chef
   a in London.
   b in France.
   c in the USA.
4 He was first on TV
   a in 1975.
   b in 1987.
   c in 1998.
5 Jamie trained 15 … people for his *Fifteen* restaurant in London.
   a successful young
   b unemployed old
   c unemployed young
6 Jamie now has *Fifteen* restaurants in … countries.
   a two
   b three
   c four
7 Jamie first met his wife … and they have …
   a in 2000 / three children.
   b at college / two children.
   c at school / two children.

P **C Finish the *How long …?* sentences about Jamie.**

	Then	Now	How long …?
1	Jamie first worked as a chef in 1992.	He works as a chef now.	He *has* worked as a chef *since* 1992.
2	Jamie was first famous in 1998.	He's famous now.	He … been famous … 1998.
3	Jamie had his first *Fifteen* restaurant in London in 2002.	He has a *Fifteen* restaurant in London now.	He … a *Fifteen* restaurant in London … 2002.
4	He had his first *Fifteen* restaurant in Australia in 2006.	He has a *Fifteen* restaurant in Australia now.	He has had a *Fifteen* restaurant in Australia for … years.
5	Jamie married Jools in 2000.	He's married to Jools now.	He has been married to Jools … years.

I **D Ask another student in your class.**

> How long has Jamie Oliver worked as a chef?

> He has worked as a chef since …

> How long has he …?

> He has …

Das present perfect		
I	have	worked
he/she/it	?	been
we		lived
you	?	had
they		

Can you give the missing forms?

▸ successful   ▸ to marry   ▸ to be married to (someone)

Success stories **61**

6 | Check-in | Training | Language | Check-out

3 We have our own firm!

R A Read about Kate, Annie and Ruth.

1. Where do they live?
2. Where were they all students?
3. What did they do after college?
4. What does their firm do?

Kate (photo), Annie (photo), Ruth (photo)

Kate, Annie and Ruth live in Danbury in England – the same town as Lukasz Nowak. They were all students – and best friends – at Danbury FE college. When they left college, they started their own firm in the town. It's called PartyPeople. The firm organises parties (with food and music) for schools, local firms and local kids.

R/P B A reporter from the Danbury newspaper is interviewing Kate, Annie and Ruth about their firm. He has these questions for them. Listen and find the answers.

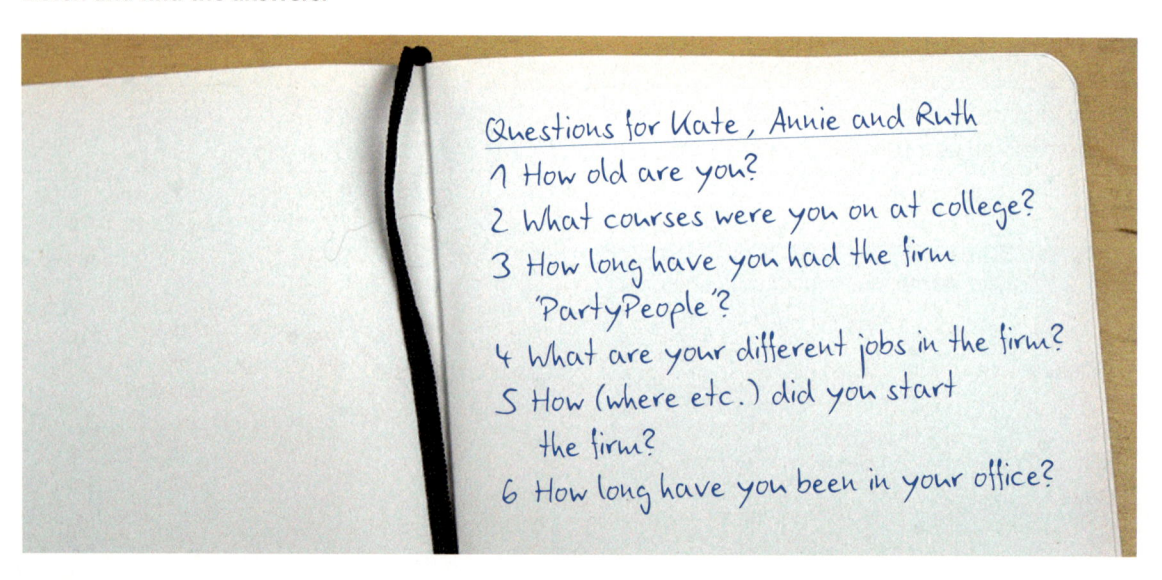

1|19

Questions for Kate, Annie and Ruth
1. How old are you?
2. What courses were you on at college?
3. How long have you had the firm 'PartyPeople'?
4. What are your different jobs in the firm?
5. How (where etc.) did you start the firm?
6. How long have you been in your office?

▶ cookery   ▶ electronics   ▶ customer

62 Success stories

> Check-in   > **Training**   > Language   > Check-out   **6**

R/P **C** You're the reporter now. Finish your article about Kate, Annie and Ruth.

Three Danbury women and their successful company

Do you want a party? Do you need food? Music? The local firm PartyPeople can organise everything for you!

Kate, Annie and Ruth are now **(1)** … years old. They were all friends and students at **(2)** … College. Kate was on a **(3)** … course, Annie on a **(4)** … course and Ruth wanted to be a **(5)** … When they left college, they started their firm, *PartyPeople*. They have had the firm now for **(6)** … years.

The three women all have different jobs in the company. **(7)** … is the 'businesswoman', **(8)** … is the disk jockey who plays the music, and **(9)** … cooks all the food for the parties.

PartyPeople is very successful now. But it was small when it started. At first, Kate, Annie and Ruth organised the parties and cooked the food in Kate's **(10)** … Now the three women use an old pizzeria in Danbury. They cook the food in the kitchen and the **(11)** … is their office. They have been in the pizzeria for **(12)** … years.

I/P **D** Interview your partner.

1 First copy and fill in the form for YOU.
2 Then interview a partner. Write in your partner's answers.
3 Write a short text about your partner.

My partner … (name) lives in …
(S)he's lived there for/since …

		YOU	Your partner
1	What street do you live in? How long have you lived there?		
2	What's your favourite band? How long have you liked it?		
3	What's your favourite piece of clothing? How long have you had it?		
4	Do you have a car, a bike or a scooter? How long have you had it?		
5	How long have you learned English?		

▶ to organise   ▶ to fill in a form   ▶ piece of clothing

So läuft's besser

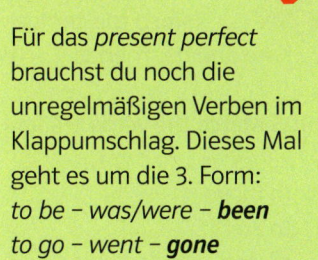

Für das *present perfect* brauchst du noch die unregelmäßigen Verben im Klappumschlag. Dieses Mal geht es um die 3. Form:
*to be – was/were – **been***
*to go – went – **gone***

Success stories

4 Language practice

Das present perfect mit *for* und *since* → Grammar summary 4

„Wie lange"-Fragen (*How long …?*) sind mit dem present perfect und *for* oder *since* zu beantworten:
How long have you lived here?
– *I have lived here **for** two years / **since** 2006.*

Merke Dir den Unterschied zwischen *for* und *since*:
Since wird mit einem Zeitpunkt (z. B. *2006*) verwendet, *for* mit einem Zeitraum (z. B. *two years*).

Bildung:
Das present perfect wird mit *have/has* und der 3. Form des Verbs gebildet.

I **have**	been
he/she/it **has**	lived
we/you/they **have**	

Fragen:
*How long **have** you **lived** here?*
*How long **has** he **had** his own firm?*
*How long **have** they **been** friends?*

P A *For* or *since*? Finish the sentences.

1 Lukasz has lived in England … 2005.
2 Jamie Oliver has been a famous chef … over 20 years.
3 He has been married to Jools … 2000.
4 Kate, Annie and Ruth have had their own firm … five years now.
5 How long have you lived here? – I have lived here … 15 years.
6 How long have you had your bike? – I have had it … August.

P B In sentences a, b and c, one verb is in the *simple present*, one in the *simple past*, and one in the *present perfect*. Give the right forms.

1 a Lukasz *lives* **(live)** in Danbury.
  b He *moved* **(move)** to Danbury in 2005.
  c He … **(live)** in Danbury since 2005.
2 a Jamie Oliver … **(leave)** college in 1992.
  b He … **(be)** a chef now.
  c He … **(be)** a chef since 1992.
3 a Kate … **(have)** her own company for five years.
  b She … **(start)** the company with two friends five years ago.
  c Kate and her friends … **(work)** together now in the firm.

P C WORDS Match the verbs 1–6 and the phrases A–F.

1	to move	A	your own company
2	to start	B	to be a plumber
3	to ring	C	school or college
4	to leave	D	to a country
5	to train	E	your boyfriend/girlfriend
6	to marry	F	someone on their mobile

Success stories

> Check-in   > Training   > Language   > **Check-out**   **6**

5 Activities

P **A** You are chatting to a buddy in England with Instant Messenger. Write your answers to her questions. Write full sentences. Think of a screen name for yourself.

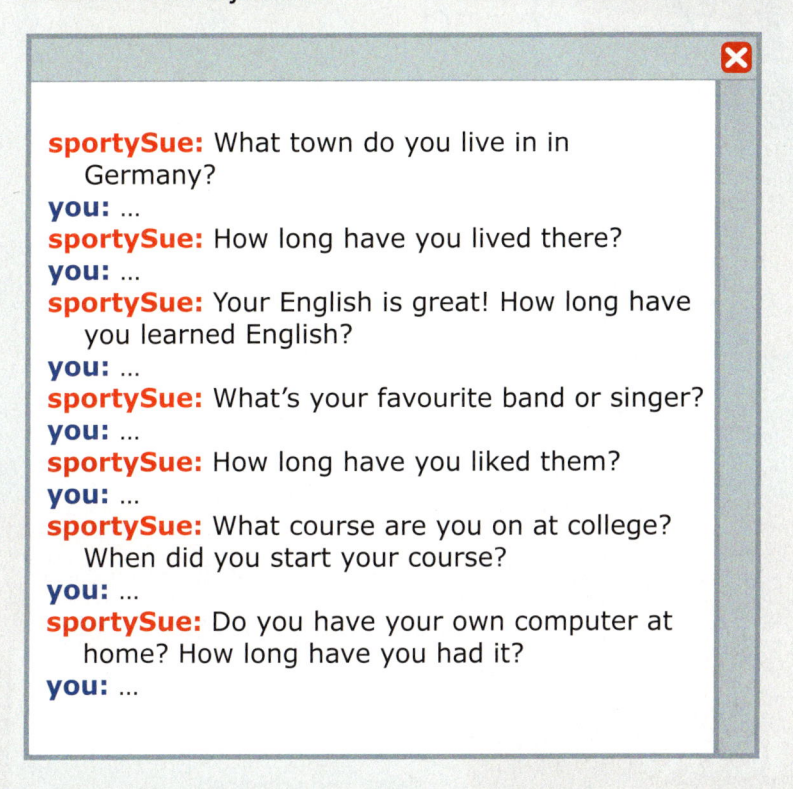

> **sportySue:** What town do you live in in Germany?
> **you:** …
> **sportySue:** How long have you lived there?
> **you:** …
> **sportySue:** Your English is great! How long have you learned English?
> **you:** …
> **sportySue:** What's your favourite band or singer?
> **you:** …
> **sportySue:** How long have you liked them?
> **you:** …
> **sportySue:** What course are you on at college? When did you start your course?
> **you:** …
> **sportySue:** Do you have your own computer at home? How long have you had it?
> **you:** …

* P **B** Do you know a success story? Write the story in full sentences in about 100 words. It can be about:

- a famous person,
- someone in your family,
- someone you know,
- a friend.

P **C REVISION** Can you give all the missing forms in the table?

to be	was/were	(1)	to go	(8)	gone
to come	(2)	come	to have	(9)	(10)
to do	(3)	done	(11)	made	made
to drink	drank	(4)	to ring	(12)	rung
(5)	ate	eaten	to sing	sang	(13)
to find	(6)	found	to speak	spoke	(14)
to fly	(7)	flown	(15)	wrote	written

→ List of irregular verbs: Klappumschlag

How do you see your life in 10 years?

1. I'll be married.
   Yes No Don't know

2. I'll have a good job.
   Yes No Don't know

3. I'll still live in the town/city where I live now.
   Yes No Don't know

Unit 7
Looking ahead

Am Ende dieser Unit kann ich …
→ über mein Leben in der Zukunft reden und schreiben,
→ über meine Pläne für die Zukunft reden und schreiben.

1 Four American teenagers look ahead

R/P **A** Maddy and her friend Isabella are college students in the US. They're answering questions in an online survey called: *How do you see your life in 10 years?* What are the girls' answers?

1. Do they think they'll be married in ten years?
2. Do they think they'll have a good job?
3. Do they think they'll still live in the town where they live now?

They think … / They don't think … / They don't …

P **B** What about YOU? Do you think you'll be married in ten years from now? Will you have a good job? What about your town or city?

▸ survey   ▸ still   ▸ in 10 years

66 Looking ahead

Check-in   Training   Language   Check-out   **7**

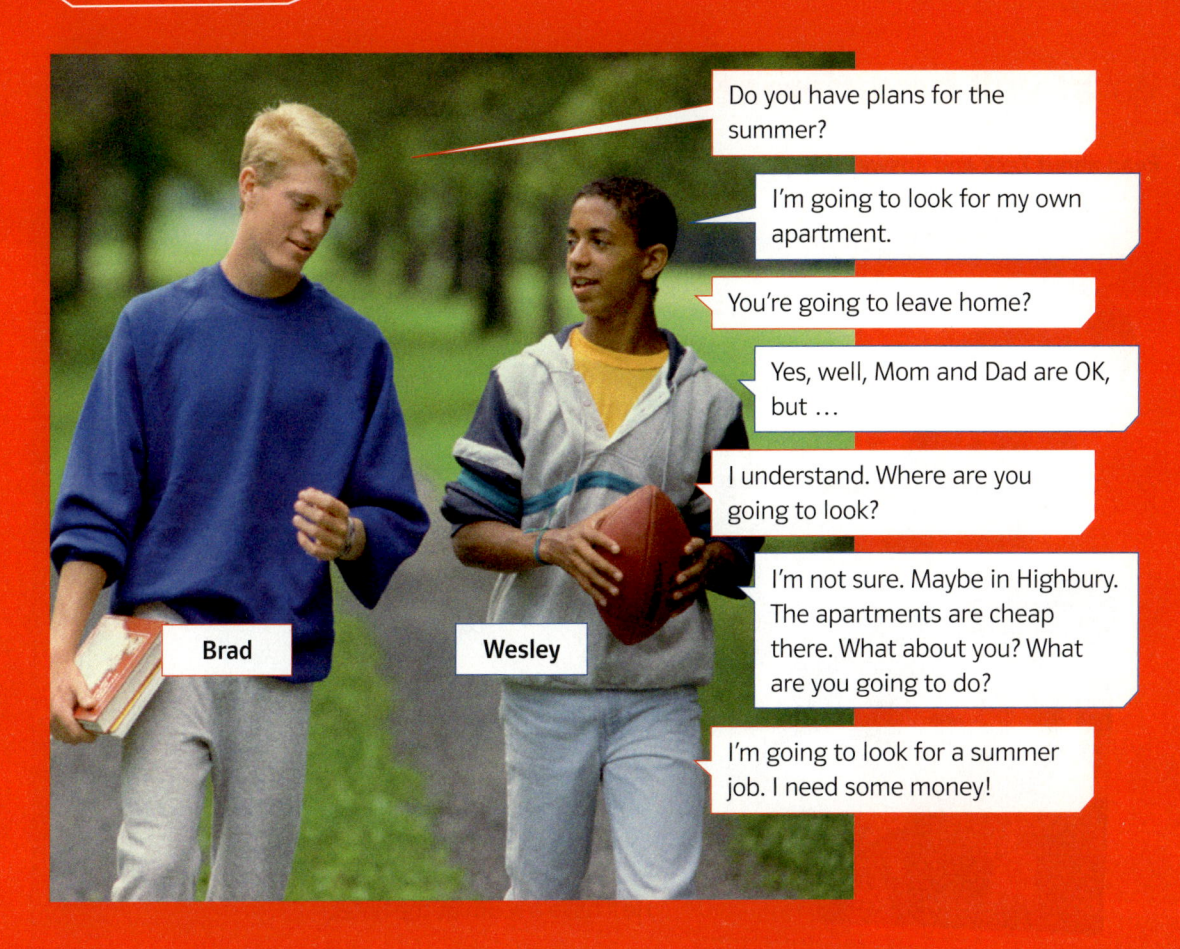

Do you have plans for the summer?

I'm going to look for my own apartment.

You're going to leave home?

Yes, well, Mom and Dad are OK, but …

I understand. Where are you going to look?

I'm not sure. Maybe in Highbury. The apartments are cheap there. What about you? What are you going to do?

I'm going to look for a summer job. I need some money!

Brad   Wesley

R C Brad and Wesley are college friends too.
They are talking about their next summer vacation.
Read the conversation. Who's this?

1. He's going to look for a summer job.
2. He isn't going to look for a summer job.
3. He's going to leave home.
4. He's going to look for his own apartment.
5. He needs some money.

Tips and tricks

to look **ahead**	vorausschauen
to look **for**	suchen
to look **at**	(etwas) ansehen
to look **after**	für jmdn./etwas sorgen
to look … **up**	(etwas) nachschlagen

P/I D What about YOU? Do you have plans for your summer vacation? What are you going to do? Tell the class. Here are some ideas.

- to do nothing (to chill out!)
- to work
- to stay at home
- to visit people in your family
- to travel

▸ apartment (US)   ▸ summer vacation (US)   ▸ to leave home

Looking ahead   **67**

7

> Check-in   > **Training**   > Language   > Check-out

2 What will be different?

R **A** Read about Zack and answer the questions below.

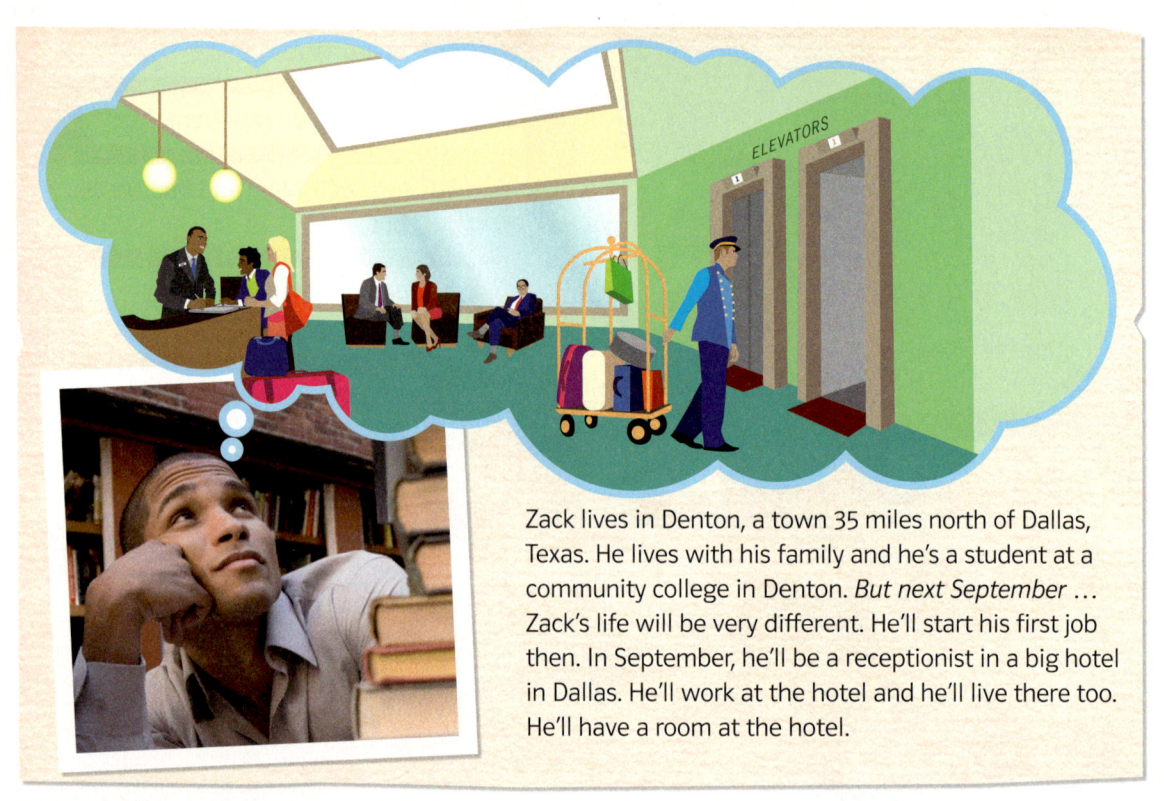

Zack lives in Denton, a town 35 miles north of Dallas, Texas. He lives with his family and he's a student at a community college in Denton. *But next September …* Zack's life will be very different. He'll start his first job then. In September, he'll be a receptionist in a big hotel in Dallas. He'll work at the hotel and he'll live there too. He'll have a room at the hotel.

1 Where does Zack live now?
2 Does he have an apartment?
3 Does he have a job now?
4 What will Zack do next September?
5 What will his job be then?

P **B** How will Zack's life be different next September? Make sentences like this.

Zack is a student now. But he won't be a student next September. He'll be a hotel receptionist.
Zack … now. But …

I **C** Zack's two college friends Jay and Hunter will also start their first job next September. But what job will they have? What will they do? Work with a partner and find out.

Partner B: Please look at page 156 now.
Partner A: You have information on the next page about Jay. Answer your partner's questions. Then ask questions and find the missing information about Hunter.

▸ north of   ▸ to be different   ▸ elevator

68 Looking ahead

> Check-in   > **Training**   > Language   > Check-out   **7**

Name	Jay Rishi
Job?	He'll be a journalist.
Where?	He'll work at a newspaper in Denton.
Live?	in an apartment in Denton
Do?	He'll interview people and he'll write articles for the paper.
Wages?	He'll earn $500 a week.
Hours?	Monday–Friday, 10 a.m. to 6.30 p.m.
Ideas about work?	He thinks he'll be a bit nervous at first. But the best thing is he'll earn his own money.

Name	*Hunter Glenn*
Job?	
Where?	
Live?	
Do?	
Wages?	
Hours?	
Ideas about work?	

- What job will Hunter have?
- When will he work?
- What does he think about work?
- Where will he work/live?
- How much will he earn?

P **D** Write a short text about Jay or Hunter. Start like this:

(Jay) is a student now but next September his life will be very different. He won't be a student, he'll be a …

I **E** Talk in class.

What are your ideas about work? Do you think you will be nervous about your first job? Will it be interesting? Hard?
What will be the best (and worst!) things about work?

Will ('ll) und *won't*		
I'll	I won't	
he'll	he **?**	
?	she won't	live
it'll	it won't	work
we'll	**?**	be
?	you won't	
they'll	**?**	

Can you give the missing forms? **?**

▸ wages ▸ to earn ($500) a week ▸ nervous

Looking ahead **69**

7

> Check-in   > **Training**   > Language   > Check-out

3 Plans for an apartment

R A Erin has a new job – and her first apartment. What are her plans for the apartment? First match the words and the pictures A–O, then listen and answer the questions below.

> a houseplant • a lamp • some candles • an exercise bike •
> a coffee table • a sofa • a wall cupboard • a mirror •
> a beanbag • a CD tower • a wardrobe • a bedside cupboard •
> an armchair • a rug • a computer desk

R B Which is right – a, b, c or d?

1 Erin's apartment has a living room, a bathroom, a kitchen and …
   a one bedroom.   b two bedrooms.   c three bedrooms.   d four bedrooms.
2 She's going to paint the walls of her apartment …
   a white.   b blue.   c green.   d red.
3 In the living room, she's going to have a sofa, a coffee table, an armchair, her CD tower and a big …
   a wall cupboard.   b TV.   c lamp.   d DVD player.
4 Erin is going to put her computer and a computer desk in the …
   a living room.   b bedroom.   c bathroom.   d kitchen.
5 Erin likes yoga and she's going to put a rug and some candles in the …
   a living room.   b bedroom.   c bathroom.   d kitchen.
6 She's going to put her … there too.
   a mirror   b lamp   c TV   d exercise bike

▸ cupboard   ▸ to paint something (red)   ▸ to put

70 Looking ahead

| Check-in | Training | Language | Check-out | **7** |

P **C** Now YOU. Imagine that you have the new apartment below.
What are your plans? What colour are you going to paint the walls?
What things are you going to put in the rooms?

1 Note down your plans. You can use the words from exercise A and the other useful words below.
2 Tell the class.

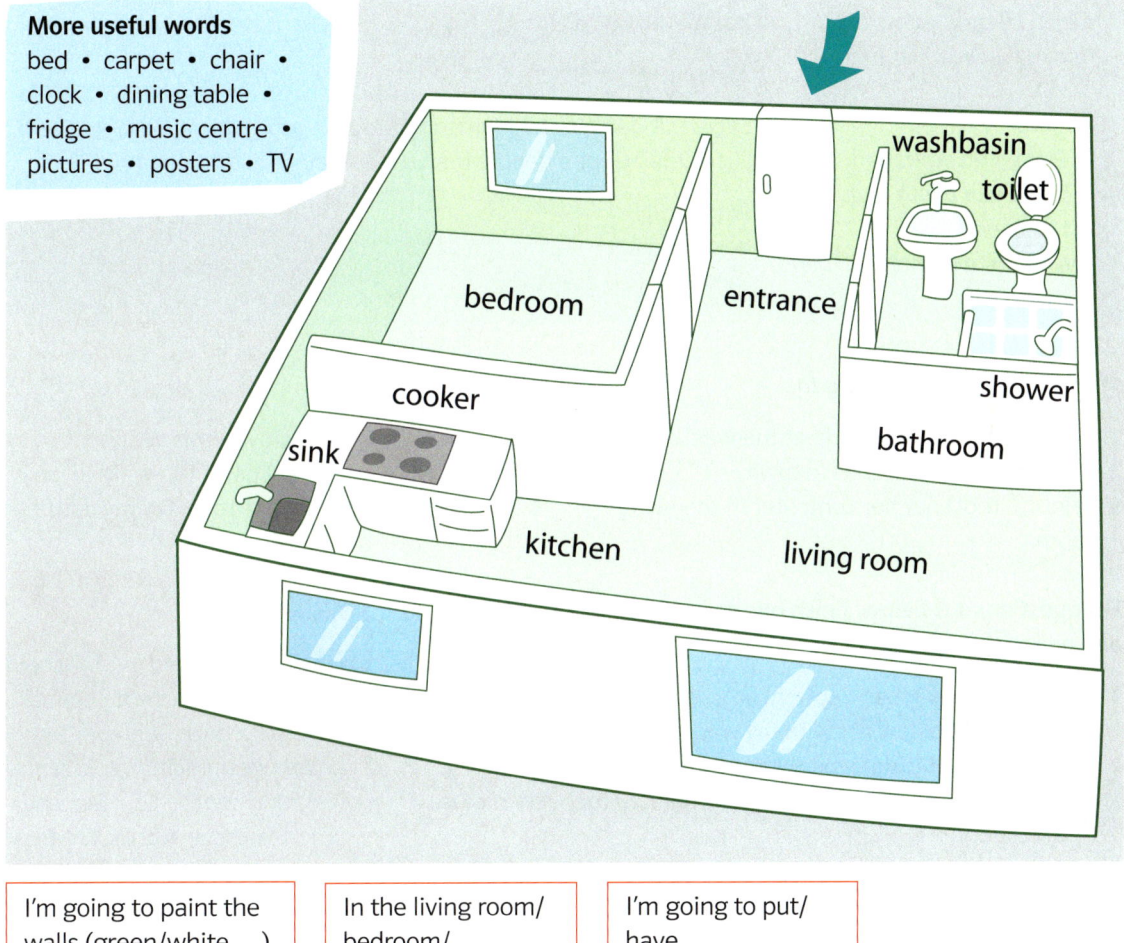

More useful words
bed • carpet • chair • clock • dining table • fridge • music centre • pictures • posters • TV

Labels on apartment diagram: washbasin, toilet, bedroom, entrance, shower, bathroom, cooker, sink, kitchen, living room

I'm going to paint the walls (green/white …).

In the living room/bedroom/…

I'm going to put/have …

going to		
I'm	I'm not	
?	he isn't	
she's	?	
it's	it isn't	going to
we're	?	
you're	?	
?	they aren't	

Can you give the missing forms?

▶ sink ▶ washbasin ▶ shower ▶ fridge

Looking ahead **71**

7 | Check-in | Training | Language | Check-out

4 Language practice

Das Futur → Grammar summary 6 7

Will
Für Tatsachen, Vorhersagen und Vermutungen:
In 2020 **I'll be** 30 years old.
I think **I'll have** a job then.

Will und won't bleiben in allen Personen unverändert:

I will ('ll)	I won't
he/she/it will ('ll)	he/she/it won't
we/you/they will ('ll)	we/you/they won't

Going to
Für Pläne und Vorhaben:
What **are you going to do** next weekend?
– **I'm going to visit** an old friend.

Sätze mit *going to* bildet man mit *to be* + *going to* + ein zweites Verb.
Für Verneinungen benutzt man die Verneinungsformen von *to be*:

I'm / I'm not he's / he isn't they're / they aren't	going to	visit

---

P A Make sentences with *going to*.

1. What *are you going to* do at the weekend?
2. I … meet some friends in town.
3. Erin … (not) put her computer in the living room.
4. … (your brother) visit you this year?
5. What colour … (they) paint the walls?
6. This evening I … cook a meal for my dad.

P B For questions 1–3 below, finish one sentence (a or b) with *going to* and one with *will*.

1. a I have a new job in September. I … **(be)** a car mechanic.
   b I … **(buy)** a new car with my wages.
2. a What … **(you/do)** next weekend, John?
   b I heard on the radio that the weather … **(be)** very nice next weekend.
3. a Juliette … **(be)** 21 on Tuesday next week.
   b We … **(organise)** a party for her.

> **Hier und dort**
>
> Einige Wörter sind in britischem und amerikanischem Englisch unterschiedlich oder werden anders geschrieben, z. B. *centre* (GB) und *center* (US). Manche amerikanische Wörter wiederum werden in britischem Englisch benutzt, z. B. *Hi* (anstatt *Hello*) oder *movie* (anstatt *film*).

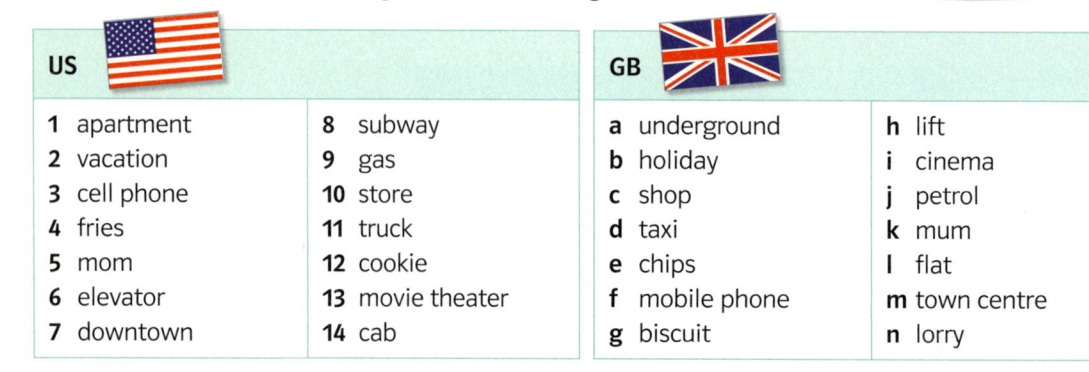

R C WORDS Match the American English and British English words.

US		GB	
1 apartment	8 subway	a underground	h lift
2 vacation	9 gas	b holiday	i cinema
3 cell phone	10 store	c shop	j petrol
4 fries	11 truck	d taxi	k mum
5 mom	12 cookie	e chips	l flat
6 elevator	13 movie theater	f mobile phone	m town centre
7 downtown	14 cab	g biscuit	n lorry

Looking ahead

| Check-in | Training | Language | **Check-out** | **7** |

5 Activities

P A You see this question in an e-zine called *Eupidoo!* It's for young people in Europe. Write an email to the e-zine about your plans. Write 50-70 words. Begin like this:

Dear Eupidoo,
My name's … and I'm from …

> One day you'll have a job – and you'll have some money! So what are you going to do with your money? Are you going to look for a flat? Buy a car? Travel? We want to hear about your plans!

✱ I/P B Look at page 66 again then do a survey in your class called: *How do you see your life in 10 (or 5) years?* Make a graph and write about the answers. Here are some ideas:

> I'll be married • I'll have children • I'll often speak English •
> I'll still live in the town where I live now • I'll travel a lot •
> I'll have my own firm • I'll live with my parents •
> I'll do lots of sport • I'll still like the music I like now • …

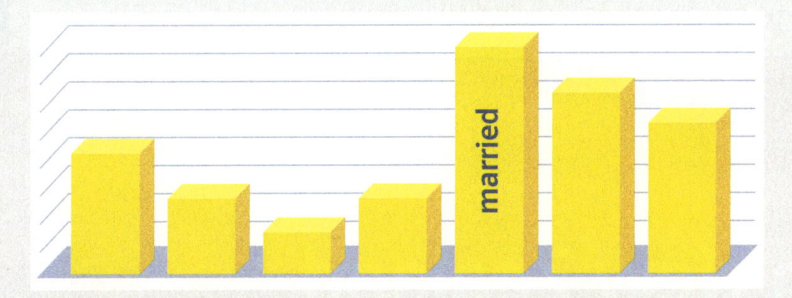

A lot of people / Most people in the class think that they …
Not many people / Only one or two people think that they …
About half / a quarter of the people in the class think that they …
(10) people in the class think that they …
Everybody / Nobody thinks that he or she …

P C REVISION Copy and complete the table with all the different forms of *to work*.

	simple present	simple past	present perfect	*will*	*going to*
I	work	?	?	will work	?
he she it	?	worked	?	?	is going to work
we you they	?	?	have worked	?	?

Looking ahead 73

Sven Heiderich and Daniela Stollenwerk are from Germany. They're apprentices with a big German car company. They usually work in Germany, of course. But their company has workshops around the world, and this month Daniela and Sven are in Christchurch, on the South Island of New Zealand. They're really happy. A month in New Zealand! In Christchurch, they're with Mr MacKenzie and his family. Mr MacKenzie is the manager of the company's workshop there. It's January. In Germany it's very cold. But in New Zealand it's summer. Right now, Daniela and Sven are at a barbecue in Mr MacKenzie's garden.

Unit 8
A month in New Zealand

Am Ende dieser Unit kann ich ...
- über Neuseeland reden und scheiben,
- wichtige Redewendungen im Alltag richtig benutzen.

1 In Christchurch

R/P **A Read about Sven and Daniela and answer the questions below.**

1. What are Sven and Daniela's jobs and where do they usually work?
2. Where are they this month? Who is the man in the photo on the next page.
3. Where are Daniela and Sven right now and what are they doing?

▶ apprentice   ▶ of course   ▶ barbecue

> Check-in   > Training   > Language   > Check-out   **8**

P/R **B** Sven and Daniela are talking to Mr MacKenzie. Read the conversation and choose the best answer a or b. (Correct answers are on page 81.)

Mr MacKenzie	So, do you like New Zealand, Sven?	
Sven	Oh yes, it's **(1)** …	**1 a** great! **b** horrible!
Mr MacKenzie	And what do you think of the Kiwis?	
Sven	**(2)** …	**2 a** They're really friendly. **b** They taste nice.
Mr MacKenzie	Would you like another burger, Daniela?	
Daniela	Oh, no thank you, Mr MacKenzie. I'm **(3)** …	**3 a** fed up! **b** full up!
Mr MacKenzie	And what about you, Sven?	
Sven	**(4)** … They're delicious.	**4 a** Yes, please. **b** No thanks.

P **C** Talk in class. Would you like to go to New Zealand? Could you survive a month in an English-speaking country? What things would be hard – the language, the food, the weather, …?

▶ to be fed up   ▶ to be full up   ▶ delicious   ▶ to survive

A month in New Zealand   **75**

2 About New Zealand

A Before Sven and Daniela went to New Zealand, they looked at this web page. Read the page. Find the best headings A–F for the paragraphs 1–6 in the text.

A Small, beautiful – and famous
B Do you speak Kiwi?
C Sport
D People
E The land of the Kiwis
F Cities

New Zealand

808236-0010

1 _____

Yes, kiwis are a kind of fruit. In fact, lots of the kiwis that we eat come from New Zealand. But a kiwi is also a kind of bird. It lives only in New Zealand. And New Zealanders use the name of the bird for themselves. They say: "I'm a Kiwi. I'm from New Zealand."

2 _____

New Zealand isn't a big country. It's just a bit smaller than Germany. But it's very beautiful, with mountains, lakes and forests. And only about four million people live here. There are 82 million people in Germany!

New Zealand's beautiful mountains are famous now. In 2000, the film director Peter Jackson started making his *Lord Of The Rings* films in New Zealand. So when you see the films, you can see lots of places in New Zealand.

3 _____

The first people in New Zealand were the Maoris. They have lived here for around 1,000 years. Today, about 8 per cent of New Zealanders are Maoris. Europeans have only been in New Zealand since 1768. The first European was Captain Cook from England. After him, lots more English people came. That's why New Zealanders speak English.

4 _____

New Zealanders love sports. There's skiing, swimming, surfing, canoeing, mountain climbing and lots more. One of the most popular sports is rugby. Before a match, the New Zealand rugby team always does a Maori war dance. It's called a 'Haka' and it's very frightening! People also come to New Zealand for another famous sport – bungee jumping.

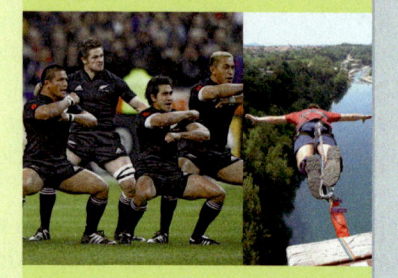

▶ heading ▶ paragraph ▶ a kind of ▶ frightening

76 A month in New Zealand

> Check-in   > **Training**   > Language   > Check-out   **8**

5 _____

. New Zealand doesn't have a lot of
. big cities. The biggest city is Auckland
. on the North Island. About
30 1.3 million people live there. But
. Auckland isn't the capital of New
. Zealand. That's Wellington. About
. 450,000 people live in Wellington.

6 _____

. When New Zealanders speak English, they have a 'Kiwi'
35 accent. It's almost the same as the accent of people from
. Australia. They have some kiwi words and phrases, too.
. *Hello* is *G'day* (like in Australia). On the beach, people often
. wear *jandals* – in Britain they're *flip-flops*. And, of course,
. everyone in New Zealand loves a *barbie*: a barbecue.

R **B** Finish the sentences below with information from the text.

1 The word 'Kiwi' is the name that New Zealanders use for themselves. It's also a bird and …
2 New Zealand isn't a big country. In fact, it's … than Germany.
3 Peter Jackson is a film director. He started making the *Lord Of The Rings* movies in New Zealand in …
4 The Maoris have lived in New Zealand for …
5 Europeans have been in New Zealand since …
6 New Zealanders speak English today because …
7 One of the favourite sports in New Zealand is … and before a match the national team does a … called a 'Haka'.
8 The biggest city in New Zealand is Auckland but the capital is …
9 The Kiwi accent is almost the same as …
10 The Kiwi word for *flip-flops* is …

R **C** Find words in the text for …

1 a kind of fruit
2 a person who makes films
3 a language
4 seven kinds of sport
5 a kind of dance
6 the most important city in a country
7 something you wear on your feet

So läuft's besser

Längere Lese- oder Hörtexte scheinen oft nur auf den ersten Blick schwierig. Keine Panik!
• Verschaffe dir zunächst einen groben Überblick über den Text: Schaue dir die Bilder und Überschriften an. Lese den ersten und letzten Satz.
• Lies (oder höre) danach den Text zweimal. Versuche, unbekannte Wörter aus dem Zusammenhang zu erschließen. Nimm erst dann das Wörterbuch zur Hand.

P **D** Talk about the text. What facts did you know already? What didn't you know? What was the most interesting thing in the text for you?

► capital   ► accent   ► match   ► team

A month in New Zealand **77**

8 | Check-in | Training | Language | Check-out

3 Be polite, please.

P **A** Sven and Daniela have to speak English every day in New Zealand. Look at the three pictures below. Where do you think they are? What are they doing?

R **B** You will hear three conversations. Listen and match the conversations (1–3) and the pictures (A–C).

1|22

P/R **C** What are the missing phrases in the three conversations? Note down your answers, then listen again and check.

1|22

1   Mrs MacKenzie   (1) … some more pancakes, Daniela?
    Daniela   Yes, please, Mrs MacKenzie. They're delicious.
    Mrs MacKenzie   Here you are.
    Daniela   (2) …
    Mrs MacKenzie   Sven? What about you?
    Sven   They're fantastic, but I'm afraid I'm absolutely full up!
    Mr MacKenzie   What about some orange juice?
    Sven   Mmm, yes, please. (3) …

2   Daniela   Excuse me, Mrs MacKenzie. (4) …
    Mrs MacKenzie   Sure. What's the problem, Daniela?
    Daniela   Well, it's really hot in the day but it's cold at night. (5) … another blanket for my bed, please?
    Mrs MacKenzie   (6) … Come on. Let's get one now.

> Could you help me, please? • Pardon? • Of course. • That would be nice. • What does … • Thank you. • Would you like … • I understand now. • Could I have … • Would you two like …

▶ pancake(s)   ▶ blanket   ▶ absolutely (full up)   ▶ Let's …

A month in New Zealand

3 Ben G'day, guys. How are you this morning?
Sven G'day, Ben. We're fine, thanks.
Ben Hey, listen. Some of us are going to go to the beach after work tomorrow. **(7)** … to come?
Daniela Yeah, cool. Thanks.
Ben Do you have togs?
Sven **(8)** …
Ben Do you have *togs*?
Sven Sorry, I don't understand. **(9)** … 'togs' mean?
Ben Sorry, yeah, it's a Kiwi word. It means, you know, a swimsuit.
Daniela Oh, right. **(10)** … Yes, I have togs.
Sven Me too.
Ben Great. See you then.

P/I **D** Work in small groups. Practise the conversations.

R **E** Match the phrases 1–5 with a correct answer A–G. There's sometimes more than one answer.

1	Would you like …?	A	It means, you know, …
2	Here you are.	B	Of course.
3	Could you help me, please?	C	Thank you.
		D	Yes, please. That would be nice.
4	Could I …?	E	Cool! Thanks.
5	What does … mean?	F	Sure. What's the problem?
		G	I'm afraid I'm absolutely full up!

P/I **F** Now YOU. Work in your groups again. Write another conversation, then read it to the class. Use the phrases on these two pages. Here are some ideas:

breakfast/lunch/dinner
toast • coffee • milk • soup • bread • dessert • potatoes

Could you help me, please?
• phone your parents
• have a shower
• borrow some 'jandals'
• go to the beach/cinema with some friends

Hier und dort

Wenn Deutsche Englisch sprechen, wird es von Muttersprachlern oft als sehr direkt und vielleicht etwas unhöflich empfunden. Um diesen Eindruck zu vermeiden, verwende so oft wie möglich die Ausdrücke *Would you like …? Could I …? Please …* usw.

Pardon?
• "Did you see the rugby match on TV yesterday? What did you think of the Haka?"
• "Kiwis are flightless birds."

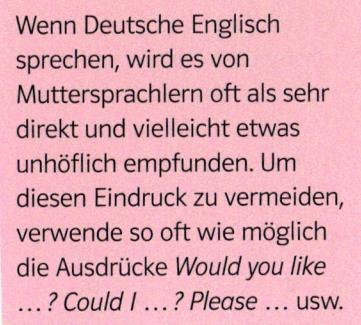

▶ to mean   ▶ See you.   ▶ to borrow

A month in New Zealand

4 Language practice

> **Höflichkeitsformen**
>
> **Could**
> Mit *Could you/Could I …?* kann man höflich um etwas bitten:
> *Excuse me. Could you help me, please?*
> *Could I phone my parents in Germany, please?*
> Eine Antwort lautet dann:
> *Sure. What's the problem? / Of course.*
>
> **Would you like …?**
> *Would you like …?* benutzt man, um etwas höflich anzubieten:
> *Would you like a cup of coffee / some more toast?*
> Darauf kann man antworten:
> *Yes, please. / Sorry, I'm afraid I'm full up. / I don't like coffee so much.*
>
> **Pardon? / Sorry, I don't understand.**
> Wenn man ein Wort oder einen Ausdruck nicht versteht, hilft die Frage:
> *Pardon? I'm sorry, I don't understand.*
> *What does … mean?*
> Und wenn man es dann verstanden hat:
> *Oh right, I understand now.*
>
> A Would you like to come to my house for a barbie?
> B Pardon?
> A A barbie.
> B Sorry, I don't understand. What does 'barbie' mean?
> A It means 'barbecue'.
> B Oh right, I understand now. Yes, please!

P A Finish the sentences with the best phrases.

1 Would you like some more soup? – … It's delicious!
2 Excuse me. … help me, please?
3 Could I borrow your dictionary, please? – …
4 Would you like some more dessert? – It's fantastic but …
5 Peter Jackson is a famous movie director.
   – … ? I … What … movie director … ?
6 Movie director? It's a person who makes films. You know, like Steven Spielberg. – Oh right. I …

R/P B WORDS Choose the correct word a, b, c or d for each number in the text.

> Sven and Daniela are from Germany but they're in New Zealand (1) … the moment. They're apprentices with a big German car company. It has workshops (2) … the world and there's a workshop in Christchurch. Sven and Daniela love New Zealand. It's smaller (3) … Germany and it's very beautiful. It's very interesting, (4) … , that New Zealanders use the name 'Kiwis' for themselves. A kiwi is a (5) … of bird. It lives only in New Zealand. About 8 per cent of people in New Zealand are Maoris. The Maoris have lived in New Zealand (6) … a thousand years.

1	a in	b on	c at	d to
2	a around	b in	c over	d about
3	a as	b than	c then	d for
4	a to	b two	c true	d too
5	a name	b kind	c word	d like
6	a for	b in	c since	d from

5 Activities

P A Your New Zealand pen friend Lucy wants to know about Germany. Write an email of about 70 words in full sentences. Here are some ideas.

- Is Germany bigger or smaller then New Zealand?
- How many people live in Germany?
- What are the names of some large cities? What's the capital?
- Are there lots of mountains and lakes?
- What are the most popular sports in Germany?
- What's the weather like in Germany?

* P B Imagine that you are in New Zealand for your company – like Daniela and Sven. You are with a family. It's your first day and you are just arriving at their house. Write a short conversation.

P C REVISION Christopher Hustert from Dresden in Germany is on holiday in New Zealand. He's writing an email to his American friend Aaron. Finish the email. Use the *simple present, present continuous, simple past, present perfect, going to* and *will*.

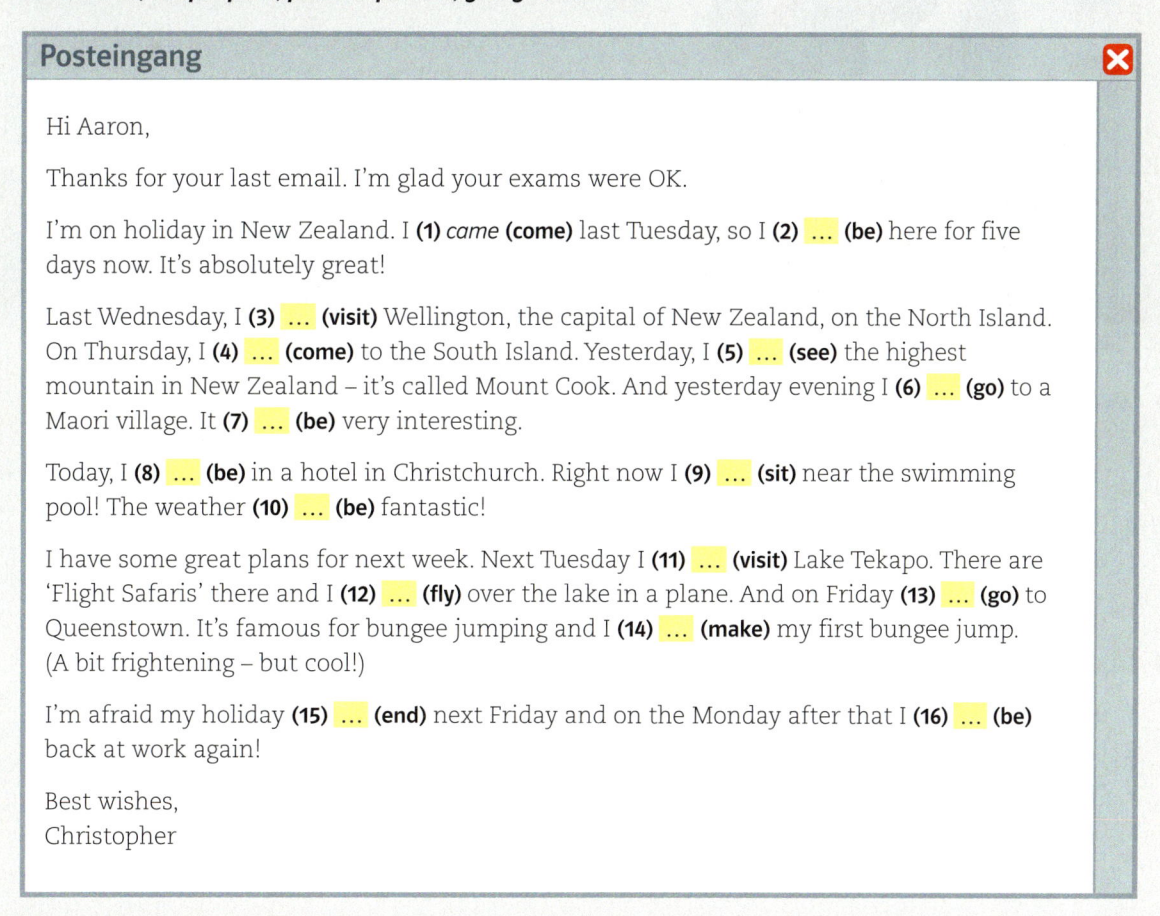

Posteingang

Hi Aaron,

Thanks for your last email. I'm glad your exams were OK.

I'm on holiday in New Zealand. I **(1)** *came* **(come)** last Tuesday, so I **(2)** ... **(be)** here for five days now. It's absolutely great!

Last Wednesday, I **(3)** ... **(visit)** Wellington, the capital of New Zealand, on the North Island. On Thursday, I **(4)** ... **(come)** to the South Island. Yesterday, I **(5)** ... **(see)** the highest mountain in New Zealand – it's called Mount Cook. And yesterday evening I **(6)** ... **(go)** to a Maori village. It **(7)** ... **(be)** very interesting.

Today, I **(8)** ... **(be)** in a hotel in Christchurch. Right now I **(9)** ... **(sit)** near the swimming pool! The weather **(10)** ... **(be)** fantastic!

I have some great plans for next week. Next Tuesday I **(11)** ... **(visit)** Lake Tekapo. There are 'Flight Safaris' there and I **(12)** ... **(fly)** over the lake in a plane. And on Friday **(13)** ... **(go)** to Queenstown. It's famous for bungee jumping and I **(14)** ... **(make)** my first bungee jump. (A bit frightening – but cool!)

I'm afraid my holiday **(15)** ... **(end)** next Friday and on the Monday after that I **(16)** ... **(be)** back at work again!

Best wishes,
Christopher

Answers to exercise B, page 75: **1** a; **2** b (Here a 'Kiwi' is a New Zealander!); **3** b; **4** a

Test Unit 1–8

Reading Part 1: Ronaldinho

Read this magazine article and answer the questions.

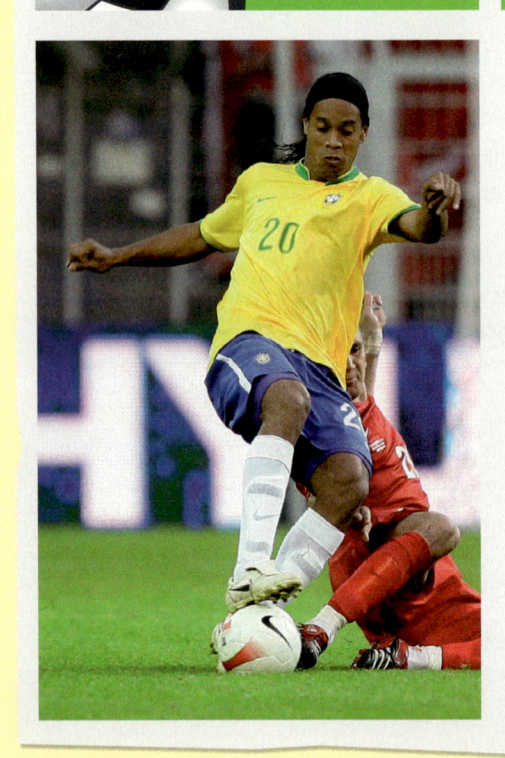

A great footballer

Ronaldo de Assis Moreira was born on 21 March 1980 in Brazil. People call him 'Ronaldinho', which means 'little Ronald'. His father died when Ronaldinho was only eight. When he was little, Ronaldinho started
5 playing futsal1 and beach football. Later he became interested in real football. When he was only thirteen years old, he scored 23 goals in a match for his local team. He became famous when he scored a lot of goals in the Egypt under-17 world championship. He is
10 also famous because he has a special style when he plays.

Ronaldinho's brother, Roberto, was also a professional football player but he stopped playing and became Ronaldinho's manager. In 1999 Ronaldinho was in the
15 Brazilian national team and he played for Brazil against Germany in the 2002 World Cup. Brazil won.

He has played for FC Barcelona since 2003. His contract with them has brought him millions of dollars. In 2005 he was FIFA World Player of the Year.

A Which is right? Note down a, b or c.

1 Ronaldinho was born in
a Egypt.
b Brazil.
c Barcelona.

2 Ronaldinho scored 23 goals
a for the Brazilian national team.
b in the Egypt under-17 world championship.
c for his home town.

3 Ronaldinho's brother
a is also a professional footballer.
b was also a professional footballer.
c wants to be a professional footballer.

B True or false? Note down T or F.

1 Ronaldinho's father died when Ronaldinho was a child.
2 Ronaldinho's style is not the same as the style of other footballers.
3 Ronaldinho played for the Brazilian national team when he was thirteen.
4 Ronaldinho played for Germany in a World Cup match.
5 In 2005, he was the worst football player in the world.

▶ **futsal** Hallenfußball   ▶ **contract** Vertrag   ▶ **score a goal** ein Tor schießen   ▶ **championship** Meisterschaft

Reading Part 2: **The right job**

Read about the jobs below and find the right job for these people. Give the letter as in the example.

He is very interested in cars and machines. = **B**

1. She's interested in keeping fit, is sporty, doesn't want to work with children.
2. He wants to work outside, but doesn't want to work full time, He can't ride a bicycle.
3. She likes fashion, she wants to work with people and she is 19 years old.
4. He likes little children, speaks English, but he isn't sporty.
5. He speaks English, likes people, but is not good with his hands. He doesn't want to work mornings, and he wants to work indoors.
6. She doesn't want to be inside all day. She can ride a bicycle and has no problems with early hours.
7. She likes sport and she likes children. She is a teacher.
8. He doesn't want to work outside. He can use a computer very well. He doesn't want to work in the evenings.

A **Sports teacher** Roseberry School is looking for a sports teacher for classes of 8–10 year olds for 20 hours per week, mornings. Please write to: Roseberry Primary School, 3 Barton Road, Bath.

B **Bob's Car Paradise** Good with your hands? Our workshop is looking for a car mechanic. 35 hours a week, 6 weeks holiday a year. Friendly atmosphere. Come and see us at 45 High Street, Bristol.

C **Fitness trainer** Tim and Sara, 30 years old, are looking for a personal fitness trainer for regular training. Interested? Please call us on 0728 45321.

D **Postman** We give you a bicycle and uniform. Hours from 6.30 a.m. to 2.30 p.m. Monday to Saturday. Call 0701 987654.

E **Gardener** We are looking for a part-time gardener to work for two families with large gardens in South London. We pay well. Phone 0208 6294888.

F **Shop assistant** Are you over 18 but under 25? Do you like people and fashion? Do you like working in a team? Bella's Young Fashions Boutique is looking for a shop assistant. Working hours: Tuesday to Saturday 10.00am to 8pm. Phone 0234 13579.

G **Do you speak English?** Do you like looking after little children 2–5 years old? The International Nursery School in Berlin is looking for a nursery assistant. Hours: 8 a.m. to 2 p.m. Phone 030 7654321.

H **Want to work in an office?** Our small construction company is looking for an office worker to work on the computer. Hours: 8.30am to 3.30pm. Monday to Friday. Call 0124 224567 or contact Brian Thorpe@construct.com

I **Interested in meeting people?** Hotel International is looking for a friendly barman for our bistro bar. You must speak English and be willing to work evenings and weekends. Send us an email: hotelinternational@internet.de

▶ willing bereit

8

Reading Part 3: New Zealand

Choose the correct word a, b, c, or d for each number in the text below.

The Land of the Kiwis

New Zealand is (1) … Germany. People (2) … New Zealand often (3) … themselves 'Kiwis'. (4) … is a bird in New Zealand called a kiwi, but kiwis are also a (5) … fruit. The first people in New Zealand were the Maoris. They (6) … there (7) … around 1,000 years. The first European in New Zealand was Captain Cook. He (8) … from England. That is why New Zealanders (9) … English.

1	a more small than	b	smaller as	c	smaller than	d	more small than
2	a from	b	off	c	out of	d	out
3	a say	b	tell	c	call	d	ask
4	a It	b	That	c	There	d	They
5	a sort	b	name of	c	type	d	kind of
6	a have lived	b	live	c	are living	d	do live
7	a in	b	since	c	on	d	for
8	a is coming	b	comes	c	will come	d	came
9	a speak	b	speaks	c	are speak	d	speaking

Listening: What's my job?

You will hear five people talking about their jobs. Write down the five jobs from the jobs in the box below.

office worker • cycle courier • pilot • fitness trainer • taxi driver • hairdresser • police officer • gardener • firefighter • fisher

Mediation: Signs

A Du bist mit Freunden im Urlaub in Neuseeland. Deine Freunde sprechen kein Englisch und wollen wissen, was diese Schilder bedeuten. Erkläre sie ihnen kurz auf Deutsch.

1. Caution Wet floor
2. In case of fire break glass
3. No mobile phones
4. SECURITY DO NOT LEAVE BAGS/PROPERTY UNATTENDED

B Now explain to an English person – in English of course – what these German signs at work mean.

1. Nichtraucherzone
2. Gehörschutz empfohlen
3. Gefahr 11,000 Volt!
4. Betreten der Baustelle verboten!

Writing: Your life and plans

Next month your class is going to visit an FE college in England for three weeks. You are going to stay with an English student there (Jack or Jenny). Write an email and tell him/her about yourself:
- your college,
- your free time,
- your part-time jobs,
- your plans.

Write 75–100 words.

▶ explain erklären

Unit 9
Travel

Am Ende dieser Unit kann ich …
- → über Reisen, Flughäfen und Hotels sprechen und schreiben,
- → Menschen, Sachen und Orte detailliert beschreiben,
- → eine ‚Mindmap' erstellen.

1 Check-in!

P/I **A** Talk in class. How do you travel? First finish the sentences with words from the box. Then make more sentences.

1 I … come to college by bike.
2 In town, I … travel by bus.
3 I … travel by tram or S-Bahn.
4 When I go on holiday, I … travel by plane.

always • often • usually/normally • sometimes • never • hardly ever

I often/hardly ever … travel by underground.
I usually walk/go on foot.
I sometimes use my inline skates.

▶ by (bike) ▶ on foot ▶ normally ▶ hardly ever

Tips and tricks

You go …
- **by** bike/train/bus/tram/underground
- **by** car (or you drive)
- **by** plane (or you fly)
- **on** foot (or you walk)

86 Travel

| Check-in | Training | Language | Check-out | 9 |

R/P **B** Herr Kreuger is a businessman. He often flies to other countries for meetings. Today, he's on a business trip to London. Right now he's checking in at the check-in desk. Finish the sentences below with *who, which* or *where*.

1 The place ... you check in at an airport is the check-in desk.
2 The man ... is checking in here is Herr Kreuger.
3 The woman ... is helping him is Frau Bliscz. She's a check-in clerk.
4 The document ... she has in her hand is Herr Kreuger's boarding card.

P **C** Finish these sentences in your own words.

1 An airport is a place where ...
2 A businessman or woman is a person who ...
3 A plane is a big machine which ...
4 A ... is ...

▸ to check in   ▸ (check-in) desk   ▸ (check-in) clerk   ▸ boarding card

Travel 87

2 How an airport works

A Look at the picture of the airport on the next page and read the text below. Then answer the questions.

`808236-0011`

BORDKARTE	BOARDING CARD
PASSENGER'S NAME	KREUGER/ROLF HERR
FROM	BERLIN TEGEL TXL
TO	LONDON HEATHROW LHR
FLIGHT NUMBER EA 4147	DAY M DATE 08 SEPT TIME 07:45
SEAT 14D GATE 2	EUROPAIR

People who travel by plane from or to an airport (like Herr Kreuger) are passengers. When passengers fly from an airport, they go to DEPARTURES. First, they check in at the check-in
5 desk. The check-in clerk gives them a boarding card. On it, passengers can see the number of the gate where their plane departs.

Next they go through the security check. Here, security officers check people's clothes and
10 their hand baggage. After that, passengers go through the passport check. Passport officers check their passports. Now passengers usually have some time before their plane departs. There are cafés, restaurants and shops where
15 they can eat, drink and buy things.

security check   *passport check*

Finally, passengers get on (or 'board') the plane – and the plane takes off. And when passengers arrive at an airport? Well, they go through the passport check, get their baggage
20 at the baggage reclaim, go through the customs check (where customs officers sometimes check their baggage) – and that's it. Easy!

B Put these words in the right order under the right heading. You can use some words twice.

cup of coffee • check-in desk • passport check • customs • gate • plane • baggage reclaim

DEPARTURE	ARRIVAL
check-in desk	

C Here are some people, places and things which you find at an airport. What are they? Finish the definitions, then make two more definitions yourself.

1 The security check is the place *where security officers* …
2 A passport officer is a person/someone …
3 A boarding pass is something/a document …

▶ passenger ▶ to depart ▶ (hand) baggage ▶ to check ▶ to arrive at (an airport)

Travel

| Check-in | **Training** | Language | Check-out | 9 |

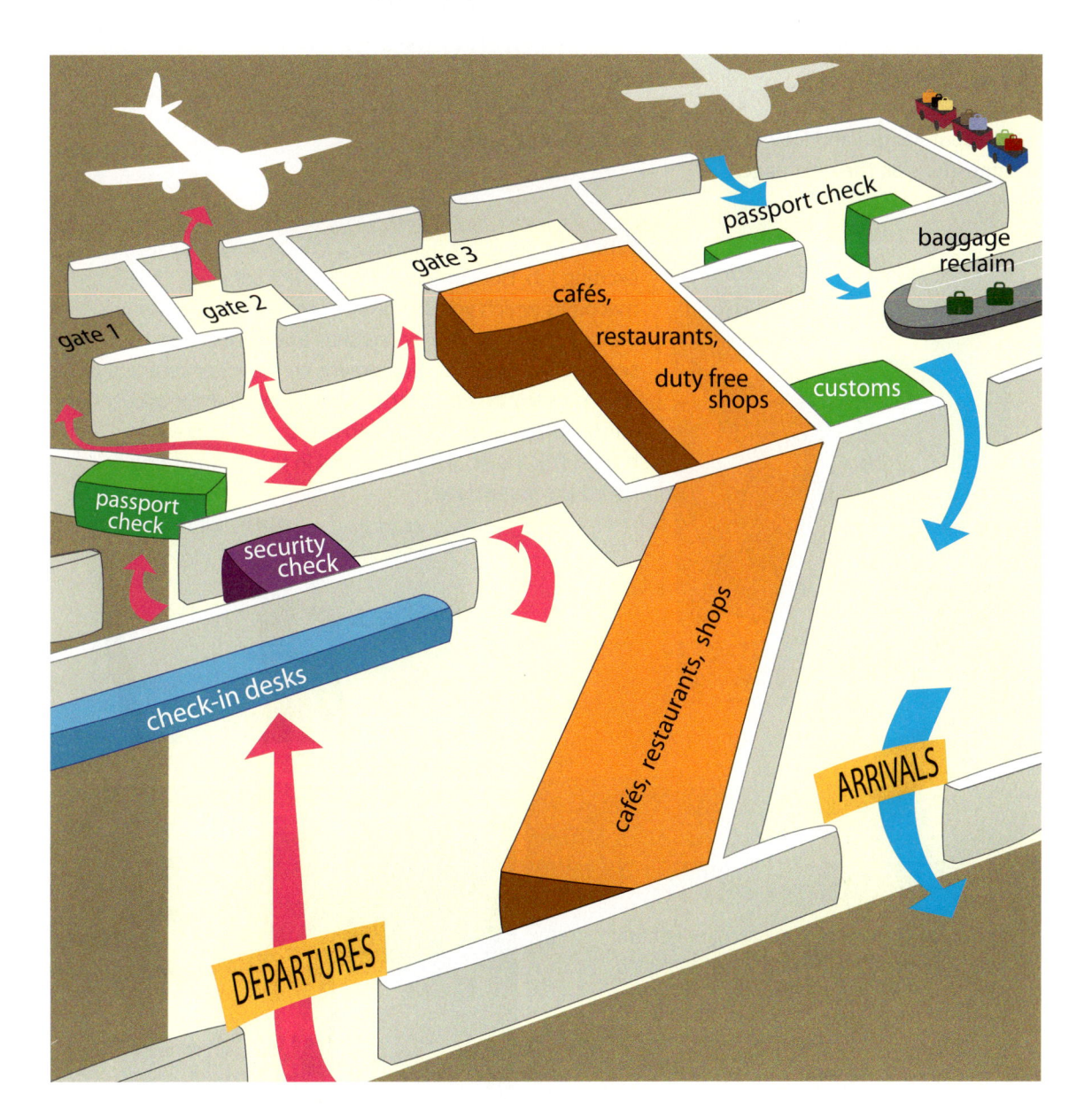

Airport map with labels: gate 1, gate 2, gate 3, passport check, security check, check-in desks, cafés, restaurants, duty free shops, cafés, restaurants, shops, passport check, baggage reclaim, customs, DEPARTURES, ARRIVALS

M **D** Your German friend has to fly to the USA tomorrow. It's his/her first time at an airport. Explain in German what he or she has to do at the airport – first here in Germany, then when he/she arrives in the USA.

Relativsätze	
People	A pilot is a person/someone … flies a plane.
Things	A plane is a big machine … can fly.
Places	A restaurant is a place … you can eat and drink.

What are the missing words?

▸ departure(s) ▸ arrival(s) ▸ baggage reclaim ▸ duty free (shop) ▸ customs

Travel **89**

9 At a hotel

> Check-in > **Training** > Language > Check-out

3 At a hotel

A Read about Sandra and look at the hotel brochure. Then answer the questions on the next page.

Sandra Kaiser is from Hamburg in Germany. She has an exciting job. Her company builds roller coasters – the big machines which you often see at theme parks and fairs. Sandra is an electrical technician. She checks and services the electrical equipment on the roller coasters. Her company builds roller coasters around the world, so Sandra often travels in her job and she often stays at hotels. This week, she's at a hotel in the north of England called the River Hotel.

Welcome To The River Hotel

The River Hotel is a quiet, friendly hotel only 10 minutes on foot from the River Towers Theme Park. Ideal for families – children under 10 stay free.

Rooms
    12 single rooms
    10 double rooms
    10 family rooms (2 adults + 2 children)

All rooms have a bathroom and shower.

Facilities
    The River Restaurant
    Bar
    Garden with children's playground
    Free parking
    TV in all rooms
    Wi-Fi Internet connection

Please note that we are a non-smoking hotel.

▶ to service (equipment)   ▶ to stay at (a hotel)   ▶ single/double room   ▶ facilities

90 Travel

> Check-in   **Training**   Language   Check-out   **9**

1 Answer the questions about Sandra and her job in full sentences.

    a Where's Sandra from?
    b What does Sandra's company build?
    c What's a roller coaster?
    d What's Sandra's job? What work does she do?
    e What does Sandra often do in her job? Why?
    f Where's Sandra this week?

> **Tips and tricks**
>
> Adverbien sowie *often*, *always*, *sometimes* stehen immer `vor` einem Vollverb:
> She `often travels` in her job.

2 True or false? Note down T or F.

    a The hotel has a total of 32 rooms.
    b You can walk from the hotel to the *River Towers Theme Park* in 10 minutes.
    c You can smoke at the hotel.
    d A mum, a dad and three children can stay in a family room.
    e Children under 10 don't have to pay for their room.
    f Parking at the hotel costs £1.00 a day.
    g You can use the Internet at the hotel.
    h The single rooms at the hotel don't have a bathroom or shower.

R   **B** Sandra is checking in at the hotel. Listen. Find the missing words from the box.

> 6 a.m. to 10 a.m. • key • the second floor • registration form • A single room • You're welcome. • 214

Receptionist	Hello. How can I help you?
Sandra	Hello. My name's Kaiser. K-A-I-S-E-R. You have a room for me.
Receptionist	Just a moment. Ah yes, Ms Kaiser. **(1)** … for four nights?
Sandra	That's right.
Receptionist	Would you fill in the **(2)** … for me, please?
Sandra	Mmm. Here you are.
Receptionist	Thanks. Here's your **(3)** … You're in room **(4)** … That's on **(5)** … There's a lift just over there. Breakfast is from **(6)** … in the restaurant over there.
Sandra	Great. Thanks very much.
Receptionist	**(7)** … Enjoy your stay with us.

P/I   **C** Now YOU. Read the dialogue with a partner. Then change the names, times, room number etc. and make a new dialogue.

▶ registration form   ▶ key   ▶ on the second floor   ▶ over there

Travel

4 Language practice

Relativsätze → Grammar summary **12**

Relativsätze: who, which und where
Wir verwenden *who*, *which* und *where*, um Menschen, Sachen und Orte genauer zu beschreiben: *who* für Personen, *which* für Sachen, und *where* für Orte.

A check-in clerk is a person/someone **who** …
A roller coaster is a big machine **which** …
A hotel is a place **where** …

⚠ Vor *who*, *which* und *where* steht kein Komma.

Das simple present und das present continuous (Wiederholung)
Das **simple present** für Aussagen, die längere Zeit gültig sind, sowie für Dinge, die wir regelmäßig tun. Häufigkeitsadverbien wie *often*, *sometimes* oder *never* stehen **vor** dem Verb:
I **usually** come to college by bus.

Das **present continuous** für Aktivitäten, die gerade im Augenblick stattfinden:
He **is checking in** at the airport **right now**.

P A Make sentences.

1	A receptionist is someone		opens a door.
2	A roller coaster is a big machine	who	travel by plane, boat, bus etc.
3	Passengers are people	which	you can get a cola or a coffee.
4	A key is something	where	works in a hotel.
5	A café is a place		you often see at theme parks.

R/P B *Simple present* or *present continuous*? Choose the correct forms.

1 What **do you do / are you doing** at the moment, Christian?
2 Right now, I **listen to / am listening to** music.
3 What **does Sandra often do / is Sandra often doing** in her job?
4 Well, her company **builds / is building** roller coasters all around the world, so she **often travels / is often travelling** to other countries.
5 Look at this picture. In the picture, a person **checks in / is checking in** at an airport.

P C WORDS Work with a partner. Look at the TRAVEL mindmap. Can you find 15 more words and phrases?

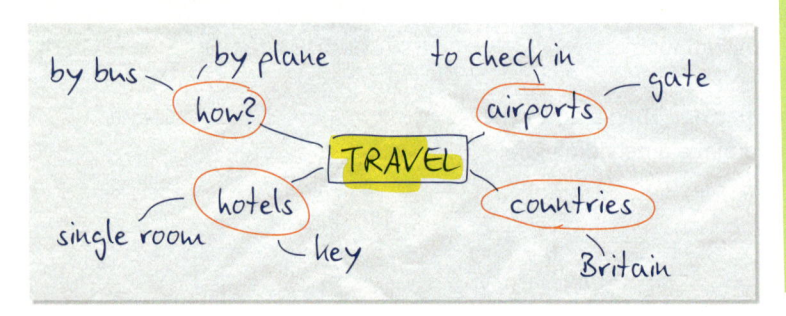

So läuft's besser

Mindmaps sind eine gute Methode, Vokabeln zu sammeln und thematisch zu lernen. In einer Mindmap werden Begriffe rund um ein Thema gesammelt. Mindmaps können einzelne Wörter sowie Redewendungen enthalten. So bekommt man einen tollen Überblick!

> Check-in   > Training   > Language   > Check-out   **9**

5 Activities

P | A **A holiday postcard.** You're on holiday. Send a postcard to an American friend. Think of the missing information yourself and finish the postcard below.

```
Dear (1) … ,

I'm on holiday in (2) … with
(3) … . The weather is (4) … .
The hotel where we are is
(5) … . Right now I'm (6) … .
Yesterday we (7) …

Best wishes,

(8) …
```

✱ P/I | B **Role-play**

1 Work in a small group.
2 Look back at the texts and conversations in this unit. Choose some situations which you think are interesting. They can be at an airport, a hotel, in a shop, in a café, …
3 Take parts and role-play the situations in your group. Then show your role-plays to the class.

P | C | PROJECT There are lots of signs at airports. Use the Internet to find more signs (in Britain or the USA). Make a poster with some of the signs.

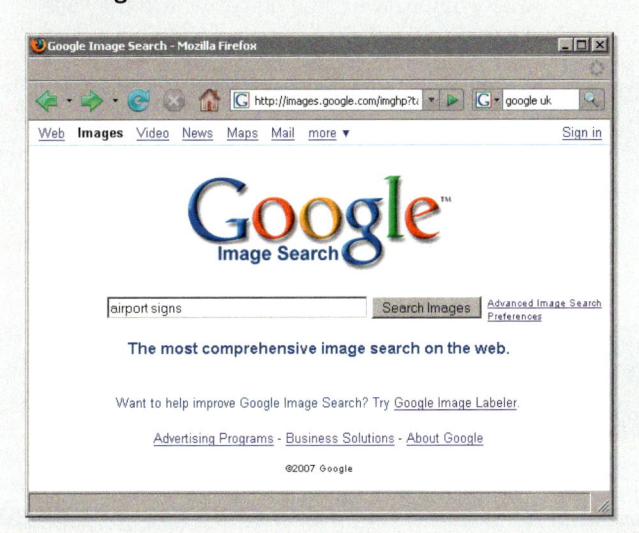

So läuft's besser

Warum nicht auf Englisch googlen!? Das geht ganz leicht: Einfach auf der deutschen Google-Seite auf „Google.com in English" klicken oder bei einer Suchmaschine deiner Wahl die Endung .com anhängen.

Travel

9

> Check-in   > Training   > Language   > **Check-out**

R **A** Look at the cover of this magazine and read the short text from inside the magazine.

1 What's the title of the magazine?
2 Who is it for?
3 How often will the magazine come out?
4 What things will always be in the magazine? What articles are there in this issue?

From your GO FOR IT! team

Hello!
... and welcome to this first issue of the new magazine **GO FOR IT!** – a magazine just for students like YOU in vocational colleges around Germany. Every month you'll find interesting articles, quizzes, competitions and useful information about jobs and the world of work. And, yes, it's all in English. But don't panic: your English is better than you think!

GO FOR IT!

The NEW magazine for college students in Germany!

This month ...
Where do people speak English?

PLUS
We want to hear about your college!

Tips to stay fit and healthy

Vote for your favourite band

And ...
JOBS, JOBS, JOBS
A profile of a different job each week.

Hong Kong

R **B** Read the article from this month's magazine which is on the next page and answer these questions.

1 How many people in the world today speak – or can understand and use – English?
2 How many will know English in 2015?
3 What is a 'native speaker'? How many native speakers are there in the world? Where do they live?
4 Why are the people in these countries native speakers?
5 Where do people speak English as a second or official language? Why do the people there know English?
6 The text says that there are millions more people around the world who also see and use English every day. Name *three* places where they use English.

P/I **C** Activities

Try the activities in the magazine – the survey and the question about Denglisch.

▶ cover (of a magazine)   ▶ issue   ▶ article   ▶ competition

94 Travel

English everywhere!

English is a world language. Of the six billion people who live in the world, around a quarter speak (or can understand and use) English every day. In the year 2015, experts say that *half of all the people in the world* will know English.

There are three sorts of people who speak English: native speakers (who speak English as their first language); people who speak English as a second or 'official' language; and then millions more like YOU who see and use English every day at college, in their jobs, on the Internet and in lots of other places.

- native speakers (about 350 million). People from Britain came to live here and brought English with them.
- places where people speak English as a second ('official') language (250–350 million). The British had colonies in these countries.

* The first language in Quebec (a region of Canada) is French.

USA, Canada, (Quebec)*, Britain, Pakistan, AFRICA, India, Australia, New Zealand

When and where do you see or use English?
Find out in your class.
Do a survey.
- Do you know a native speaker?
- Where and when do you see or use English: in songs? magazines? on the Internet? ...?

Could I borrow your 'handy', please?

Pardon? You mean my mobile.

Denglisch

'Denglisch' is the word which we use for English words in German: like *joggen* or *brainstorming*. How many words like this do YOU know? But remember: some Denglisch is wrong! For a British person, 'handy' means 'praktisch'!

▶ billion (= 1000 million) ▶ a quarter ▶ sort of ▶ native speaker ▶ to borrow

Travel

Unit 10
A visit to a company

Am Ende dieser Unit kann ich . . .
→ über Unternehmen schreiben und sprechen,
→ andere höflich begrüßen,
→ sagen, *wie* man Dinge macht (schnell, langsam etc.).

1 A week in England

R **A** Read the short text below and look at the pictures above and on the next page.

> The four people on the left in the photo – Tobias, Patricia, Iris and Melanie – are from Germany. They're apprentices in a German chemicals company. They all want to be laboratory technicians. The man on the right is their trainer, Herr Wolf. This week, they're spending a week in England. They're visiting some British companies. Today,
> 5 they're visiting a company which makes paint. It's called Rolac Paints PLC. Right now, it's almost 9 a.m. and they're just arriving at the company. They have an appointment with someone at the company at 9 o'clock, so they're walking quickly.

▶ chemicals company   ▶ laboratory technician   ▶ appointment

96   A visit to a company

| Check-in | Training | Language | Check-out | 10 |

R **B Answer the questions.**

1 Who are all the people in the picture above?
2 Where are they this week? What are they doing there?
3 What are they doing today?
4 How are they walking at the moment (quickly? slowly? …?) Why?

P **C How do you do these things? Choose the best word.**

1 In the morning, I always get up …   quickly   slowly
2 I usually arrive for my lessons at college …   punctually   not very punctually
3 I speak English …   well   quite well   OK   badly

▸ quickly   ▸ slowly   ▸ punctually   ▸ quite well   ▸ badly

A visit to a company

| 10 | > Check-in | > **Training** | > Language | > Check-out |

2 Welcome to Rolac

R **A** Before their visit, the apprentices read a brochure about Rolac Paints PLC. Look at this page from the brochure. Find out:

1 How old is the company?
2 How did the company grow in the 1950s and 60s. How important is it today?
3 Where are the company's head office and main factory?
4 How do many processes in the Rolac factory happen?
5 What different sorts of paint does the company make? What sorts of people buy them?

Welcome to
ROLAC PAINTS PLC

808236-0012

About Rolac and the factory
ROLAC PAINTS started in 1876. In the 1950s and 60s, the company grew very quickly and it is now one of the world's largest manufacturers of paint. Our main factory and our
5 head office are here in England, but we also have factories and offices in the USA, Russia, Australia and China. The factory which you are visiting today is very modern. Many processes happen automatically with computers and robots. But they can't do everything! Over 1,000 people work here, too.

10 **Who uses our paint?**
Rolac makes many different sorts of paint – for people's homes, for buildings, for cars, lorries and tractors – even for bridges. So lots of different people buy our paints, from customers in DIY shops to big companies.

15 Today, you can walk slowly around our factory and see exactly how we make our paints. We are very happy that you are here – enjoy your visit!

Adjektive	Adverbien
This old bus is very **slow**.	It travels **?**
But this new bus is **quick**.	It travels **?**
The process is **automatic**.	The process happens **?**
Here's an **exact** diagram of the factory.	On it, you can see **?** how we make our paints.

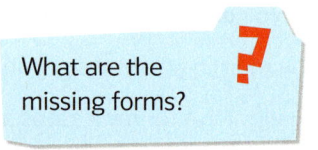

What are the missing forms? **?**

▶ head office ▶ factory ▶ to grow ▶ manufacturer ▶ DIY (Do It Yourself) shop

98   A visit to a company

| Check-in | Training | Language | Check-out | **10** |

R/I **B** Tobias, Patricia, Iris, Melanie and Herr Wolf are just arriving at Rolac Paints PLC. Ms Roberts, from the company, is waiting for them at the reception desk. Listen, then read the conversation in a group.

2|4

`808236-0013`

Ms Roberts	Herr Wolf? Hello. I'm Christine Roberts.
Herr Wolf	How do you do, Ms Roberts.
Ms Roberts	Welcome to Rolac Paints.
Herr Wolf	Thanks. It's great to be here. Can I introduce our apprentices? This is Melanie Seiler.
Melanie	How do you do, Ms Roberts.
Herr Wolf	Tobias Schuhmann.
Tobias	Nice to meet you, Ms Roberts.
Herr Wolf	Patricia Schwarz.
Patricia	How do you do.
Herr Wolf	And Iris Büchsel.
Iris	Nice to meet you, Ms Roberts.
Ms Roberts	OK. Let's go to the cafeteria. We can have a cup of coffee, then you can look round the factory with me. How's your English?
Apprentices	Mmm!
Herr Wolf	I think we all speak English quite well, but perhaps you can speak slowly for us?
Ms Roberts	Sure. OK. Please come this way …

P/I **B** Now YOU. Work in your groups again. Imagine that you are visiting a company. One of you is a trainer (like Herr Wolf), and one of you is from the company (like Ms Roberts). Make a conversation, then act your conversation for the class.

Hier und dort

How do you do?
Beim ersten Treffen mit jemandem aus Großbritannien ist der übliche Gruss *How do you do*. Darauf antwortest du : *How do you do* oder *Nice to meet you*. (**Nicht** ~~Very well thank you!~~) Wenn man jemanden wieder trifft, sagt man aber *How are you?*

Die Hand geben in GB
Britten geben sich seltener die Hand als Deutsche. Es ist in GB nicht üblich, dass sich Freunde und Arbeitskollegen täglich die Hände schütteln.

▶ to introduce   ▶ apprentice   ▶ How do you do?   ▶ to imagine

A visit to a company **99**

10 > Check-in > **Training** > Language > Check-out

3 A tour of the factory

R **A** The German group is looking around the factory with Ms Roberts. Here's a plan of the factory. Look at it first and find the English for:

> Labor • Büros • Herstellung • Lagerhalle • Eingang •
> Kantine • Rohstoffe • Qualitätssicherung • Rezeption •
> Abfertigung

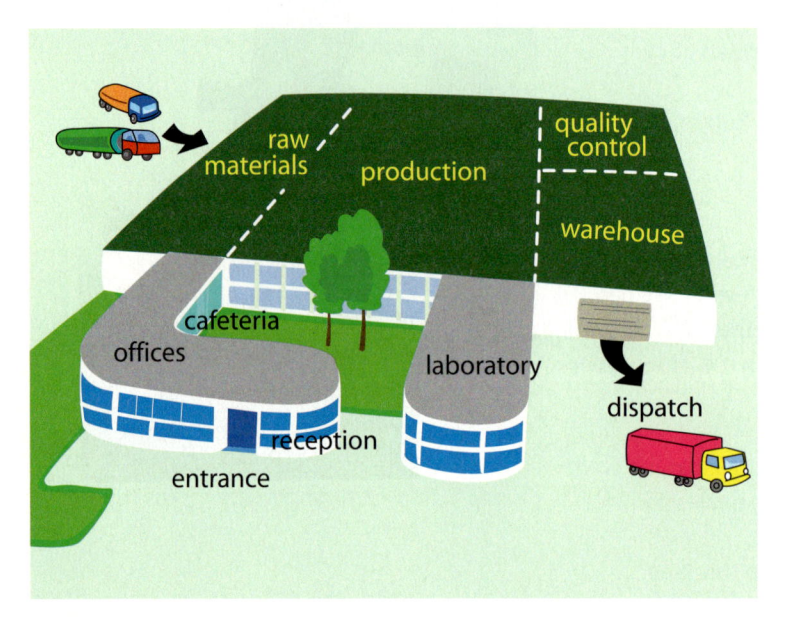

Labels on the factory plan: raw materials • production • quality control • warehouse • cafeteria • offices • laboratory • dispatch • reception • entrance

B Now listen to Ms Roberts. Look at the plan above. Which parts of the factory do they visit first, second, third, …?

First they go to …
Then/next they visit …
After that …
Finally, …

R/I **C** Listen again. Write down the missing words and phrases. Compare your answers with a partner.

Part 1: Raw materials

Ms Roberts: OK. Are you all ready? Let's start our factory tour. Making paint begins with the raw materials. We use lots of different powders, water, oils and other chemicals. They all arrive at the factory **(1)** … We store them here, in these big tanks. Every day, we use about **(2)** … kilograms of powder.

Image labels: powder • tanks

▶ powder   ▶ to store   ▶ tank

100 A visit to a company

Part 2: Production and quality control

Ms Roberts: OK. Let's go now to **(3)** ... part of the factory, the production area. This is the place where we make the paint. We make it in these big tanks. We do this all automatically. Can you see those people up there, with the **(4)** ...? They're mixing the different powders and chemicals for the different paints. When the paint is ready, something very important happens. It's called Quality Control. Now, here we are. Oh, hi, Rachel. This is Rachel, everybody. She's a quality control technician. What are you doing at the moment, Rachel?

Rachel: Hi. I'm checking some paint. We don't want **(5)** ... with our products, so we check all the paints carefully before they go out of the factory.

Part 3: Warehouse and dispatch

Ms Roberts: OK, so we have the paint and we know that it's good quality. Now we put the paint into cans and we store it here, in the warehouse. **(6)** ..., we send the paint to shops or companies. We call this 'dispatch'. This big robot can load the paint quickly and easily onto lorries.

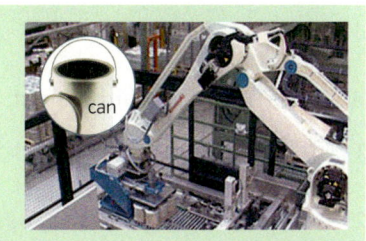

Part 4: Research and development and the offices

Ms Roberts: Just two more places now. Let's go here first. This is the laboratory. This is where we **(7)** ... new paints.

OK, and finally, here we are again in the offices. All the business and the administrative people work here – the people who **(8)** ... the raw materials, **(9)** ... the paints, look after the company's money and so on. So, that's it. I hope you enjoyed your quick tour!

P/M **D** After the visit to Rolac Paints, Herr Wolf asked the apprentices some questions. Can you answer them? Give the answers in German.

1. Welche Rohstoffe benutzt man bei der Herstellung von Farben?
2. Welche Rolle spielen Computer im Herstellungsprozess?
3. Welche Abteilung im Unternehmen ist für die Qualität der Produkte verantwortlich? Warum ist diese Abteilung so wichtig?
4. Wo werden a) die Produkte vor der Abfertigung gelagert und b) neue Produkte entwickelt? Verwende bitte die englischen Begriffe.
5. Welche Rolle spielen die kaufmännischen Angestellten im Unternehmen? Bitte Beispiele nennen.

▶ area ▶ to mix ▶ to put into ▶ to load onto ▶ administrative

A visit to a company

4 Language practice

Adjektive, Adverbien und das present continuous → Grammar summary 2 11

Adjektive und Adverbien
- **Adjektive** beschreiben Personen und Sachen:
 A **slow** bus.
 An **automatic** process.
 This question is **easy**.

- **Adverbien** sagen mehr über Verben aus.
 Sie sagen uns, *wie* etwas passiert:
 The bus travels **slowly**.
 The process happens **automatically**.
 You can answer the questions **easily**.

Das present continuous für befristete Aktivitäten
Wir verwenden das present continuous auch für längere, befristete Aktivitäten, die bereits begonnen haben, aber noch nicht beendet sind:
We **are spending** a week in England.
We **are visiting** factories this week.

R/P **A** *Adjective or adverb?* What's right, a or b?

1 I'm from Germany. Could you speak a) slow b) slowly for me, please?
2 You're English is great! You speak it very a) good b) well .
3 Lots of doors in shops, factories and other places open and close a) automatic b) automatically .
4 Henry always arrives on time. He's a very a) punctual b) punctually person.
5 Can you play tennis?
 – Well, a little bit. But I play very a) bad b) badly .
6 I can't do this.
 – Of course you can! It's a) easy b) easily .
 You can do it a) easy b) easily .

P **B** *Simple present or present continuous?* Give the missing forms.

1 Tobias is a German apprentice. He usually … **(work)** every day in his company in Germany.
2 In Germany, he … **(speak)** German, of course.
3 But he isn't in Germany this week. This week he … **(spend)** a week in England.
4 And he … **(speak)** English a lot every day.
5 It's 9 o'clock in the morning right now. Tobias, some other apprentices, and their trainer Herr Wolf … **(arrive)** at a factory in England which makes paint.

P **C** WORDS The mindmap on the right is about companies. How many more words and expressions can you find? Copy and complete the mindmap.

Mindmap: COMPANIES — paint, products, office worker, people, buildings, warehouse, processes, to manufacture

102 A visit to a company

| Check-in | Training | Language | Check-out | **10** |

5 Activities

P A You are Tobias or Patricia. It's the day after your visit to Rolac. Finish the email below to your Irish friend about your week in England. (You must invent some details yourself).

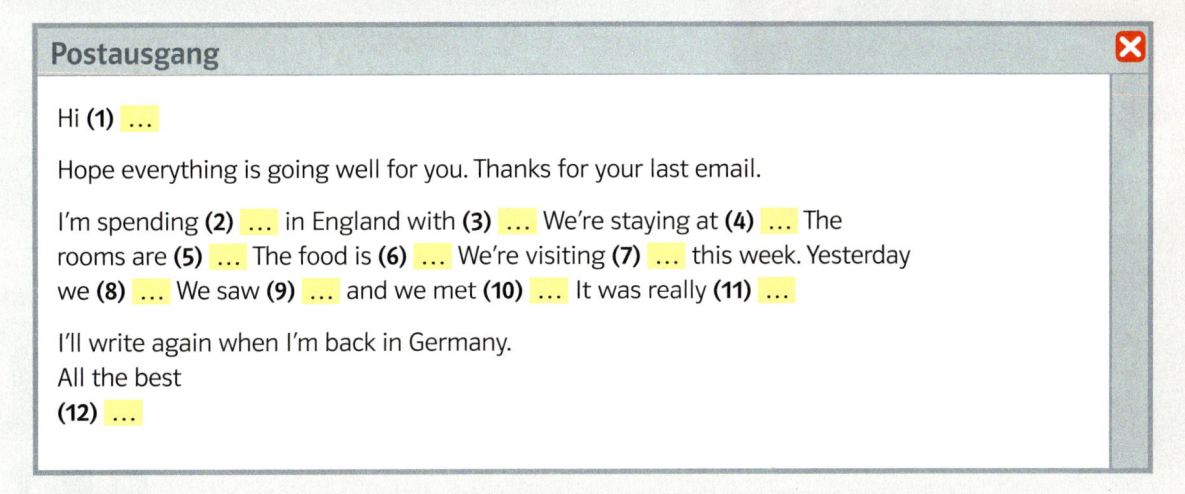

Postausgang   ✕

Hi **(1)** …

Hope everything is going well for you. Thanks for your last email.

I'm spending **(2)** … in England with **(3)** … We're staying at **(4)** … The rooms are **(5)** … The food is **(6)** … We're visiting **(7)** … this week. Yesterday we **(8)** … We saw **(9)** … and we met **(10)** … It was really **(11)** …

I'll write again when I'm back in Germany.
All the best
(12) …

---

* **P B** The apprentices have to write a report for Herr Wolf. You're one of the apprentices. Copy the form below and write a short report. Write about 100 words.

VISIT REPORT

Apprentice's name: _____   Date of visit: _____
Company: _____
Contact person at company: _____

Please write a short report in English about the visit. Include the following information:
- the company's product(s)
- a short description of the main processes in the company
- a worker who you met at the company and her/his job
- the most interesting thing which you saw/learned

R/P C PROJECT Find out about a company. It can be small or large, in the USA, Japan etc. or in your town. Make a poster.

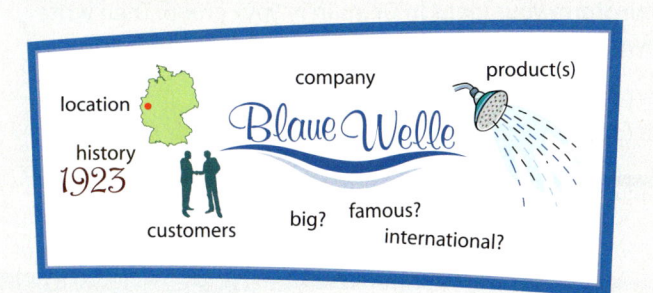

Poster example: Blaue Welle — location, company, product(s), history 1923, customers, big?, famous?, international?

So läuft's besser

Sehr viele Unternehmen haben Websites in mehreren Sprachen. Tipp: Vergleiche die englische und die deutsche Website eines Unternehmens. So kannst du leicht die wichtigsten Vokabeln lernen.

A visit to a company

10

> Check-in   > Training   > Language   > **Check-out**

GO FOR IT!

The magazine for college students in Germany!

This month ...
How hard should you work?

PLUS
Tell us about your hobbies!
My favourite day of the week

R/I A Work in a small group. Read the article now and answer the following questions.

1. Who are the people in the pictures? Do we learn their names?
2. Where's the girl at the top of the page from and what's her job?
3. What cities are the guys at the bottom of the page from? What are their jobs?
4. Which of the people …
   a. starts work at nine in the morning and goes home again at nine in the evening?
   b. works hard from Monday to Friday?
   c. usually goes home about 6 p.m.?

R/P/I B In your group, copy and fill in the table below with information from the article. (Tip: sometimes there isn't an answer for all three countries.)

According to the article …	Germany	Japan	USA
how long each day/week/year does a typical person work?			
how important are work colleagues?			
what do people think about work?			
what do they think about free time?			

I/P C What do YOU think? How hard should you work? Brainstorm your ideas in German in your group. Then write down five ideas in English and tell the class your ideas.

We (don't) think that …   In our opinion, …
We (don't) agree that / with (person) …

▶ according to   ▶ to brainstorm   ▶ in (our) opinion

104   A visit to a company

> Check-in   > Training   > Language   > **Check-out**   **10**

How hard should you work?

808236-0014

Hi! I'm **Lilli Weiss** and I'm a secretary in an office in Germany. I guess I'm a 'typical' German office worker. I love my job. I work hard from Monday to Friday. My colleagues are great. And, of course, my career is really important to me. But work isn't everything in my life. I also have friends, a boyfriend, and my family. I need my free time and my holidays. For me, work and free time are important.

Do people in other countries agree with Lilli? Let's go to Japan and the USA. What do people think there?

Working in Japan

Workers in Japan work longer hours than workers in Europe. But most important, they also always go out together with their work colleagues in the evening.
"For Japanese workers," says **Toshi**, an office worker from Tokyo, "our company is our family. Here's a typical day for me. I get up at 6.30 and at 7.30 I commute to my office. I arrive at 8.50 and work starts at 9. I work until 7 p.m. Lunch is a sandwich at my desk. Then from 7 p.m. to about 9 p.m. I go out with my colleagues. Then I go home and go to bed!

Working in the USA

Larry Zydel is a bit tired today! He's an office worker from Chicago, Illinois, in the USA. In a year Americans work more hours than Japanese workers. Larry's day isn't so bad – he usually goes home at about 6 p.m. But Americans don't have long holidays. Larry gets 12 days a year – yes, that's everything, just 12 days in total. "People often say that Americans are workaholics", says Larry. "But for us, work is the most important thing in our lives. The first question which people always ask you in the States is: 'What's your job?'"

So what do YOU think? Who's right?

▶ to go out with (somebody) ▶ to commute to (work) ▶ to arrive at (a place or time) ▶ the States

A visit to a company

This ...

Unit 11
Future technology

Am Ende dieser Unit kann ich ...
→ über das Leben in der Zukunft sprechen und schreiben,
→ sagen, was unter gewissen Bedingungen passiert (wenn),
→ mit längeren Texten arbeiten.

1 Future technology – will it be good or bad for us?

R **A Read the short text below and answer the questions on the next page.**

In the Terminator movies, the world's biggest computer (called Skynet) becomes self-aware in the year 2029. And 'the machines' take over the world. In lots of sci-fi movies, future technology will be frightening and horrible. Computers will kill people, cities will be dirty and dangerous, or we'll meet aliens on other planets (and
5 they'll usually want to kill us, too!). For other people, future technology will bring a better life for everybody. We'll have beautiful green cities, we'll live and work in high-tech buildings, and, with new drugs, we'll all be healthier and live longer. So who's right? Will future technology be good or bad for us?

▸ to take over (the world)   ▸ to kill   ▸ to be good/bad for (us)

106 Future technology

| Check-in | Training | Language | Check-out | **11** |

... or this?

R **B Finish the sentences.**

1 In lots of science fiction movies, future technology will be …
2 These movies show us cities which will be …
3 And computers which …
4 But other people have different ideas. They think that cities will be … and that we'll live longer because we'll have …

R/P **C What do you think? Choose the best answers for YOU.**

1 I think that life in the future will be
   a) better than life today b) worse than life today.
2 If we have robots in the future,
   a) they'll want to kill us b) they won't want to kill us.
3 If we have lots of new technology in the future, our cities a) will be dirty and dangerous b) our cities will be green and beautiful.
4 If I meet aliens one day, a) they'll be friendly b) they'll be dangerous.

▸ science fiction   ▸ drug(s)   ▸ dirty

Future technology   **107**

11

> Check-in > **Training** > Language > Check-out

2 20 years from now   `808236-0015`

R **A** Nobody really knows about the future. But here are some ideas from experts about life in 20 years. Read them now. What are the missing words 1, 2 and 3? Use the words in the box.

homes • shopping • clothes

20 years from now. If the experts are right ...

(1) ... in 20 years from now will be very different. There'll be new textiles. The girl's jacket, for example. The jacket will
5 change with the weather. It'll become cool in hot weather and warm in cold weather. There'll be lots of technology in clothes, too. The boy's T-shirt
10 will have electronics in it so that he can choose and change the colours. And if he meets a friend, his shirt will show the word 'hi!'. We'll have electronic things
15 like mobiles, MP3 players and so on in our clothes. Jackets (and earrings or watches) will also be computers.

(2) ... in the future will be very 'green' – people will think a lot about energy. There'll be lots of electronics, too. Maybe there'll be an 'information wall'. This big screen will be your TV and a computer where you can get information and read or
5 send messages. You don't want to watch TV? There'll be virtual reality games with *real* aliens! Is your home dirty? No problem. Your little house robot will clean it quickly and automatically. And no, it won't kill you!

▶ electronics ▶ electronic ▶ screen

108 Future technology

| Check-in | **Training** | Language | Check-out | **11** |

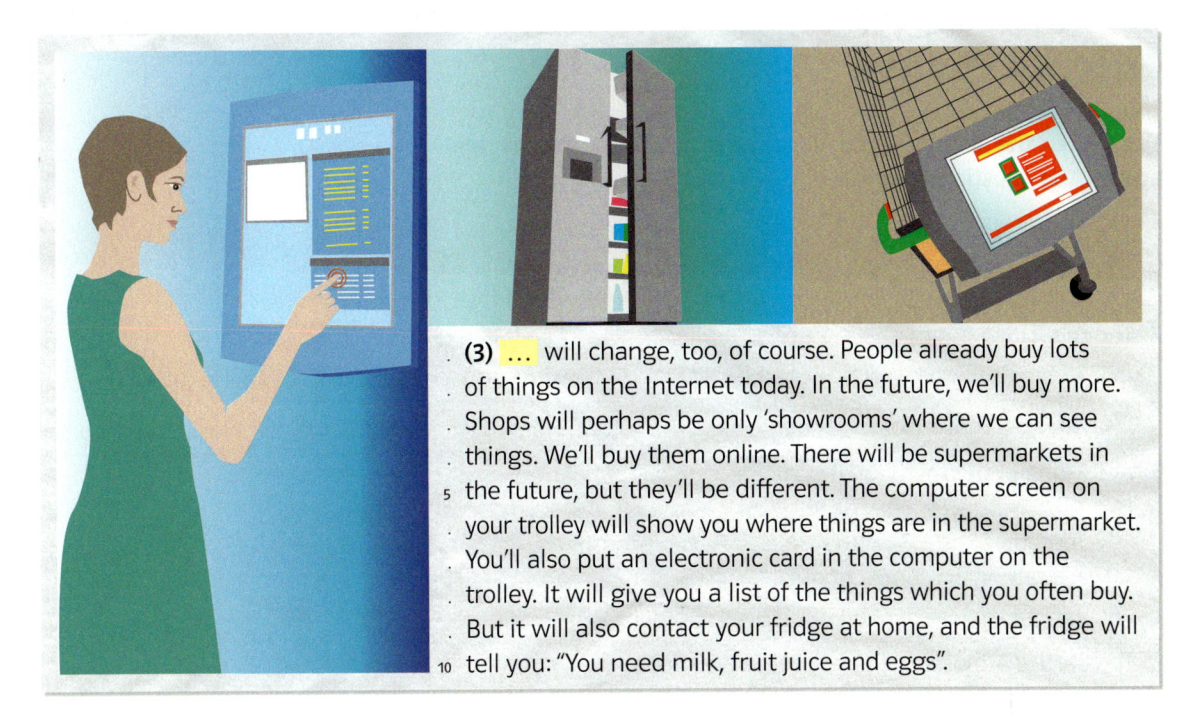

(3) … will change, too, of course. People already buy lots of things on the Internet today. In the future, we'll buy more. Shops will perhaps be only 'showrooms' where we can see things. We'll buy them online. There will be supermarkets in
5 the future, but they'll be different. The computer screen on your trolley will show you where things are in the supermarket. You'll also put an electronic card in the computer on the trolley. It will give you a list of the things which you often buy. But it will also contact your fridge at home, and the fridge will
10 tell you: "You need milk, fruit juice and eggs".

P/R B **The girl in the picture at the top of last page is Kia, and the guy's name is Jayden. It's a typical day for them in the year 2030. Answer the questions.**

1 If it's hot today, what will Kia's jacket become?
   If it's hot today, her jacket will become cool.
2 If Jayden meets a friend, what word will the friend see on Jayden's T-shirt?
   If he … , the friend will see …
3 If Jayden wants to phone a friend, where will his mobile be?
   If he … , his mobile …
4 If Kia wants to watch TV today, where will the TV be?
   If she …
5 What if she doesn't want to watch TV? What will she perhaps do?
   If she doesn't … , she'll perhaps …
6 What will Kia's house robot do if her home is dirty today?
7 If Jayden needs some new trainers, where will he buy them?
8 If Kia goes to the supermarket, what will she put in the computer on her trolley?
9 What will happen if Kia doesn't have apples and yoghurt in her fridge at home?

If-Sätze Typ 1	
If Jayden **meets** a friend,	his T-shirt ? (show) the word 'hi!'.
If Kia ? to watch TV,	she'**ll look** at the big 'information wall'.

What are the missing forms?

▶ to put (something) in   ▶ to show (somebody) where   ▶ to tell (somebody)

Future technology **109**

11 | Training

3 Climate change

R/P A The text on the next page is a magazine article. Read the text and answer the questions below.

1. The article is about
   - a) cities in the future.
   - b) weather in the future.
   - c) a big storm in the USA.
   - d) energy from the sun.

2. The main idea of the text is that
   - a) life in the future will be very difficult.
   - b) we don't have to change our lives in the future.
   - c) we mustn't change our lives in the future.
   - d) we must change our lives in the future.

3. According to the text, climate change
   - a) is happening already.
   - b) will happen soon.
   - c) happened in the 1800s.
   - d) will never happen.

4. CO_2 is a gas which comes from
   - a) the earth's atmosphere.
   - b) global warming.
   - c) fossil fuels.
   - d) the sun.

5. The earth's atmosphere has become warmer in the last 200 years because …

6. Some parts of the earth will become deserts and others will be under water if …

7. The text says that we can do two things now to help with the problem of climate change. What are they?

8. What will we perhaps find in the future which will help even more with the problem?

9. According to the text, in cities in the future there'll perhaps be
   - a) lots of cars.
   - b) lots of trains.
   - c) lots of trees, grass and water.
   - d) lots of streets.

10. Finish this definition:
    An SPS (Solar Power Satellite) is …

So läuft's besser

Mit längeren Texten umgehen

- Bevor du einen Text liest, versuche anhand der Bilder und Überschriften zu erraten, worum es geht. Stelle dir diese Fragen: Was ist das Thema? Was weiß ich selbst schon darüber? Was will der Text vielleicht sagen?
- Lies den Text einmal durch und suche die Hauptpunkte: Ist er für oder gegen etwas? Enthält er eine oder zwei Hauptideen?
Tipp: Texte beginnen häufig mit einer kurzen Zusammenfassung des Inhalts.
- Lies den Text noch einmal (zwei- oder sogar dreimal). Du wirst unbekannten Wörtern begegnen, aber du kannst während des Lesens anfangen zu überlegen, was sie bedeuten.
- Einige Tipps, wie du die Bedeutung eines Wortes erschließen kannst:
  a) Wenn das unbekannte Wort z. B. ein Substantiv ist: Kennst du ein ähnliches Verb?
  (*product* → *to produce*)
  b) Kennst du ein ähnliches Wort im Deutschen oder in einer anderen Sprache?
  (*disaster* = Desaster)
  c) Versuche aus dem Zusammenhang zu erschließen, was die Bedeutung sein könnte.
  (*to* damage *the environment:* der Umwelt *schaden*)

▸ storm   ▸ main   ▸ global warming   ▸ fossil fuels   ▸ according to

| Check-in | Training | Language | Check-out | 12 |

We are looking for
A FULLY-QUALIFIED KINDERGARTEN ASSISTANT
to work full-time in our friendly kindergarten. The kindergarten currently has 52 children aged from 3–5 years and is open from 8 a.m. to 6 p.m. Mon–Fri. For further information please contact:
Ms F Hernandez
Green Park Kindergarten
Tel: 910-764 4433.

Kindergarten Manager
$30K per year
The First Steps Kindergarten is seeking a manager for its two city kindergartens. Applicants must be fully-qualified and have at least five years' experience in kindergarten work. For further details please phone us on **910-875 1248**

WANTED
Apple Tree Kindergarten
15 Duke Street
A PART-TIME KINDERGARTEN ASSISTANT FOR A BUSY DOWNTOWN NURSERY. THE JOB WOULD SUIT SOMEONE WHO IS CURRENTLY TRAINING FOR A QUALIFICATION.
CONTACT: INFO@APPLETREE.EDU

R/P **C** Look at the ads above again. If you were Richie, which job would you apply for?

If I was Richie, I would apply for the job at the … Kindergarten.

R/P **D** If you were Richie again, why would you choose that job? Match the sentence halves below.

If I worked at the Apple Tree Kindergarten, …	I would be a manager. (But I don't have five years' experience.)
If I worked at The First Steps Kindergarten, …	the job would be full time and I would be an assistant. (That's perfect!)
If I worked at the Green Park Kindergarten, …	I would work only part time. (That's no good for me.)

▶ (fully) qualified ▶ qualification ▶ to suit ▶ further information

Job hunting

2 Looking at job ads

R/I **A** Some big, international German companies have job ads in English. You and your partner are looking at two ads for jobs in Germany.

PARTNER A: Please go now to page 157.
PARTNER B: Look at your ad below. Copy and complete the table with information from the ad. Next, answer your partner's questions about your ad. Then ask your partner questions and complete the table about her/his ad.

KARL BOSSMANN

Sales Assistant, Berlin

Karl Bossmann is Germany's biggest retailer of fashion clothing for men and women. The company also has stores in 34 countries around the world. We are currently looking for a sales assistant to work in our store in Berlin.

5 The job would suit a young person who is fully qualified to work in retail (Kaufmann/-frau im Einzelhandel). The applicant must be friendly, must enjoy meeting people and working in a team, and must speak English well (many customers in our Berlin store are English-speaking). Hours are Monday to Friday
10 9:30 a.m. to 7:00 p.m. and Saturday 10:00 a.m. to 4:00 p.m. Holidays: 3 weeks per year. Salary: €2000.

Interested? For further information, phone (030) 414 71 86 or email us at careers@karl.bossmann.de. We look forward to hearing from you!

	My ad	My partner's ad
Company	Karl Bossmann	
Job	sales assistant	
Place of work		
Qualifications		
Knowledge of English		
Hours		
Holidays		
Salary		

- What company is the job with?
- What qualifications do you need?
- What's the job?
- Where …?
- What holidays do you get?
- Do you need English?
- When …?
- How much do you earn?

▶ place of work ▶ knowledge (of English) ▶ salary

118 Job hunting

| Check-in | Training | Language | Check-out | **12** |

R/P **B** Compare the two jobs. Finish the sentences below.

1. If you got the job with Karl Bossmann, you **would be** a sales assistant.
2. If you got the job with Deutsche Mobil, you … (be) a secretary.
3. If you got the job with Karl Bossmann, you … (work) in …
4. If you got the job with Deutsche Mobil, you … (work) in …
5. If you wanted the job with Karl Bossmann, you … (need) to be a *Kaufmann/-frau im Einzelhandel*.
6. If you … (want) the job with Deutsche Mobil, you … (need) a … qualification.
7. You … (need) English if you … (work) for Karl Bossmann in Berlin.
8. You … (need) English if you … (work) for Deutsche Mobil, too.
9. When would you work if you worked for Karl Bossmann? If you … (work) for Karl Bossmann, you … (work) from …
10. And if you worked for Deutsche Mobil? Well, you … (work) … if you worked for them.

P **C** What do you know about jobs? Look at these jobs. How many sentences can you make? Use your dictionary if necessary.

- Where would you work?
- What would you do in your job?
- What sort of people would you meet?
- What places (countries etc.) would you perhaps travel to?

If you were a …
If you worked as a …, you would …

make-up artist

travel tour guide

computer games developer

If-Sätze Typ 2	
If you ❓ (be) a travel guide,	you ❓ (meet) lots of tourists.
You ❓ (need) English	if you ❓ (work) for this company.

What are the missing forms: **simple past** or ***would***?

▶ to get a job (with)   ▶ sort of   ▶ to need (English)

Job hunting **119**

3 A job interview

R **A** Last week, Meryem Gulec from Bremen in Germany saw this job ad in a magazine. She was interested in a traineeship as a flight attendant. She contacted Mr Werner, wrote her CV and sent it to Air Deutschland. Answer the questions below about the CV.

AIR DEUTSCHLAND currently has a number of **TRAINEESHIPS** for flight attendants, check-in clerks, computer technicians and sales people. For further information, please contact Heiko Werner, Personnel Manager, on

1 Where in Bremen does Meryem live?
2 Where did she go to primary school?
3 When did she start and finish secondary school?
4 What qualification did she get at the end of secondary school?
5 Where does she go to college and what qualification does she want to get there?
6 Does Meryem have a part-time job? What does she do?
7 What computer programs can she use?
8 How well does she speak Turkish? And English?
9 What does she like doing in her free time?

CURRICULUM VITAE

Personal details
Name: Meryem Gulec
Address: Findorffstraße 20
 28215 Bremen
Date of birth: 1992

Education and qualifications
Primary school: 1998–2003 Grundschule Burgdamm, Bremen
Secondary school: 2003–2008 Schulzentrum Findorff, Bremen
 Qualification: Hauptschulabschluss
College: 2008– Kaufmännische Schule Findorff, Bremen
 Qualification: Kauffrau für Touristik und Freizeit
 (management assistent for tourism and leisure)

Work experience 2008– Part-time job at Hapag-Lloyd Travel Agents, Bremen

Skills
Computer: Microsoft Word, Microsoft Excel
Languages: German (fluent), Turkish (mother tongue), English (good)

Interests travel, making clothes, singing

▶ traineeship ▶ education ▶ work experience ▶ skill(s) ▶ quite

> Check-in   > **Training**   > Language   > Check-out   **12**

R **B** It's one month later, and Meryem is having a job interview at Air Deutschland with Mr Werner. You'll hear three parts of the interview. Listen and answer the questions.

Part 1
First, Mr Werner asks Meryem some questions about her CV. Listen and choose the correct answer a, b or c.

1 Meryem loves
   a going to airports.
   b flying.
   c staying in hotels.

2 Two years ago she flew to
   a London.
   b the USA.
   c Turkey.

3 Meryem sings in
   a a club for young people.
   b a rock band.
   c her bathroom at home.

Part 2
Mr Werner is talking to Meryem now about the work of a flight attendant. Listen and finish the sentences.
1 Meryem thinks that she would be a good flight attendant because
   – she loves travel and …
   – she also likes …
   – she also likes being …
2 If Meryem worked for Air Deutschland, she would only be at home …

Part 3
Listen to the end of Meryem's interview with Mr Werner. True or false? Note down T or F.
1 If Meryem got the traineeship, her training would last six months.
2 She would be in Bremen the first month.
3 After that, she would fly on normal flights but she wouldn't work as a flight attendant.
4 Mr Werner will contact Meryem tomorrow about the traineeship.

I **C** Talk in class. What do YOU think? Did Meryem give good answers in her interview? Why (not)? Do you think that she will get the traineeship?

▶ to have an interview   ▶ to be away from home   ▶ to last   ▶ to contact (someone)

Job hunting **121**

4 Language practice

If-Sätze Typ 2 → Grammar summary 9

Wir benutzen *if*-Sätze Typ 2, um über eventuelle Situationen zu sprechen:
What would you do if you were Richie?
– *If I was Richie, I would apply for a job in the Apple Tree Kindergarten.*

Wir bilden *if*-Sätze Typ 2 mit *if* + simple past and *would*.

if + simple past	*would*
If I **got** the job,	I **would be** very happy.

Wir können auch mit dem *would*-Teil beginnen:
I would be very happy if I got the job.

Vorsicht! *Would* wird nie zweimal in einem *if*-Satz benutzt:
I would be happy if I ~~would get~~ *the job.*

P A Answer the questions about the pictures.

1. Where would you be if you saw the Eiffel Tower?
If I saw the Eiffel Tower, I would be in …
2. Where would you be if you saw the Brandenburg Gate?
3. What would you be if you had this job?
4. What would you eat if you went to this restaurant?
5. What *wouldn't* you do if you saw this sign?

P B Give the answers from A again. Start with the *would* part:

I would be in … if I saw the Eiffel Tower.

R/P C WORDS Can you find the 'job hunting' words and phrases from the unit? Explain them in German.

primaryschoolcurriculumvitaetraineeshipqualificationsfullyqualifiedwantedparttimeskillsfurtherinformationknowledgeofenglishexperiencefulltimecurrentlysecondaryschooltoapplyforajob

> Check-in   > Training   > Language   > Check-out   **12**

5 Activities

P **A** Write about 50 words about the cartoon below.

- What people can you see?
- Where are they and what's happening?
- What do you think? What would an interviewer say if someone did this in an interview?

Speech bubble: I'm fine thanks. I'm just having a job interview. How are you?

* P **B** Here are some questions which interviewers often ask in interviews. What answers would YOU give? Write 70–100 words in full sentences.

1 "What are your favourite subjects at college? Why?"
2 "Have you had a job before? What sorts of things did you do?"
3 "Give me an example of a time when you worked in a team. What happened?"

P **C** PROJECT Write a CV for YOU. Look at Meryem's CV on page 120 for ideas. If possible, use a computer and print your CV. Think about layout and headings.

CURRICULUM VITAE

Personal details
Name:
Address:
Date of birth:

Education and qualifications
Primary school:
Secondary school:

Job hunting

12 Check-out

GO FOR IT
The magazine for college students in Germany
This month ... **job interview tips**

From your GO FOR IT! team
Hello!
This month, **GO FOR IT!** has an article with tips for job interviews.

R **A** Copy the table below. Then read the article and write the *do's* and *don'ts* of interviews into your table.

TIPS FOR THE PERFECT JOB INTERVIEW	
DO'S	DON'TS
1 Find out about the company.	1 Don't go to bed late!
2 ...	

I **B** Talk in class.

- What do you think about the tips? Do you agree or disagree with the ideas?
- Which *three* tips do you think are the most important?
- The article talks about clothes for an interview. What are your ideas about 'good' and 'bad' clothes for an interview?
- "Have one or two questions which you can ask at the end". Can you think of some good questions?

I **C** Role-play

Work in a small group and role-play a job interview in English. It's fun! First, think of a job or write a job ad. Then take the parts of an interviewer (or two interviewers) and an applicant.

▶ to agree (with someone)   ▶ to disagree   ▶ applicant

Job spot

What do you think? Who would get the job?

Hi! I'm here for the job interview.

Me, too.

OK, you don't have to be a genius to answer that question. If you went to a job interview in a baseball cap, you probably wouldn't get the job – or only if the job was for a baseball player. But there are lots more do's and don'ts for job interviews. This month we give you …

15 hot tips for the perfect job interview!

Before the interview …

1. Find out about the company. Look on the Internet and in local newspapers.
2. Find out where the company is and plan your journey to the interview.
3. Think: what questions will they perhaps ask me? What will I say if they ask me those questions?
4. Go to bed early and sleep!

At the interview …

5. Don't be late! Things can always go wrong with buses etc. So plan to arrive 15–20 minutes early.
6. Yes, wear nice, clean, simple clothes. You don't have to be a fashion model or a rich business person, but be smart.
7. Shake hands with the interviewer and smile. Be positive and friendly.
8. Sit upright. You're in an interview – you aren't at home on the sofa in front of the TV!
9. Look at the interviewer when (s)he asks questions and when you answer. It's called 'eye contact' and it's very important.
10. Answer the questions but don't talk too much. The interviewer has lots of questions, so don't give 20-minute answers!
11. Speak clearly.
12. Tell the truth!
13. If you don't understand a question, say so.
14. Have one or two questions which you can ask at the end.
15. Thank the interviewer, smile again, and leave the room quietly.

▶ smart ▶ eye contact ▶ to tell the truth ▶ quiet(ly)

Job hunting

Unit 13
Global business

Am Ende dieser Unit kann ich …
→ über internationale Unternehmen sprechen und schreiben,
→ sagen, wo und wie Produkte hergestellt werden,
→ etwas über die Vor- und Nachteile der Globalisierung sagen.

1 Goods in a supermarket

R **A Read the short text below.**

1 What is the lorry in the picture delivering? Where to?
2 You can buy food in British supermarkets, of course. But what other goods can you often buy there?
3 Where are goods in a typical British supermarket made?

> This delivery lorry is delivering goods to a British supermarket. The truck is
> delivering food, but supermarkets are often very big and they also sell other
> things like clothes, electronic goods and books. Lots of the things are made
> in Britain, perhaps even in the store. The bread in many supermarkets is
> 5 made in a bakery in the store, for example. But lots of other things aren't
> from Britain. They're made in other countries around the world.

▶ (delivery) lorry ▶ to deliver ▶ goods ▶ a store

> Check-in   > Training   > Language   > Check-out   **13**

R/P **B** The products above are all on sale in a British supermarket. But they aren't from Britain. Where are they made? What do you think? Can you finish the sentences with the countries from the box?

1 The cheese is made in …
2 The pepperoni sausage is made in …
3 The beer is made …
4 The Hershey's chocolate …
5 The T-shirts are …
6 The TVs in the store …
7 The coffee is produced in …

> Africa • China • France • Germany • Italy • Japan • the USA

I **C** Talk in class. Do you have something with you today which is made in another country – a mobile, for example? Where are those products made?

▶ to be made in   ▶ to be produced in   ▶ sausage

Global business **127**

13

> Check-in > **Training** > Language > Check-out

2 Thorben's new computer

R **A** Read about Thorben. Why is he happy today? What did he do two weeks ago? What happened this morning?

Thorben Stalke lives in Göttingen. Two weeks ago, he ordered a new computer online, and this morning the computer company delivered it to his flat. The new computer is brilliant – much better than his old one. And it wasn't too expensive. Now he can play games much more quickly and surf the Internet a lot more easily. Thorben is really happy.

R **B** Thorben's computer is a typical desktop PC. But how does the company make its PCs? Look at the diagram on the next page and answer the questions below.

1 Different parts of the computer are made in different countries. Where are the monitors made?
   They're made in …
2 What about the mice? Where are they made?
3 Another important part of a computer is the keyboard. Where are the keyboards manufactured?
4 The computer tower is the place where you find all the electronics – the hard drive, the mother board and the CPU (central processing unit), for example. Where are the towers and all the things in them produced?
5 Before customers buy a computer, the company assembles all the different parts – it builds a computer. Where are the company's computers assembled?

P **C** Now look at the diagram below. How was Thorben's new computer assembled? Finish the sentences.

1 First, all the parts *were made* (make) around the world.
2 The parts … (transport) to Ireland.
3 Thorben's computer … (assemble).
4 Next, it … (transport) to Germany.
5 It … (store) in a warehouse.
6 Finally, the computer … (deliver) to his flat.

▶ to manufacture   ▶ to produce   ▶ to assemble   ▶ to transport

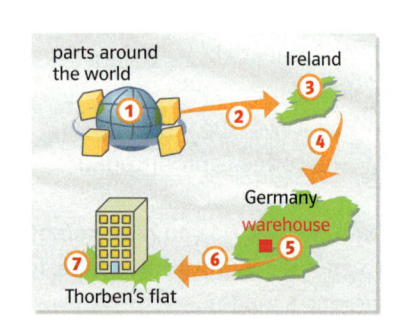

128 Global business

| Check-in | **Training** | Language | Check-out | **13** |

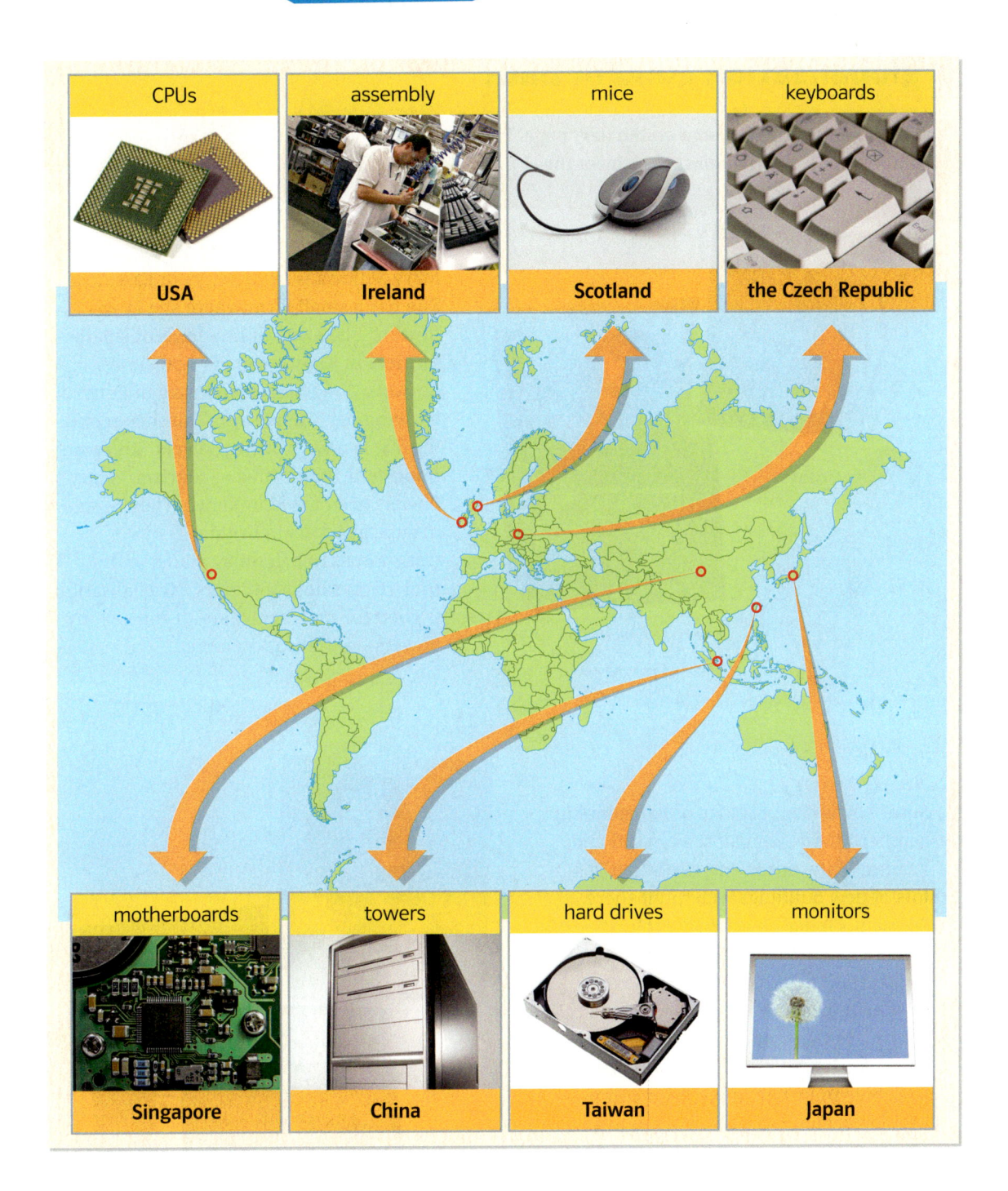

CPUs — USA
assembly — Ireland
mice — Scotland
keyboards — the Czech Republic

motherboards — Singapore
towers — China
hard drives — Taiwan
monitors — Japan

Das Passiv		
	simple present	simple past
the computer/it	❓ made	❓ produced
the monitors/they	❓ manufactured	❓ transported

What are the missing forms? ❓

Global business

3 Is globalisation good or bad?

A Read the three texts below and on the next page. Two are *for* globalisation and one is *against*. Which are they?

808236-0018

Mary's story

Mary Makusa is from Kenya in East Africa. She has a small farm where she grows flowers. She's one of hundreds of small
5 farmers in Kenya who are now flower growers. "The biggest industry in Kenya is growing tea," Mary says. "But the second biggest is now growing flowers. It's more important than coffee or tourism." Mary's
10 flowers aren't sold in Kenya. They're sold in supermarkets in Britain. They're transported to Britain by plane, and they're on sale in 24 hours. "Globalisation is good for me," says Mary. "I can sell my
15 flowers on the world market."

Flowers in a British supermarket. Over 70% of the flowers are imported from Kenya.

Sunil's story

Sunil Roy is from the city of Bangalore in southern India. Bangalore is an old and beautiful city, but in the 1980s and 90s
5 lots of new buildings were built there. Today, it's India's most high-tech city – it's sometimes called the 'Silicon Valley of India'. Like thousands of other young people in Bangalore, Sunil works in a call
10 centre. He's a computer technician, and every day he talks on a telephone helpline to people in Britain about their computer problems. Most of Sunil's friends also work in call centres for big banks and
15 other companies in Europe or the USA. "Globalisation is good for me," says Sunil. "We all speak English in India so the language isn't a problem. I earn a good salary and my life is much better than the
20 life of my parents."

▶ (to be) on sale   ▶ the world market   ▶ technician

130 Global business

| Check-in | Training | Language | Check-out | **13** |

Amjad's story

Amjad lives 2300 kilometres from Sunil in a town in Pakistan. He's 10 years old but he doesn't go to school. He works every day in a small factory. He makes footballs. Amjad can make one football a day. For a football, he earns about one euro. Amjad *has* to work. His family is very poor and they need his money. Around the world today, there are about 250 million – yes, 250 million! – children like Amjad. They work in factories, in mines, and lots work on farms. Big companies in Europe and the USA want to make their products very cheaply. The products (footballs, clothes, trainers, carpets and many other things) are made by children in poor countries like Pakistan. Then they are sold in shops in Europe – where they're often expensive. Globalisation is good for big, global companies. But for Amjad it isn't so good.

Pakistan
India
Bangalore

R/P **B** Finish the sentences with information from the three texts.

1 Growing flowers is more important in Kenya than …
2 Mary's flowers aren't sold in … They're transported to supermarkets in …
3 Globalisation is good for Mary because …
4 The city of Bangalore changed in the 1980s and 90s when …
5 Today, one name for the city is …
6 Globalisation is good for Sunil because …
7 Amjad can't go to school because …
8 There are … children like Amjad around the world today.
9 Globalisation is bad for Amjad but good for …

P **C** Is globalisation good or bad? Write a short text. Use the three stories as examples, and the useful phrases below.

Globalisation is good for some people but bad for others …

Useful phrases
on the one hand … but on the other (hand) • one reason (why globalisation is good/bad) is that … • another/a second/ a third reason … • for example, … • from this we can see that … • finally, we can say that … • on the whole …

Hier und dort

Diese Beispiele der modernen, globalen Geschäftswelt zeigen, warum Englisch *die* Weltsprache geworden ist. Wenn beispielsweise Chinesen mit Deutschen Geschäfte machen, sprechen sie Englisch. Ohne eine gemeinsame Sprache könnten sie sich nicht verständigen. Außerdem ist English für Millionen von Menschen weltweit die offizielle Amtssprache – wie für Mary aus Kenya und Sunil aus Indien. (Mehr Informationen findest du in *Go for it!* auf Seite 134.)

Das Passiv mit *by*

Footballs are often made **by** children in poor countries.
These products were made **by** young girls in Pakistan.

Give the German for *by*.

▶ (one) a day ▶ to earn ▶ on the one hand / on the other hand ▶ on the whole

Global business **131**

4 Language practice

Das Passiv → Grammar summary 10

Du kannst Passivsätze als 'umgedrehte' Aktivsätze ansehen. Das Objekt des Aktivsatzes wird zum Subjekt des Passivsatzes:
The company makes its (products) in China. **Aktiv**
The (products) are made in China. **Passiv**

Wenn du sagen willst, von wem etwas gemacht wird/wurde, verwendest du in Passivsätzen das Wort *by*:
*These footballs were made **by** children in Asia.*

Bildung:
Passivsätze werden mit *to be* und dem Partizip Perfekt (3. Form) gebildet. Die verschiedenen Zeiten werden mit den entsprechenden Zeiten von *to be* gebildet:
*The computer **is made** in Ireland.*
(simple present)
*My trainers **were manufactured** in Pakistan.*
(simple past)

P A Make *passive* sentences. Use the *simple present* or the *simple past*.

1. All our T-shirts *are made* (make) in China.
2. The flowers … (transport) to London yesterday.
3. A lot of coffee in our supermarkets … (produce) in Africa.
4. The office … (build) in 1995.
5. The computer company assembled my computer last week. Two days ago, it … (deliver) to my flat.
6. "Globalisation is good for me because my products … (sell) on the world market."
7. Do people in India speak English?
   – Sure. English … (speak) all over India.

P B Give the *active* sentences again as *passive* sentences. Use *by*.

1. Amjad made this football.
   This football was made by Amjad.
2. A Chinese company makes our motherboards.
3. Lots of young people buy these jeans.
4. Lots of young people play computer games.
5. The dog ate my chocolate!

R/P C WORDS Find words and phrases from the unit and make a GLOBAL BUSINESS mindmap.

5 Activities

I/P **A** Make a survey in your class then write about the results.

1. How many of the things which you have in class (or at home) were made in Germany? How many were made in another country? Where? Find out about as many things as you can.
2. In class, make a survey and a graph. Then write about the results:
   About 80% of our clothes/jeans/trainers were made in another country.
   Only about 20% of our clothes were made in Germany.
   Over 90% of all our electronic goods were made in another country/overseas.

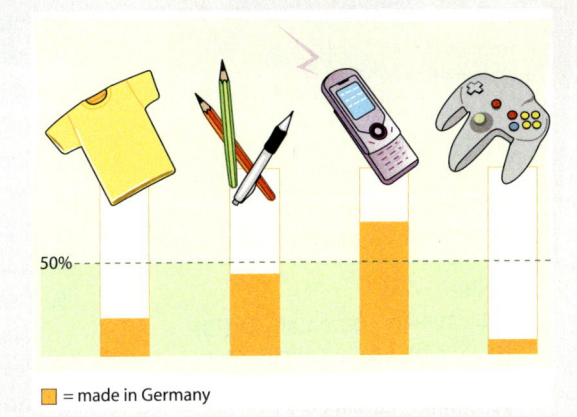

☐ = made in Germany

✱ **M** **B** You find this article about the Indian city of Bangalore on the Internet. Your friend is interested, but doesn't speak English. Give the main ideas of the article in German.

Bangalore: India's boomtown

The city of Bangalore is now so successful that flats and offices here are more expensive than in Manhattan! There are new buildings everywhere. One of the most amazing is the *Infosys*
5   building. *Infosys* is an Indian IT company which has workers around the world. The building in Bangalore is its global headquarters. In fact, it's a small city where the company's 20,000 workers all work. It also has shops, restaurants, a fitness club – and even a golf course for them! The building is so big
10 that inside it there are free bicycles for the workers! All over Bangalore, there are more cafés and shops for the city's thousands of IT workers. They earn good money and have a good lifestyle. But there are many other people in Bangalore who are still poor. Next to the big office buildings you can often see the small, dirty
15 places where they live. It's a big contrast!

P **C** **PROJECT** Make a poster. Choose *one* of the ideas below.

1. Find out how something is made and make a poster. Even simple, everyday things like toothpaste are often very complicated! Use pictures and words and show a diagram of the process.
2. FAIRTRADE is an idea to help workers like Amjad in Pakistan and other poor people around the world. Find out more about it on the Internet and make a poster.

13 Check-in   Training   Language   **Check-out**

GO FOR IT

The magazine for college students in Germany

This month …
Other countries, other customs

From your GO FOR IT! team

Hello!
This month's edition of **GO FOR IT!** has an article called 'Other countries, other customs'. What do you think that means? Can you give an example?

R A Read the texts about India and China. True, false or not in the text? Note down T, F or NT.

1. Young people in India today always use the traditional 'Namaste' greeting with people from other countries.
2. In China, young people speak English well.
3. Something which is very important for people in India is hospitality.
4. If you visit an Indian person's home, they will always first give you a cup of tea.
5. Younger people in China are more important than older people.
6. Peter Chen's boss is called Mr Wu.
7. Indian people often say 'yes' – but that doesn't always mean 'yes'.
8. It's impolite in China to say "That's a mistake" or to eat everything on your plate.

I B Look at the text about Britney Miller. What do you think of her ideas? Are German people 'funny' or 'rude'? Talk in class.

P/I C Give a short presentation to the class about the customs in another country. It can be a country which you know, or you can find information on the Internet. Remember to use 'visual aids'. Other students can ask questions at the end.

So läuft's besser

Referate *(presentations)*
- I'd like to talk today about …
- First, I'll talk about …, then I'll say something about …
- Here's a picture of …
- Here's a list of …
- Here you can see …
- For example, …
- Does everybody understand … (word/expression)?
- Thanks for listening!
- Do you have any questions?

▸ greeting   ▸ hospitality   ▸ custom

134 Global business

Other countries, other customs

808236-0019

Andere Länder, andere Sitten. In our global world, people at work now often meet other people from many different countries in their jobs. So different customs are more important. Words and actions which are very polite in one country can be very impolite in another. Let's look at two countries, India and China ...

India

Young people in India today often shake hands with visitors from other countries – like in Europe. But they will be very happy if you use the traditional Indian greeting. Put your hands together and say: "Namaste". For Indian people, hospitality is *very*
5 important. They often invite visitors to their families at home. And if you are the visitor, they will be *very* friendly. If you visit an Indian family, take a small present – but not in black or white paper. Black and white mean 'bad luck'. Another thing in India is that it is very impolite to say 'no'. So you will find that
10 Indian people often say 'yes' but mean 'no'!

China

China today is an important country in the global business world. Young Chinese people speak English well and want to understand European visitors. But China is also an old country, with lots of traditions and customs. "Older people are really important in
5 China," says Peter Chen, who works in a company in Beijing. "I'm young, so when I'm with my boss, I don't say much." Respect for other people is also really important. "Never, never say: 'That's a mistake!'" says Peter. "People in China have to 'keep face'". There are also lots of customs when people eat. Peter: "Don't eat
10 everything on your plate. That means: 'I'm still hungry and you're a bad host'. And don't drop your chopsticks. It's bad luck!"

Those funny Germans!

So what do people from other countries think about us, the Germans? Britney Miller from England is working in an office in Germany this year. What does she think?
5 "The people in my office are really nice, really friendly. But some things in Germany are different. Two secretaries in my office have worked here for ten years, but they still say: 'Frau Hübner' and 'Frau Dahmen'. I think that's funny! Another thing here is queues. In England we always stand in queues, say, for a bus. In
10 Germany, everybody runs! And in shops, people sometimes don't say 'please' or 'thank you'. For me, that's *very* rude!"

▶ impolite   ▶ present   ▶ bad luck   ▶ to stand in a queue   ▶ rude

Global business

Unit 14
Job satisfaction

Am Ende dieser Unit kann ich ...
→ meine Berufswahl begründen,
→ sagen, was – unter anderen Umständen – hätte geschehen können.

1 Why become a firefighter?

R **A** Read the text below and look at the pictures on these two pages. Then answer the questions.

On September 11, 2001, terrorists flew two planes into the World Trade Center in New York. Minutes after the planes had crashed into the two towers, firefighters from the New York Fire Department arrived. The young men and women of the
5 NYFD worked for three days. 343 of them died.

So why do people choose such a dangerous job? The most important reason is that they want to help the people in their cities. That's what the NYFD firefighters did on 9/11. And if they hadn't been there, hundreds more people would have died.
Just think of it!

▶ to crash (into) ▶ to choose ▶ such a ▶ reason

Hier und dort

Amerikaner schreiben das Datum anders als Europäer.
In den USA ist die Reihenfolge:
| **Monat** | **Tag** | **Jahr** |
| *September* | *11* | *2001* |

Dieser denkwürdige Tag wird deshalb *9/11* und nicht *11/9* genannt.

136 Job satisfaction

14

> Check-in   Training   Language   Check-out

R   B   Find words on the last page which mean:

> hineinfliegen • (Feuerwehrmann/-frau) werden •
> der wichtigste Grund • überlegen Sie mal

R/P   C   Finish the sentences.

1. On September 11, 2001, two planes crashed into …
2. Firefighters arrived there minutes …
3. How many days did the firefighters work? They …
4. How many died? …
5. The text says that people often become firefighters because …

R   D   Look at this sentence. Can you say it in German?

> If the firefighters **hadn't been** there, hundreds more people **would have died**.

▶ just think   ▶ the text says (that) …

Job satisfaction   **137**

14 › Check-in › **Training** › Language › Check-out

2 My job

R A Below, three people are talking about their jobs. Read what they say and find out …

1 their jobs,
2 *one* reason why each person likes her or his job.

808236-0020

KINGSTON TAYLOR, LONDON, ENGLAND

I was bad at school. I mean bad, man! I had trouble with my teachers, with the police, with my mum and dad. I left school when I was sixteen. I didn't want to work. A year later, I
5 was homeless. I just lived on the streets. Then one day I met a youth worker. He found a room for me in a hostel. After I had been there about six months, one of the workers at the hostel said: "Hey, you're good with the other kids here. Why not be a youth worker yourself?" I went to 10 college, got some qualifications, and now I work at the hostel. It's fantastic. I understand the kids here and I can *help* them. If I had stayed on the streets, I would have died or become an alcoholic. But I didn't. And I'm glad! 15

TONI CROFT, SYDNEY, AUSTRALIA

When I was a kid at school, I had no idea about a job. I mean absolutely *no* idea. One week I wanted to be a nurse, the next week a famous swimmer, the week after that a singer in a rock
5 band. Then one day I went to the zoo with some friends. There was a notice. It said: *Wanted. Part-time workers to help with the animals.* I got the job! And after I had finished school, I became an apprentice at the zoo. Now I work here full time. The job is so interesting. I love 10 the animals, and my work colleagues are really friendly. If I hadn't seen that notice at the zoo, I would have found another job, I'm sure. But this is the best job in the world for me.

▶ to have trouble with ▶ homeless ▶ to have (absolutely) no idea

138 Job satisfaction

14

> Check-in   > **Training**   > Language   > Check-out

GREG MACKENZIE, ONTARIO, CANADA

In my last year at school, my class visited the Canadian Pacific Railway company here in Ontario. The CPR is amazing: it's a railway which goes from the east coast of Canada to the west
5 coast, nearly 4,000 kilometres. That day with my class, I knew: I wanted to work on the railway. After I had finished high school, I became an apprentice. Now I'm a track worker. I check and repair the railway tracks. I really
10 like the job because it's important, because I work with some great guys, and because the CPR is a great company. Of course, I work outside and in Canada it can be very cold. And the work is hard. After I had worked a week, I was tired. I mean I was dead tired! If I hadn't 15 loved the job, I would have given up.

I/P B Who's this? Give the names (Kingston, Toni or Greg).

1 *Kingston* was homeless after he had left school.
2 ... would have died if he had stayed homeless on the streets.
3 ... got a part-time job after she had seen a notice at a zoo.
4 ... chose his job after he had visited a company with his class.
5 ... has really friendly colleagues.
6 ... can help young people who have problems.
7 ... was dead tired after he had worked a week in his job.
8 ... would have given up his job if he hadn't loved it.
9 ... had had absolutely no idea about jobs at school.

P C Look at the sentences below about Kingston. Can you finish the sentences about Toni and Greg?

*Kingston chose his job **after** a worker at his hostel **had said**: "Why not be a youth worker yourself?"*
*If a youth worker **hadn't found** Kingston on the streets, Kingston **would have died**.*

1 Toni chose her job after ... (see/notice)
2 If Toni ... the notice, she ... (find/another job)
3 Greg chose his job after ... (class/visit)
4 He was dead tired after the first week. If he ... (the job/give up)

What are the missing forms?

Das past perfect			
After	I	had	been finished worked
	he/she/it	?	
	we/you/they	?	

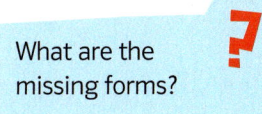

If-Sätze Typ 3	
if + past perfect	**would have**
If I ? (stay) on the streets,	I ? (die).

▶ railway   ▶ east/west coast   ▶ to check

Job satisfaction **139**

3 Be different!

R A The text below is from a brochure.

1 What do the graphs in the brochure show?
2 According to the brochure, which is right, a) or b)?
   a) Men must do men's jobs and women must do women's jobs.
   b) Men and women don't always have to do 'typical' jobs.

Why not be different?

Very often, young men choose jobs which are 'typical' for men, and young women choose jobs which are 'typical' for women. Here are some statistics.

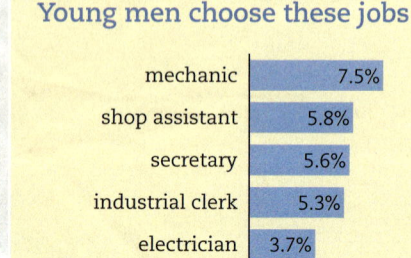

Young men choose these jobs

mechanic	7.5%
shop assistant	5.8%
secretary	5.6%
industrial clerk	5.3%
electrician	3.7%
painter and decorator	3.4%

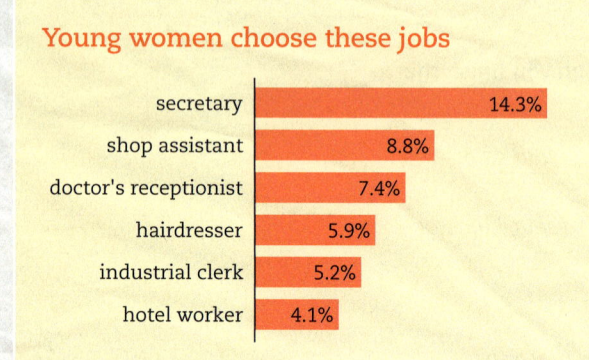

Young women choose these jobs

secretary	14.3%
shop assistant	8.8%
doctor's receptionist	7.4%
hairdresser	5.9%
industrial clerk	5.2%
hotel worker	4.1%

But what does 'typical' mean? Why choose a job just because you think that it's a *man's* or a *woman's* job? Just think! YOU *can* be different!

R B Look at the statistics in the brochure again.

1 Which jobs do a) only men usually do and which do b) only women usually do?
2 Which jobs are popular with men *and* women?
3 Which job is the most popular with a) men and b) women?

▸ graph   ▸ statistics   ▸ popular (with)

140 Job satisfaction

| Check-in | **Training** | Language | Check-out |

R 2|14 **C** You'll hear a radio programme from New Zealand called *Jobs around the world* with the presenter Mike Smith. In the programme, you'll hear two interviews with young people from Germany. You'll hear both interviews twice.

Interview 1
Listen to Julia Lammert and choose the right answer.
1 Julia is
   a a kindergarten teacher.
   b an electrician.
   c a carpenter.
   d a hairdresser.
2 Why did she choose her job?
   a Her dad is a carpenter.
   b She loved making things as a kid.
   c It was the idea of one of her teachers.
   d Her boyfriend works for a building firm.
3 What did Julia do after she had finished school?
   a She went to college full-time.
   b She got a job.
   c She was unemployed.
   d She got an apprenticeship and went to college part time.
4 What do her friends think about her job?
   a They were surprised at first, but now they think it's great.
   b They think she's crazy.
   c They all say: "You must do what you want to do."
   d They think it's a very bad idea.
5 If Julia hadn't chosen this job, she would maybe have become
   a a fashion model.
   b a secretary.
   c a fashion designer.
   d a shop assistant.

Interview 2
Listen to Hasan Samsek. True or false? Note down T or F.
1 Hasan is a care worker who looks after disabled people.
2 At school, he didn't want to be a care worker.
3 After he had finished school, he was an apprentice electrician for six months.
4 He wanted to be a care worker after he had visited a home with his class at college.
5 He's on a college course at the moment.
6 He thinks that men are better care workers than women.

I/P **D** Work in a small group. Brainstorm your ideas about these questions. Then give the class a short report.

1 Why do men and women often choose 'typical' jobs?
2 Is this situation changing? Will it change more in the future?
3 Are there *any* jobs which a) men and b) women really can't do?

> We think that …
> In our opinion, …
> The reason that …

▸ surprised ▸ care worker ▸ disabled people ▸ old people's home

Job satisfaction **141**

4 Language practice

Das past perfect und *If*-Sätze Typ 3 → Grammar summary **5 9**

Das **past perfect** wird für ein Ereignis in der Vergangenheit verwendet, das noch vor einem zweiten Ereignis in der Vergangenheit stattfand. Für das länger zurückliegende Ereignis verwendet man das past perfect, für das nicht so lang zurückliegende das simple past.
*After I **had eaten** my breakfast* (erstes Ereignis), *I walked to the bus stop* (zweites Ereignis).

Bildung: Das past perfect wird mit *had* + Partizip Perfekt (3. Form) gebildet.

***If*-Sätze Typ 3** schildern Ereignisse in der Vergangenheit, die hätten passieren können:
*If I **had seen** you yesterday, I **would have said** 'hello'.* (Aber ich habe dich nicht gesehen.)

Bildung:

if + past perfect	*would(n't) have* + Partizip Perfekt (3. Form)
If I **had seen** you,	I **would have said** 'hello'.
If I **hadn't gone** to that party,	I **wouldn't have spoken** to you.

P A Make two sentences with the *past perfect* for 1–4. Like this:

Tim got up. He ate his breakfast. He went to work.
After Tim had got up, he ate his breakfast.
After he had eaten his breakfast, he went to work.

1 Josie phoned her friend Maria. She changed her clothes. She went into town to meet Maria.
2 Jens heard a song on the radio. He downloaded it online. He listened to it on his MP3 player.
3 Hank got in his car. He started the engine. He drove to his friend's house.
4 Daisy watched a movie at the cinema. She ate a burger in town. She came home.

R B Match the sentence halves.

1 If I had seen you yesterday,
2 If you had given me your number,
3 If I had had 50 euros,
4 If I hadn't done my homework,
5 If I hadn't eaten all those cakes,

a I would have bought that nice jacket.
b I wouldn't have been ill!
c my teacher would have been angry.
d I would have phoned you.
e I would have said 'hello'.

P C Now finish this sentence in your own words.

If I hadn't chosen the college course which I'm on now, I …

R/P D WORDS Which is the 'odd word out'? Why?

1 plane	airport	bus	train
2 student	school	college	university
3 fantastic	nice	wonderful	terrible
4 to arrive	to work	to understand	important
5 elevator	subway	cinema	downtown

Check-in | Training | Language | **Check-out**

5 Activities

P A Read about Will then write a short text about YOU. Write 60–70 words.

Will went to primary school in Toronto in Canada. After he had left primary school, he went to secondary school – also in Toronto. After he had finished secondary school, he went to college. He's on a retail course. He wants to be a shop assistant. He chose his course after he had visited a big store one day with his class at school.

- primary school?
- secondary school?
- college?
- course?
- career plan?
- reason why you chose your course?

✱ I/P B Role-play

1 Work in a group of 3–4 students. You are at an international meeting of college students from around the world.
2 Look at the role card below. On page 158 you can see some more role cards. Choose one card each. First, introduce yourself to the other people in your group, then ask questions to find out about them.

ROLE CARD
- **Name** . . . . John/Jane Peterson
- **Country** . . . England
- **Course** . . . business communication
- **Reason** . . . You chose your course after you had worked for a week with your older brother/sister who has a job in an office.
- **Career plans** . You're going to be a secretary.
- **Reason** . . . You think the work is important and interesting. Also, you like working in a team with other people.

Hi. I'm … / My name's …

Where are you from?
What course are you on?
What are your career plans?

Why do you want to do that?
When did you …?
Why did you …?

I/P C PROJECT A radio interview

Work with a partner or in a small group and make a radio interview. Think of a title. In the programme, interview a student. You can ask about:
- which job they want to have,
- why and when they chose that job,
- their ideas about their career in the future.

Job satisfaction **143**

| Check-in | Training | Language | **Check-out** |

GO FOR IT!

The magazine for college students in Germany!

This month ...

EXAMS — EXAM SPECIAL

DON'T PANIC! WE HAVE TIPS FOR THE BEST RESULTS!

From your GO FOR IT! team

Hello!
This month, **GO FOR IT!** has an 'exam special' with tips for the best results.

R A Read the exam tips on the next page. Find these important words and phrases in English.

1. Note(n)
2. keine Panik!
3. Wörterbuch
4. (Zeit) einteilen
5. eine Prüfung ablegen
6. Teil (einer Prüfung)
7. Aufgabe (in einer Prüfung)
8. Uhr/Armbanduhr
9. Punkte (umsonst) verlieren
10. simple
11. überprüfen
12. Fehler

R/P B Don't be Susie! She did everything wrong in her exam last week. Can you find her mistakes?

1. She arrived at college at 9.59. Her exam started at 10.00.
2. Then she went to Room 10. The exam was in Room 12.
3. In the writing part, she had to write *two* emails. After 30 minutes, Susie had written one. Then she had only four minutes for the second email.
4. One task in Susie's exam was: 'Answer question A **OR** question B.' Susie answered question A *and* question B.
5. In her German exam, there was a reading text. There were 10 words in it which she didn't know. She thought: "I can't understand this!" So she just wrote crazy answers!
6. The last question in the German exam was a 'letter to a penfriend in Germany'. Susie wrote long, complicated sentences.
7. Then she read her letter quickly, thought: "Great!", and finished the exam.

I C Talk in class. Do you have more tips for exams? Tell the class. Write a list on the board.

GOFORIT!

▶ exam   ▶ result   ▶ grade   ▶ mark

144 Job satisfaction

> Check-in   > Training   > Language   > **Check-out**

Get the best grades in your exam! OUR TIPS.

Your course at college is almost finished. And now you have exams. They're important, of course. But remember – you can only do your best! So don't panic, and follow the tips below.

1. Be there
Find out *where* (Room 114?) and *when* (Thursday, 10 a.m.?) the exam is and the things which you need for it (pens, pencils, a dictionary). Make a CHECKLIST. Sleep well the night before, get up and have a good breakfast, and be at college *early* (not two minutes before the exam!).

2. Plan your time
OK. Now you're doing your exam. Look at *all* of it first. How many parts are there? What are the tasks? Now think: how much time do you have? *Plan your time!* A good tip is: take a small clock to college, or put your watch on the table where you can see it.

3. Read the questions
That sounds so easy, but it's really important. If the task is: 'Write 50 words', then write 50 words – not 30 or 100! (But 55–60 is OK.) If the task is: 'Listen and finish the sentences', then don't write 'True' or 'False'! You must get all the marks you can in your exam. Don't lose marks because you don't answer the questions correctly.

4. Reading and listening – don't panic
There *will* be words and expressions which you don't know at first. That's normal. Your English is OK! Read texts more than once. *You'll understand more each time.* In the listening tasks, you'll usually hear everything twice too.

5 Writing: KISS (= Keep It Short and Simple)
English isn't German! Don't think: "Wie würde ich es auf Deutsch sagen, dann erst übersetze ich es ins Englische." Do this: first, plan your ideas. Then write short, clear English sentences where you know the words and the grammar. Then *check, check, check*! He 'go' or he 'goes'? I 'life' in Germany or I 'live' in Germany?

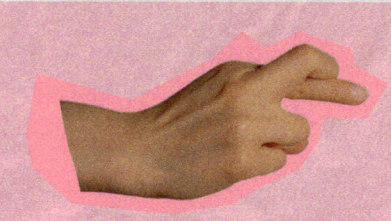

In German you say: "Ich drücke dir die Daumen". In Britain and other English-speaking countries, people 'keep their fingers crossed'.

SO – GOOD LUCK IN YOUR EXAM!
We'll keep our fingers crossed for you!

▶ to do your best   ▶ to lose marks   ▶ to keep your fingers crossed

Job satisfaction

Grammar summary

1 Das simple present

A Allgemein
Das simple present wird verwendet:
- für Aussagen, die längere Zeit gültig sind,
- um auszudrücken, was jemand regelmäßig tut.

I go to college five days a week.

I live in Germany.

B Mit *sometimes, often* usw.
Da man mit dem simple present ausdrückt, was man regelmäßig tut, wird es oft mit Wörtern wie *usually, normally, sometimes, often, always, never* verwendet. Diese Wörter (Adverbien) stehen immer:
- **vor** einem Vollverb,
- **nach** *to be*.

*I **usually** get up at 7 a.m.*

*I **often** watch TV in the evenings.*

*I'm **always** happy on Fridays.*

C Bildung: Aussagen
Das simple present wird aus der Grundform des Verbs (Infinitiv ohne *to*) gebildet. Nach *he/she/it* endet das Verb immer auf *-s* oder *-es*!

a An die meisten Verben wird einfach *-s* angehängt.
b Die Endung *-es* wird bei Verben benutzt, die auf *s, ss, x, ch,* oder *sh* enden (z. B. *to finish*), da es schwer wäre, nur ein *-s* auszusprechen.
c Auch *to go* und *to do* enden mit *-es*.
d Ein Sonderfall sind Verben, die auf *-y* enden: *to tidy* → *he tid**ies**.*

a TO WORK	b TO FINISH
I work	I finish
he/she/it work**s**	he/she/it finish**es**
we work	we finish
you work	you finish
they work	they finish

c TO GO	d TO TIDY
I go	I tidy
he/she/it go**es**	he/she/it tid**ies**
we go	we tidy
you go	you tidy
they go	they tidy

D Bildung: Fragen und Verneinungen
- Fragen im simple present werden mit *do* (bei *he/she/it*: *does*) gebildet.
- Verneinungen bildet man mit *don't* (nach *he/she/it*: *doesn't*).

Vorsicht!
Nach *does/doesn't* kommt immer die Grundform des Verbs:
Does he work? (! Does he ~~works~~?)
She doesn't work. (! She doesn't ~~works~~.)

Fragen	Verneinungen
Do I work?	I don't work
Does he/she/it wor**k**?	he/she/it doesn't wor**k**
Do we work?	we don't work
Do you work?	you don't work
Do they work?	they don't work

Grammar summary

2 Das present continuous

A Allgemein
Das present continuous benutzt man für Aktivitäten, die gerade im Augenblick des Sprechens stattfinden. Oder auch um ein Bild zu beschreiben. Es wird häufig mit Zeitangaben wie *at the moment* und *right now* verwendet.

> I'**m reading** this text at the moment.
>
> What can you see in this photo?
> – A hairdresser. Right now, she'**s cutting** a customer's hair.

B Mit *this week*, *this month* usw.
Das present continuous kann auch für längere, befristete Handlungen verwendet werden, die gerade stattfinden, benutzt werden, z. B. *this week*, *this month*.

> We'**re visiting** some friends in England this week. Julia **is learning** English on a course in London.

C Bildung: Aussagen
Das present continuous wird mit *to be* und Verb + *-ing* gebildet.

D Bildung: Fragen und Verneinungen
Fragen und Verneinungen werden mit den Frage- und Verneinungsformen von *to be* gebildet.

I'm he's/she's/it's we're you're they're	working	I'm not working she isn't working
		Am I working? Are you working? Are they working?

Verb + *-ing*: Schreibregeln
- An die meisten Verben wird einfach *-ing* angehängt: wor**k** – work**ing**, d**o** – do**ing**.
- Verben, die auf *-e* enden, verlieren das *-e*: us**e** – us**ing**, danc**e** – danc**ing**.
- Kurze Verben, die auf einen Vokal und einen Konsonanten (außer *-y*, *-w* und *-x*) enden, verdoppeln den Konsonanten: cu**t** – cu**tting** (aber pla**y** – pla**ying**).
- Längere Verben, die auf einen Vokal und einen Konsonanten enden, verdoppeln den Konsonanten nicht: visi**t** – visi**ting**, delive**r** – delive**ring**.
(Ausnahmen: trave**ll**ing, begi**nn**ing)
- Bei Verben, die auf *-ie* enden, wird *-ie* zu *-y*: d**ie** – d**ying**

Simple present oder present continuous?

> This is Patrick. He lives in England. He goes to an FE college five days a week.

> It's 8.30 in the morning. Patrick is going to college by bus.

3 Das simple past

A Allgemein

Das simple past wird verwendet, um Ereignisse in der Vergangenheit zu schildern, die jetzt abgeschlossen sind. Es wird häufig mit Zeitangaben wie *then*, *in 1970*, *last week* und *30 years ago* benutzt.

Cool shorts, Gary. Where did you get them?

I bought them yesterday in town.

B Bildung: Aussagen

- Regelmäßige Verben bilden das simple past mit *-ed*. Diese Form bleibt in allen Personen gleich.
- Unregelmäßige Verben haben Sonderformen im simple past (eine Liste findest du auf dem Klappumschlag). Diese Formen (außer bei *to be*) bleiben ebenfalls in allen Personen gleich.

regelmäßig	unregelmäßig	
TO WORK	TO GO	TO BE
I worked	I went	I was
he worked	he went	he was
she worked	she went	she was
it worked	it went	it was
we worked	we went	we were
you worked	you went	you were
they worked	they went	they were

C Bildung: Fragen und Verneinungen

- Fragen im simple past werden in allen Personen mit *did* gebildet.
- Verneinungen bildet man durchgehend mit *didn't*.
- *to be* bildet Fragen und Verneinungen im simple past mit eigenen Formen.

Vorsicht!
Nach *did/didn't* steht immer die Grundform des Verbs:
Did he work? (**!** *Did he* ~~worked~~*?*)
She didn't work. (**!** *She didn't* ~~worked~~.)

Fragen	Verneinungen
Did I work?	I didn't work
Did he/she/it work?	he/she/it didn't work
Did we work?	we didn't work
Did you work?	you didn't work
Did they work?	they didn't work
TO BE	
Was I?	I wasn't
Was he/she/it?	he/she/it wasn't
Were we/you/they?	we/you/they weren't

Verb + *-ed*: Schreibregeln

- An die meisten Verben wird einfach *-ed* angehängt: *work – worked*.
- An Verben, die auf *-e* enden, hängt man nur *-d* an: *use – used, dance – danced*.
- Kurze Verben, die auf einen Vokal (*a, e, i o, u*) und einen Konsonanten (außer *-y, -w* und *-x*) enden, verdoppeln den Konsonanten: *shop – shopped, jog – jogged*.
- Längere Verben, die auf einen Vokal und einen Konsonanten enden, verdoppeln den Konsonanten nicht: *visit – visited, deliver – delivered*. (Ausnahme: *travelled*)
- Bei Verben, die auf *-y* enden, wird *-y* zu *-i*: *study – studied*.

Grammar summary

4 Das present perfect

A Allgemein
Mit dem present perfect und *since/for* kann man 'Wie lange'-Fragen *(How long …?)* beantworten.
- *Since* wird mit einem Zeitpunkt (z. B. *2001, 3 January, last year*) benutzt.
- *For* verwendet man für einen Zeitraum (z. B. *two years, six months*).

How long has Julie had that electric guitar?
For about two days

B Bildung: Aussagen
Das present perfect wird mit *to have* und der 3. Form (Partizip Perfekt) gebildet.
- Regelmäßige Verben (wie *to work*) bilden ihre 3. Form mit *-ed*.
- Unregelmäßige Verben (wie *to go*) haben Sonderformen, die in der Liste auf dem Klappumschlag zu finden sind.

I have (I've) he has (he's) she has (she's) it has (it's) we have (we've) you have (you've) they have (they've)	worked gone

C Bildung: Fragen und Verneinungen
Fragen und Verneinungen werden mit Frage- und Verneinungsformen von *to have* + 3. Form des Verbs gebildet.

Have you worked?
Has he worked?

I haven't worked
he/she/it hasn't worked
we/you/they haven't worked

5 Das past perfect

A Allgemein
Das past perfect wird für ein Ereignis in der Vergangenheit verwendet, das noch vor einem zweiten Ereignis in der Vergangenheit stattfand. Für das länger zurückliegende Ereignis verwendet man das past perfect, für das nicht ganz so lange zurückliegende das simple past. Wir verwenden das past perfect häufig mit *after*.

*She **chose** her job after she **had visited** an interesting company.*

B Bildung
Das past perfect wird mit *had* + 3. Form (Partizip Perfekt) des Verbs gebildet. Fragen werden auch mit *had*, Verneinungen mit *hadn't* gebildet.

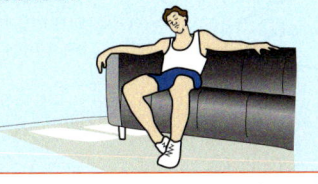

Aussagen	Verneinungen
I had worked he/she/it had worked we/you/they had worked	I hadn't worked he/she/it hadn't worked we/you/they hadn't worked

Fragen

Had I worked?
Had he/she/it worked?
Had we/you/they worked?

After Jamie had run in the marathon, he went home and went to sleep!

Grammar summary

6 Das Futur: *will*

A Allgemein
Will wird für feststehende Ereignisse in der Zukunft sowie für Vorhersagen und Vermutungen verwendet.

> I'**ll have** a family in 10 years.
> She **won't leave** her job when she has a family.

B Bildung
- **Aussagen** werden mit *will* + Grundform des Verbs gebildet. Die Kurzform (*'ll*) wird fast immer beim Sprechen und häufig auch beim Schreiben verwendet.
- **Fragen** bildet man, indem man *will* und das Subjekt tauscht. Hier sind die Kurzformen nicht möglich.
- **Verneinungen** werden mit *won't* + Grundform des Verbs gebildet.

I will (I'll) come	Will I come?
he will (he'll) come	Will he come?
she will (she'll) come	Will she come?
it will (it'll) come	Will it come?
we will (we'll) come	Will we come?
you will (you'll) come	Will you come?
they will (they'll) come	Will they come?

I won't come
he/she/it won't come
we/you/they won't come

7 Das Futur: *going to*

A Allgemein
Going to verwendet man, um über Pläne und Vorhaben zu sprechen: *I'm going to buy a new jacket* entspricht etwa auf Deutsch: „Ich habe vor, eine neue Jacke zu kaufen."

> I'**m going to** move to a new appartment next month.
> **Are** you **going to** leave home?

B Bildung
- **Aussagen** bildet man mit *to be* + *going to* + Hauptverb.
- **Fragen** bildet man mit den Frageformen von *to be* + *going to* + Hauptverb.
- Für **Verneinungen** benutzt man die Verneinung von *to be* + *going to* + Hauptverb.

I'm he's/she's/it's we're/you're/they're	going to	work
Am I Is he/she/it Are we/you/they	going to	work?
I'm not he/she/it isn't we/you/they aren't	going to	work

Will und *going to*

> It won't rain tomorrow.

> When I'm big, I'm going to be a footballer!

Grammar summary

8 Modale Hilfsverben: *must, have to, mustn't* und *don't/doesn't have to*

A Allgemein
Mit den modalen Hilfsverben *must, have to, mustn't* und *don't/doesn't have to* wird ausgedrückt, was man tun muss, nicht tun darf und nicht zu tun braucht (nicht tun muss).

must/have to	mustn't	don't/doesn't have to
In England you must/have to drive on the left.	You mustn't drive on the right!	He doesn't have to drive! He has a driver.

Must und *have to* haben etwa die gleiche Bedeutung. Sie drücken aus, was man tun **muss**.

Mustn't drückt aus, was man **nicht darf**.
Vorsicht! *mustn't* bedeutet **nicht** ‚nicht müssen'.

Don't/Doesn't have to drückt aus, was man **nicht zu tun braucht**.
Vorsicht! *don't have to* = nicht müssen

B Bildung: *must* und *have to*
- *Must* bleibt in allen Personen gleich. Auf *must* folgt die Grundform des Verbs.
- *Have to* bildet man mit *to have* + Grundform des Verbs.

must	have to
I must go he/she/it must go we/you/they must go	I have to go he/she/it has to go we/you/they have to go

C Bildung: *mustn't*
Mustn't bleibt ebenfalls bei allen Personen gleich. Auf *mustn't* folgt die Grundform des Verbs.

I mustn't he/she/it mustn't we/you/they mustn't	go

D Bildung: *don't/doesn't have to*
Die Verneinungsform von *have to* bildet man mit *don't/doesn't have to* + Grundform des Verbs.

I don't have to he/she/it doesn't have to we/you/they don't have to	go

Grammar summary

9 If-Sätze (Bedingungssätze)

A Allgemein
- Ein Bedingungssatz besteht aus einem *if*-Teil und einem Hauptsatz. Der *if*-Teil beschreibt eine Bedingung und der Hauptsatz drückt aus, was passieren wird oder passieren könnte (oder hätte passieren können), wenn diese Bedingung erfüllt wird.
- Bedingungssätze können entweder mit dem *if*-Teil oder mit dem Hauptsatz beginnen. Wenn der *if*-Teil beginnt, steht immer ein Komma vor dem Hauptsatz.
- Es gibt drei Grundtypen von *if*-Sätzen: Typ 1, 2 und 3.

B If-Sätze Typ 1:
*If you **ask** the robot, it **will clean** the house.*

- Typ 1 drückt aus, was unter bestimmten Bedingungen in der Zukunft geschehen wird oder nicht geschehen wird.

If + simple present	will + Verb
If you go to the party,	you'll see Mitch.

C If-Sätze Typ 2:
*If I **worked** for that company, I **would need** a good qualification.*

- Wir benutzen Typ 2, um über eventuelle Situationen zu sprechen oder wenn du zweifelst, dass eine Bedingung erfüllbar ist.
- **Vorsicht!** Anders als im Deutschen darf *would* nur im Hauptsatz, nicht im *if*-Teil stehen.

If + simple past	would(n't) + Verb
If you went to the party,	you would see Mitch.

D If-Sätze Typ 3:
*If he **had stayed** on the streets, he **would have died**.*

- Typ 3 schildert Ereignisse in der Vergangenheit, die hätten passieren können – die aber nicht passiert sind.

If + past perfect	would(n't) have + Partizip Perfekt (3. Form)
If you had gone to the party,	you would have seen Mitch.

If you get this answer right, Mr Davis, you'll win €500,000. But if you get it wrong, you'll lose everything.

Sorry, Mr Davis, that's the wrong answer. If you had said 'B', you would have won €500,000. But you said 'C'.

What would you do if you had €500,000?

Typ 1: Für Sachen, die passieren werden, wenn …

Typ 2: Für imaginäre, schwer vorstellbare Situationen

Typ 3: Für Sachen, die hätten passieren können

Grammar summary

10 Das Passiv

A Allgemein: Aktiv- und Passivsätze

- Aktivsätze betonen, **wer** etwas tut. Passivsätze betonen, **was** getan wird – die Handlung steht im Vordergrund.
- Bis Unit 13 in *Kickoff* findest du nur **Aktivsätze**. In einem Aktivsatz steht das Subjekt vor dem Verb. Gibt es ein Objekt, so steht dieses nach dem Verb.
- **Passivsätze** kann man als ‚umgedrehte' Aktivsätze ansehen: Das Objekt des Aktivsatzes wird zum Subjekt des Passivsatzes.

Aktivsatz

Subjekt	Verb	Objekt
The man	bought	the flowers.

Passivsatz

The man	bought	the flowers.
The flowers	were bought	by the man.

B Bildung

- Das Passiv wird mit *to be* + 3. Form des Verbs (Partizip Perfekt) gebildet.

simple present	simple past
I'm he's she's it's **made** we're you're they're	I was he was she was it was **made** we were you were they were

C Mit oder ohne *by*?

Meist wird das Subjekt des Aktivsatzes in einem Passivsatz nicht genannt. Wollen wir aber das Subjekt besonders betonen, können wir man es mit Hilfe von *by* am Satzende anfügen. In Satz **a** ist der Name des Regisseurs besonders wichtig. In Satz **b** ist es uninteressant, von wem die Blumen angebaut werden.

a *The film was made **by Steven Spielberg**.*
b *These flowers are grown in **Kenya** (by …).*

They delivered oranges to the supermarket yesterday.

Too many oranges were delivered to the supermarket yesterday!

Anhang

Grammar summary

11 Adjektive und Adverbien

A Allgemein
- **Adjektive** beschreiben Personen und Sachen. Sie stehen meist vor einem Substantiv oder nach *to be*.
- **Adverbien** sagen etwas über Verben aus. Sie sagen uns, **wie** etwas passiert.

*a **big** robot*
*The robot is **big**.*

*The robot loads the lorries **quickly**.*

B Adverbien: Bildung

- Ein Adverb wird gebildet, indem *-ly* an das Adjektiv angehängt wird.
- Bei Adjektiven mit der Endung *-y* wird das *-y* zu *-ily*.
- Die Endung *-le* wird zu *-ly*.
- *-ic* wird zu *-ically*.
- Das Adverb von *good* ist *well*.

Adjektiv	Adverb
quick	quick**ly**
easy	eas**ily**
simple	simp**ly**
automatic	automat**ically**
good	**well**

12 Relativsätze

A Allgemein
Relativsätze sind Sätze, die eines der Relativpronomen *who*, *which* oder *where* enthalten. Sie beschreiben das Wort, auf das sie sich beziehen, näher.

*The woman **who** is helping him is Frau Bliscz.*
*The document **which** she has in her hand is Herr Krueger's boarding card.*

B *who*, *which* oder *where*?
- *who* für Personen
- *which* für Sachen
- *where* für Orte

*A passenger is a person **who** travels by plane.*
*A plane is a machine **which** carries people.*
*The place **where** passengers check in is the check-in desk.*

Vorsicht! Anders als im Deutschen steht kein Komma vor *who*, *which* und *where*.

Adverbien	Relativsätze
Boris can do things very quickly.	The guy who goes to a fitness club every day is A or B?

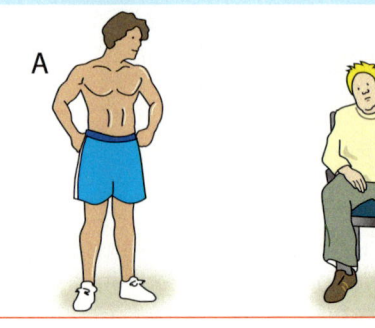

Partner files / role cards

Unit 4 5B

Partner B: Ask your partner questions to find your missing information 1–3. Then answer your partner's questions.

Where …?   When …?   What …?

A German called Levi Strauss invented today's most popular trousers – JEANS. But what do you know about him and his famous product?

rivet

Levi Strauss was born in Bavaria in Germany but in … (1) – when he was 18 years old – he went with his family to New York. In 1853, Levi went to … (2) . He wanted to sell tents to the gold miners there. But the gold miners didn't want tents. They wanted … (3) . Levi used the canvas from the tents for his new product.

The new trousers were great but they weren't very comfortable. Levi used denim (a blue cloth from France). In 1873, Levi and a friend called Jacob Davis also started using rivets. 'Jeans' were now very strong. At first, jeans were for workers. But in the 1950s some American movie stars wore jeans in movies and jeans became fashionable. Today, of course, millions of people around the world wear jeans.

Entry 4A   Answers to quiz

John Travolta
1 True
2 False. He's a pilot and one of his planes is a Boeing 707. But he doesn't have three private planes. He has *five*.
3 True.
4 True.

Victoria and David Beckham
5 c
6 c They have three sons, Brooklyn, Romeo and Cruz.
7 a
8 b

Madonna
9 False. Her real name is Madonna Louise Ciccone.
10 False. Her father's family is from Italy, but Madonna is American.
11 True. Sisters: Melanie, Paula, Jennifer. Brothers: Martin, Mario, Christopher, Anthony.
12 True.
13 True. In London.
14 False. They have an apartment in New York and a house in Los Angeles.

Anhang **155**

Partner files / role cards

Unit 7 2C

Partner B: You have information below about Hunter. Ask your partner questions and find the missing information about Jay. Then answer your partner's questions.

Name	Jay Rishi
Job?	…
Where?	…
Live?	…
Do?	…
Wages?	…
Hours?	…
Ideas about work?	…

Name	Hunter Glenn.
Job?	He'll be a cowboy.
Where?	He'll work on a ranch.
Live?	He'll have a room in the ranch house.
Do?	He'll work on the ranch, he'll look after the cattle *(Vieh)*.
Wages?	He'll earn €650 a week.
Hours?	In the summer, he'll often work 7 days a week from 6 a.m. to 7 or 8 p.m.
Ideas about work?	He thinks that it'll be very hard at first but that it'll be very exciting.

- What job will Jay have?
- When will he work?
- What does he think about work?
- Where will he work/live?
- How much will he earn?

Partner files / role cards

Unit 12 2A

PARTNER A: Look at your ad below. Copy and complete the table with information from the ad. Next, ask your partner questions and complete the table about her/his ad. Then answer your partner's questions about your ad.

DEUTSCHE MOBIL

Secretary, Münster

Deutsche Mobil is not only one of Germany's biggest companies, but also one of the world's most important companies in the telecommunications industry. We are currently seeking a

secretary

to work in our office in Münster. The job would suit a young person who is fully qualified in office work (Bürokaufmann/-frau). The applicant must have excellent computer skills, enjoy working in a team, and speak English well. A lot of the correspondence and telephoning in the office is in English. Hours are Monday to Thursday 7:30 a.m. to 5:00 p.m. and Friday 7:30 a.m. to 1:00 p.m. Holiday: 4 weeks per year. Salary: €3000.

For further details, phone 05192 100500 or email us at careers@deutschemobil.de

	My ad	My partner's ad
Company	Deutsche Mobil	
Job	secretary	
Place of work		
Qualifications		
Knowledge of English		
Hours		
Holidays		
Salary		

- What company is the job with?
- What qualifications do you need?
- What's the job?
- Where …?
- What holidays do you get?
- Do you need English?
- When …?
- How much do you earn?

Anhang **157**

Partner files / role cards

Unit 14 5B

Name	Sam / Sally Jefferson
Country	USA
Course	health and beauty
Reason	Your best friend is a hairdresser and he/she loves his/her job. You worked at your friend's salon in the summer vacation last year.
Career Plans	You're going to be a hairdresser.
Reason	You like working with your hands. You enjoy meeting people.

Name	Liam / Laura Walker
Country	Australia
Course	social studies
Reason	You chose your course after your had read an interesting article about social work in a magazine.
Career Plans	You're going to be a social worker.
Reason	You think the work is important because you can help people.

Name	Alan/Anne MacDonald
Country	Canada
Course	cookery
Reason	You chose your course after you had had a part-time job in a restaurant.
Career Plans	You're going to be a chef.
Reason	You love cooking. And you think that in your job you can travel and work in different countries.

Name	Peter/Petra James
Country	New Zealand
Course	construction
Reason	You always loved making things when you were a kid. You chose your course after you had visited a college in your town – it had an 'open day'.
Career Plans	You're going to be a carpenter/bricklayer.
Reason	You like working with your hands. You don't want to work inside in a boring office!

Vocabulary

Grundwortschatz und Zahlen

Wochentage, Monatsnamen, Subjektpronomen (he, she, it usw.) und Wörter, die im Deutschen und Englischen ähnlich oder identisch sind (z. B. jeans), werden als bekannt vorausgesetzt und sind im Folgenden nicht aufgeführt.

A
a/an ein(e)
about über; ungefähr
activity Aktivität
address Adresse
after nach
afternoon Nachmittag
again wieder
against gegen
age Alter
airport Flughafen
all alle(s)
already schon, bereits
also auch
always immer
a.m. vormittags *(nur nach Uhrzeiten)*
America Amerika
American amerikanisch; Amerikaner/in
and und
animal Tier
another noch eine(r, s), ein(e) andere(r, s)
answer; to answer Antwort; beantworten
any irgendein(e)
apple Apfel
to arrive ankommen
as als
to ask (questions) fragen, (Fragen) stellen
at an, auf, in, bei
at home zu Hause
autumn Herbst
away weg

B
back zurück
bad schlecht, schlimm
bathroom Badezimmer
to be (was/were, been) sein
beach Strand
beautiful schön
because weil
bed Bett
bedroom Schlafzimmer
to begin (began, begun) anfangen
below unter, unten
best beste(r, s)
better besser
big groß
bike/bicycle Fahrrad
bird Vogel
birthday Geburtstag
bit (a bit) (ein) bisschen
black schwarz
blue blau
book Buch
boring langweilig
bottle Flasche
box Schachtel, Kiste, Kasten, Kästchen
boy Junge
boyfriend Freund
bread Brot
breakfast Frühstück
Britain Großbritannien
British britisch
brother Bruder
bus Bus
but aber
to bring (brought, brought) bringen
to buy (bought, bought) kaufen
by von; mit

C
cake Kuchen
called namens
can können
car Auto
cat Katze
centre Zentrum
chair Stuhl
child, children Kind(er)
cinema Kino
city (Groß)stadt
class (Schul)klasse, Kurs
clock (Wand)uhr
coffee Kaffee
coke Cola
cold kalt
colour Farbe
to come (came, come) kommen
to cook kochen
to copy kopieren, abschreiben
correct; to correct korrekt, richtig; korrigieren
to cost (cost, cost) kosten
to count zählen
country, countries Land, Länder
to cover decken, bedecken, abdecken
cupboard Schrank

D
dad Papa
to dance tanzen
dancer Tänzer/in
date Datum
daughter Tochter
day Tag
desk Schreibtisch
dialogue Dialog
dictionary Wörterbuch
different verschieden, unterschiedlich
difficult schwierig, schwer
dinner Abendessen
to do (did, done) machen, tun
dog Hund
door Tür
drink; to drink (drank, drunk) Getränk, Trinken; trinken

E
ear Ohr
early früh
east Ost
easy leicht
to eat (ate, eaten) essen
egg Ei
English Englisch; englisch
evening Abend
every jede(r,s)
everywhere überall
example; for example Beispiel; zum Beispiel
Excuse me! Entschuldigung!
exercise Übung
expensive teuer
eye Auge

F
false falsch
family Familie
famous berühmt
far weit, fern
fast schnell
father Vater
favourite lieblings-
to feel (felt, felt) fühlen
to fill in ausfüllen
to find (found, found) finden
to find out herausfinden
fine fein, schön
finish beenden, abschließen, fertigstellen
firm Firma
first erste(r, s)
fish Fisch
flower Blume, Blüte
to fly (flew, flown) fliegen
food Essen, Nahrung
foot, feet Fuß, Füße
football Fußball
for für
to forget (forgot, forgotten) vergessen
form Form; Formular
free frei, kostenlos
free time Freizeit
friend Freund
friendly freundlich
from von
fruit Obst
full voll, vollständig
fun Spaß

G
game Spiel
garden Garten
German Deutsch; deutsch
Germany Deutschland
to get (got, got) bekommen, erhalten
to get up aufstehen
girl Mädchen
girlfriend Freundin
to give (gave, given) geben
glass Glas
to go (went, gone) gehen
good gut
good morning guten Morgen
goodbye auf Wiedersehen
grass Gras, Rasen

Vocabulary: Grundwortschatz

great großartig
green grün
guitar Gitarre
guy Typ, Kerl
guest Gast

H
hair Haar
half halb
hand Hand
to happen geschehen, passieren
happy glücklich
hard hart, schwierig
hat Hut
to hate hassen, gar nicht mögen
to have (had, had) haben
head Kopf
to hear (heard, heard) hören
hello hallo
help; to help Hilfe; helfen
her ihr(e)
here hier
hi hallo
high hoch
him ihm, ihn
his sein(e)
holiday Urlaub, Ferien
home Zuhause
homework Hausaufgabe
hot heiß, scharf
hour Stunde
house Haus
how many wie viele
how old wie alt
hungry hungrig
husband Ehemann

I
idea Idee, Vorstellung
if wenn, falls, ob
important wichtig
in; into in; in … hinein
in front of vor
interested (in) interessiert (an)
interesting interessant
its sein(e), ihr(e)

J
job Arbeit, Beruf
just einfach, nur, gerade

K
kid Kind
kilometre Kilometer
to know (knew, known) wissen, kennen

L
language Sprache
large weit, groß
last letzte(r, s)
late (zu) spät
to learn lernen, erfahren
left links
lesson Unterrichtsstunde
Let's … Lass/lasst uns …
letter Brief
light Licht; leicht
like wie
to like mögen
life, lives Leben
to listen (zu)hören
little klein, wenig
to live leben, wohnen
living room Wohnzimmer
long lang
to look at betrachten, ansehen
lots of, a lot of viel(e)
loud laut
to love lieben, sehr gern mögen
lunch Mittagessen

M
magazine Zeitschrift
to make (made, made) machen
man, men Mann, Männer
many viele
map (Land)karte
me mir, mich
to mean (meant, meant) bedeuten
meal Mahlzeit
to meet (met, met) treffen, kennen lernen
metre Meter
midday Mittag
middle Mitte; mittlere(r, s)
midnight Mitternacht
mile Meile
milk Milch
minute Minute
mistake Fehler
(at the) moment (im) Moment
money Geld
month Monat
more mehr
morning Morgen
most die meisten
mother Mutter
motor bike Motorrad
movie *(US)* Kinofilm
Mr Herr (Anrede)
Mrs Frau (Anrede für verheiratete Frau)
Ms Frau (Anrede)
mum Mama
music Musik
must müssen
my mein(e)

N
name Name
near nahe
never nie(mals)
new neu
next nächste(r, s)
nice nett, schön, hübsch
night Nacht
no nein; kein/e
noise Lärm, Geräusch
north Nord
not nicht
nothing nichts
now jetzt
number Zahl, Nummer

O
o'clock Uhr
of von, aus
of course natürlich
office Büro
often oft, häufig
old alt
on an, auf, bei, in
one day eines Tages
only nur, erst
open; to open offen, geöffnet; öffnen
or oder
other andere(r,s)
our unser(e)

P
p.m. nachmittags (nur nach Uhrzeiten)
page Seite
paper Papier
parents Eltern
part Teil
partner Partner(in)
to pay (paid, paid) (be)zahlen
pen Stift, Füller
people Leute, Volk
perhaps vielleicht
person Person
phone Telefon
photo(graph) Foto(graf)
picture Bild
place Platz, Ort, Stelle
plane Flugzeug
to play spielen
please bitte
police Polizei
potato Kartoffel
pound Pfund
price Preis
to put (put, put) setzen, legen, stellen

Q
quarter Viertel
question Frage
quick(ly) schnell
quiz Ratespiel

R
rain; to rain Regen; regnen
to read (read, read); read out lesen; vorlesen
really wirklich
red rot
remember sich erinnern, daran denken
rich reich
to ride (rode, ridden) reiten; fahren *(mit dem Auto, Fahrrad)*
right richtig; rechts
right now gerade jetzt
river Fluss
road Straße
room Zimmer, Raum
to run (ran, run) laufen, rennen

S
sad traurig
same der-/die-/dasselbe
to say (said, said) sagen
school Schule
Scotland Schottland
secretary Sekretärin
sea Meer
second zweite(r, s)
to see (saw, seen) sehen, verstehen
to sell verkaufen
to send (sent, sent) schicken, senden
sentence Satz
sheep Schaf
shoe Schuh
shop Geschäft, Laden
shopping Einkaufen
short kurz
to shut (shut, shut) schließen
to sing (sang, sung) singen
sister Schwester
to sit (sat, sat) sitzen
to sleep (slept, slept) schlafen
slow langsam
small klein
snow Schnee
so so
some einige
something etwas
sometimes manchmal
son Sohn
song Lied
soon bald

Vocabulary: Grundwortschatz

(I'm) sorry. Tut mir Leid.
south Süden
to speak (spoke, spoken) sprechen
spring Frühling
to stand (stood, stood) stehen
to start anfangen, beginnen
story Geschichte
street Straße
strong stark, kräftig
student Schüler(in), Student(in)
suddenly plötzlich
sugar Zucker
summer Sommer
sun Sonne
sure sicher
to swim (swam, swum) schwimmen

T

table Tabelle, Tisch
to take (took, taken) nehmen, brauchen, dauern
to talk reden, sprechen
tall groß
tea Tea
teacher Lehrer(in)
television Fernsehen
to tell (told, told) erzählen, sagen
thanks; thank you danke
that der/die/das

their ihr(e)
them sie, ihnen
then dann
there dort
there is/are es gibt
these diese
thing Ding, Sache
to think (thought, thought) denken, glauben, meinen
third dritte
this diese(r, s)
those diese
time Zeit
times Mal
tired müde
to an, auf, nach, zu
today heute
tomorrow morgen
too auch; zu
town Stadt
train Zug
to travel reisen, fahren
tree Baum
trousers Hose
true wahr, echt
to try versuchen

U

under unter
to understand (understood, understood) verstehen
to use benutzen, verwenden
usually gewöhnlich

V

very sehr
to visit besuchen

W

to wait warten
to wake up (woke, woken) aufwachen, aufwecken
to walk gehen, laufen, spazieren
wall Wand
to want wollen
to wash waschen
to watch beobachten, zuschauen
water Wasser
to wear (wore, worn) tragen
weather Wetter
week Woche
weekend Wochenende
welcome willkommen
well gut; gesund; also
west Westen
what was
what time um wie viel Uhr
when wann
where wo
which welche(r, s)
white weiß
who wer, wem, wen
why warum
wife, wives Ehefrau, Ehefrauen

to win (won, won) gewinnen
window Fenster
winter Winter
with mit, bei
without ohne
woman, women Frau, Frauen
wonderful herrlich, traumhaft, wundervoll
word Wort
work; to work Arbeit; arbeiten
world Welt
to write (wrote, written) schreiben
wrong falsch

Y

year Jahr
years old Jahre alt
yellow gelb
yes ja
yesterday gestern
young jung
your dein(e), euer/eure

Zahlen

Cardinal numbers				Ordinal numbers			
1	one	17	seventeen	1st	first	17th	seventeenth
2	two	18	eighteen	2nd	second	18th	eighteenth
3	three	19	nineteen	3rd	third	19th	nineteenth
4	four	20	twenty	4th	fourth	20th	twentieth
5	five	21	twenty-one	5th	fifth	21st	twenty-first
6	six	22	twenty-two	6th	sixth	22nd	twenty-second
7	seven	30	thirty	7th	seventh	30th	thirtieth
8	eight	31	thirty-one	8th	eighth	31st	thirty-first
9	nine	40	forty	9th	ninth	40th	fortieth
10	ten	50	fifty	10th	tenth	50th	fiftieth
11	eleven	60	sixty	11th	eleventh	60th	sixtieth
12	twelve	70	seventy	12th	twelfth	70th	seventieth
13	thirteen	80	eighty	13th	thirteenth	80th	eightieth
14	fourteen	90	ninety	14th	fourteenth	90th	ninetieth
15	fifteen	100	a hundred	15th	fifteenth	100th	hundredth
16	sixteen	110	a hundred and ten	16th	sixteenth		

- 1,000 a thousand • 1,000,000 (1m) a million • 1,000,000,000 (1bn) a billion
- 1.5 one point five • 2.73 two point seven three • 27% twenty-seven per cent
- ½ a half • ¼ a quarter • ¾ three quarters • ⅓ a third • ⅕ a fifth
- £1.50 one pound fifty • 99p ninety-nine p/pence • $12.20 twelve dollars twenty

Vocabulary

Unitbegleitendes Vocabulary

Abkürzungen und Zeichen

etw	= etwa	L	= links	**1A**	Vor den Vokabeln findest du immer die jeweiligen Übungsnummern der Unit.
pl	= Plural, Mehrzahl	R	= rechts		
sb	= somebody	P	= Partner files		
sth	= something				
BE	= britisches Englisch	=	entspricht		
AE	= amerikanisches Englisch	↔	ist das Gegenteil von		
AustrE	= australisches Englisch	→	verwandt mit	**blue**	Vokabel aus Hörtext
NewZE	= neuseeländisches Englisch	!	Achtung		

Entry English, English everywhere

	entry ['entri]	Zugang, Aufnahme	
1A	**festival** ['festɪvl]	Festival	
	Cologne [kə'ləʊn]	Köln	
	band [bænd]	(Musik-)Band	Peter plays in a band.
	Europe ['jʊərəp]	Europa	Britain is in Europe, so is Germany.
	USA [ju:es'eɪ]	Vereinigte Staaten von Amerika	the United States of America
1B	**What about you?** [ˌwɒt əbaʊt 'ju:]	Und du?	
1C	**Illinois** [ɪlɪ'nɔɪ]	US-Bundesstaat	
	to take it in turns [ˌteɪk ɪt ɪn 'tɜːnz]	sich abwechseln	There's only one bathroom. We must take it in turns.
1E	**London** ['lʌndən]	*Hauptstadt Englands*	! Aussprache
2A	**native speaker** [ˌneɪtɪv 'spiːkə]	Muttersprachler/in	Are you a native speaker of English? – No, German is my first language.
	Canada ['kænədə]	Kanada	
	worker ['wɜːkə]	Arbeiter/in	
	construction worker [kən'strʌkʃn]	Bauarbeiter/in	
	G'day [g'deɪ]	Guten Tag! *(AustrE:)*	
	nurse [nɜːs]	Krankenschwester, -pfleger	Nurses work in hospitals.
	Australia [ɒs'treɪlɪə]	Australien	
	technician [tek'nɪʃn]	Techniker/in	-ician für Berufe *(electrician, musician)*
	New Zealand [ˌnjuː 'ziːlənd]	Neuseeland	
2C	**twins** [twɪnz]	Zwillinge	
	painter ['peɪntə]	Maler/in, Anstreicher/in	painter → to paint
	decorator ['dekəreɪtə]	Maler/in, Tapezierer/in	
	doctor ['dɒktə]	Arzt, Ärztin	You go to the doctor when you are ill.
	receptionist [rɪ'sepʃənɪst]	Empfangsdame, -mitarbeiter	
	doctor's receptionist	Sprechstundenhilfe	receptionist → reception
3	**Montana** [mɒn'tænə]	US-Bundesstaat	
3A	**walking** ['wɔːkɪŋ]	Wandern, Spazierengehen	walking ↔ running
	cycling ['saɪklɪŋ]	Fahrradfahren	They love walking and cycling.
	canoeing [kə'nuːɪŋ]	Kanufahren	
	to go on holiday (to) ['hɒlɪdeɪ]	Urlaub machen (in)	They go on holiday to Italy every year.
3B	**hostel** ['hɒstl]	Herberge	
	brochure ['brəʊʃə]	Prospekt, Broschüre	! Betonung
	on the phone [ˌɒn ðə 'fəʊn]	am Telefon	
	warden ['wɔːdn]	Herbergsvater/-mutter	
	to complete [kəm'pliːt]	vervollständigen	Complete the sentences with a partner.

Unitbegleitendes Vocabulary

	to check [tʃek]	überprüfen, kontrollieren	Can you check the time? Isn't it late?
	mountain ['maʊntɪn]	Berg	
	speaking ['spi:kɪŋ]	am Apparat	
	facilities [fə'sɪlətɪz]	Einrichtungen	The hotel has fantastic facilities.
	dining room ['daɪnɪŋ rʊm]	Esszimmer, Speisesaal	
	washing machine ['wɒʃɪŋ məʃi:n]	Waschmaschine	There's a washing machine for dirty T-Shirts.
	much [mʌtʃ]	viel	
	thanks very much [ˌθæŋks veri 'mʌtʃ]	vielen Dank	Thank you very much for the book.
	You're welcome. [jɔː 'welkəm]	Bitte. Gern geschehen.	
	bye [baɪ]	tschüs	→ bye-bye
	access ['ækses]	Zugang	
	to contact ['kɒntækt]	sich in Verbindung setzen mit	If you want to contact her, write an email.
3C	swimming pool ['swɪmɪŋ pu:l]	Schwimmbad	I can go swimming in the swimming pool.
	movie theater ['mu:vi θɪətə]	(AE:) Kino	(BE:) cinema
4A	English-speaking ['ɪŋglɪʃ ˌspi:kɪŋ]	englischsprachig	Australia is an English-speaking country.
	star [stɑː]	Star	There are a lot of stars in this film.
	singer ['sɪŋə]	Sänger/in	singer → to sing
	musician [mjʊ'zɪʃn]	Musiker/in	musician → music → musical
	face [feɪs]	Gesicht	a happy face, an angry face
	poster ['pəʊstə]	Plakat	
	on TV [ɒn ˌtiː'viː]	im Fernsehen	on TV – on the radio
	to note down [ˌnəʊt 'daʊn]	notieren, aufschreiben	Can you note down this information?
	pilot ['paɪlət]	Pilot/in	! Betonung
	private ['praɪvət]	privat	! Betonung
	Florida ['flɒrɪdə]	US-Bundesstaat	
	posh [pɒʃ]	piekfein, todschick (hier:) Name	She always wears posh hats.
	England ['ɪŋglənd]	England	! Aussprache
	million ['mɪljən]	Million	! Betonung
	tattoo [tæt'uː]	Tätowierung	
	Italy ['ɪtəli]	Italien	! Betonung
4C	questionnaire [ˌkwestʃə'neə]	Fragebogen	The questionnaire has 100 questions.
	motor bike ['məʊtə baɪk]	Motorrad	
	scooter ['sku:tə]	Motorroller	He can ride a scooter to work.
	mobile phone [məʊbaɪl 'fəʊn]	Handy	! Es heißt nicht handy in Englisch.
	album ['ælbəm]	Album, CD, Schallplatte	If there are lots of songs on a CD, it's an album.
	musical instrument [ˌmju:zɪkl 'ɪnstrəmənt]	Musikinstrument	
4D	LA [ˌel 'eɪ]	Los Angeles	
	terrible ['terəbl]	furchtbar, fürchterlich	Rap songs are terrible.
5A	to match [mætʃ]	zuordnen	
	past [pɑːst]	(Uhrzeit:) nach	! half past twelve = halb eins
	to [tə]	(Uhrzeit:) vor	
	a quarter to [ə 'kwɔːtə tə]	(Uhrzeit:) Viertel vor	Quarter wird wie four ausgesprochen.
5B	to point to [pɔɪnt tə]	auf etw zeigen	Point to the right number.
	What time is it? [ˌwɒt 'taɪm ɪz ɪt]	Wie spät ist es?	
5C	missing ['mɪsɪŋ]	fehlend	There is a letter missing.
	fashion ['fæʃn]	Mode	
	company ['kʌmpəni]	Unternehmen, Firma	= firm
	to jog [dʒɒg]	joggen	She is jogging with her friend.
	subway ['sʌbweɪ]	(AE:) U-Bahn	(BE:) underground
	to say hello to sb [ˌseɪ həˌləʊ tə]	jdn begrüßen	Say hello to my mother.
	apartment [ə'pɑːtmənt]	(AE:) Wohnung	(BE:) flat
	supper ['sʌpə]	Abendessen	We eat supper at 6 o'clock.
5D	tip [tɪp]	Tipp, Hinweis	
	trick [trɪk]	Trick, Kniff	
5E	vocational college [vəʊˌkeɪʃnl 'kɒlɪdʒ]	Berufsbildende Schule	

Anhang **163**

Unitbegleitendes Vocabulary

	to surf [sɜːf]	surfen	
	to work out [wɜːk ˈaʊt]	trainieren	
	fitness club [ˈfɪtnəs klʌb]	Fitnessklub	
6A	waiter [ˈweɪtə]	Kellner	waiter → waitress (Kellnerin)
	bus driver [ˈbʌs draɪvə]	Busfahrer/in	
	shoe shop [ˈʃuː ʃɒp]	Schuhgeschäft	
	shop assistant [ˈʃɒp əsɪstənt]	Verkäufer/in	A shop assistant sells things in a shop.
	mechanic [mɪˈkænɪk]	Mechaniker/in	A mechanic often works with cars.
	backpacker [ˈbækpækə]	Rucksacktourist/in	
6B	conversation [ˌkɒnvəˈseɪʃn]	Gespräch, Unterhaltung	a conversation **with** sb **about** sth
	trainers [ˈtreɪnəz]	Turnschuhe	
	size [saɪz]	Größe	What size shoes do you have?
	Just a minute! [ˌdʒʌst ə ˈmɪnɪt]	Einen Moment!	
	to try [traɪ]	(Kleidung:) anprobieren	Try these shoes.
	should [ʃʊd]	sollte/n	It's cold. You should take a pullover.
	thanks a lot [ˌθæŋks ə ˈlɒt]	vielen Dank	
	youth [juːθ]	Jugend	= young people
	youth hostel [ˈjuːθ hɒstl]	Jugendherberge	A youth hostel is a cheap place to stay.
	ticket [ˈtɪkɪt]	Fahrschein	You must get a ticket, then take the bus.
	euro [ˈjʊərəʊ]	Euro	! Aussprache
	to sit down [sɪt ˈdaʊn]	sich (hin)setzen	to sit down ↔ to stand up
	to go off [gəʊ ˈɒf]	losgehen	
	most of the time	meistens	= usually
	maybe [ˈmeɪbi]	vielleicht	= perhaps
	to stop [stɒp]	anhalten, stehen bleiben; (Motor:) ausgehen	The bus always stops here.
	engine [ˈendʒɪn]	Motor	Most cars have the engine in front.
	to start [stɑːt]	starten	to start ↔ to stop
	electrical [ɪˈlektrɪkl]	elektrisch	
	to test [test]	testen, ausprobieren	
	ready [ˈredi]	bereit, fertig	Are you ready? – Yes, let's go!
	to order [ˈɔːdə]	bestellen	Let's order steaks.
	sir [sɜː]	(mein) Herr	Good morning, sir.
	yeah [jeə]	ja	
	menu [ˈmenjuː]	Speisekarte	! Nicht verwechseln mit ‚Menü'.
	steak [steɪk]	Steak	
	fries [fraɪz]	(AE:) Pommes	(BE:) chips
	vegetables [ˈvedʒtəblz]	Gemüse	! Betonung
	pea [piː]	Erbse	
	carrot [ˈkærət]	Karotte, Möhre	
	bean [biːn]	Bohne	
	medium rare [ˌmiːdiəm ˈreə]	(Steak:) medium	rare – medium – well done
	certainly [ˈsɜːtnli]	gewiss, sicherlich	I certainly want to come to your birthday party.
	to book [bʊk]	reservieren, buchen	I want to book a holiday in Italy.
	single room [ˈsɪŋgl ˌruːm]	Einzelzimmer	
	double room [ˈdʌbl ˌruːm]	Doppelzimmer	
	credit card [ˈkredɪt ˌkɑːd]	Kreditkarte	
	to reserve [rɪˈzɜːv]	reservieren	Can I reserve a table?
	to call [kɔːl]	anrufen	= to phone
	to look forward to doing sth [ˌlʊk ˈfɔːwəd tə]	sich auf etw freuen	I look forward to hearing from you.
	to choose (chose, chosen) [tʃuːz, tʃəʊz, ˈtʃəʊzən]	wählen, auswählen, aussuchen	! Doppel ‚o'
	to watch TV [ˌwɒtʃ tiːˈviː]	fernsehen	to **watch** TV – to **see** a film

Unitbegleitendes Vocabulary

Unit 1 At college

	college ['kɒlɪdʒ]	Hochschule, Berufsbildende Schule, Universität	Lots of 16 year-olds go to college when they leave school.
1	California [kælɪ'fɔːniə]	Kalifornien	
1A	above [ə'bʌv]	oben(stehend)	above ↔ below
1B	ocean ['əʊʃn]	Ozean	! Aussprache
	community [kə'mjuːnəti]	Gemeinde	Our village is just a small community.
	course [kɔːs]	Kurs, Lehrgang	
	business course ['bɪznəs kɔːs]	Betriebswirtschaftslehrgang	
	cool [kuːl]	kühl, cool	
	to hope [həʊp]	hoffen	I hope I get a good job.
1C	phrase [freɪz]	Wendung, Ausdruck	'Morning' is a word, 'good morning' is a phrase.
2A	marketing company	Vertriebsgesellschaft	
	break [breɪk]	Pause	After two lessons we always have a break.
	lunch break ['lʌntʃ breɪk]	Mittagspause	
	cafeteria [ˌkæfə'tɪəriə]	Cafeteria, Kantine	! Betonung
	to hang out with [ˌhæŋ 'aʊt wɪð]	sich mit jdm rumtreiben	
2C	straight away [ˌstreɪt ə'weɪ]	sogleich, unverzüglich	I liked her straight away.
3A	high school ['haɪ ˌskuːl]	Oberschule	A school in the USA for kids from 15 and 18.
	almost ['ɔːlməʊst]	fast, beinah	Emma is still 17, but she's almost 18.
	to leave (left, left) [liːv, left, left]	weggehen, verlassen	
	one day [wʌn 'deɪ]	eines Tages	
3B	to offer ['ɒfə]	bieten, anbieten	Can I offer you a drink?
	to train [treɪn]	eine Ausbildung machen	I'm training to be a mechanic.
	to last [lɑːst]	dauern	Hot weather doesn't usually last very long.
3C	over ['əʊvə]	über	
	everyone ['evrɪwʌn]	jeder, alle	= everybody
	whether ['weðə]	ob	Nicht verwechseln mit *weather*.
	hairdresser ['heəˌdresə]	Friseur/in	Hairdressers cut people's hair.
	credit ['kredɪt]	(etw:) Leistungspunkte	
	enough [ɪ'nʌf]	genug, genügend	! Die zweite Silbe wird ‚aff' gesprochen.
	even ['iːvn]	sogar, noch	If you are early you can even stay to dinner.
	between [bɪ'twiːn]	zwischen	We always have a break between lessons.
	to need [niːd]	brauchen, benötigen	Tom needs lots of food for his birthday party.
	details ['diːteɪlz]	Einzelheiten, Angaben	
	toll free [təʊl friː]	(AE:) gebührenfrei	
	subject ['sʌbdʒɪkt]	Fach; Thema	
	subject area ['eəriə]	Fachgebiet	
	art [ɑːt]	Kunst, Grafik	! Nicht mit ‚Art' verwechseln.
	design [dɪ'zaɪn]	Gestaltung, Design	
	automotive mechanics [ɔːtəˌməʊtɪv miː'kænɪks]	Kraftfahrzeugmechanik	
	administration [ədˌmɪnɪ'streɪʃn]	Verwaltung	
	business administration	Betriebswirtschaftslehre	
	information technology [ɪnfəˌmeɪʃn tek'nɒlədʒi]	Informationstechnologie	IT is short for information technology.
	construction [kən'strʌkʃn]	Baugewerbe	
	health [helθ]	Gesundheit	
	beauty ['bjuːti]	Schönheit, Kosmetik	beauty → beautiful
	media ['miːdɪə]	Medien	! Steht meist im Plural: *The media are* …
	retail services ['riːteɪl sɜːvɪsɪz]	Einzelhandel	
	social work [ˌsəʊʃl 'wɜːk]	Sozialarbeit	
	child care ['tʃaɪld keə]	Kinderbetreuung	
	electronics [ɪˌlek'trɒnɪks]	Elektronik	California has a strong electronics industry.
4	practice ['præktɪs]	Praxis, Übung	
4A	simple present [ˌsɪmpl 'preznt]	einfaches Präsens	
5A	subject ['sʌbdʒɪkt]	(Brief:) Betreff	
	capital letter [ˌkæpɪtl 'letə]	Großbuchstabe	Sentences begin with capital letters.

Unitbegleitendes Vocabulary

	Dear …, [dɪə]	(Brief:) Liebe/r …,	
	Yours, … [jɔːz]	(Brief:) Dein/e …, Ihr …	
	Best wishes, [ˌbest ˈwɪʃɪz]	(Brief:) Alles Gute,	
	All the best, [ˌɔːl ðə ˈbest]	(Brief:) Alles Gute,	
5B	group [gruːp]	Gruppe	
	information [ˌɪnfəˈmeɪʃn]	Auskunft, Information(en)	! Immer im Singular: The information is …
	typical [ˈtɪpɪkl]	typisch, normal	
5C	revision [rɪˈvɪʒn]	Wiederholen (von Lehrstoffen)	
	bottom [ˈbɒtəm]	Ende, (Seite:) Fuß	

Unit 2   People and jobs

1	career [kəˈrɪə]	Beruf, Laufbahn, Karriere	a career as (a singer)
1A	right now [ˌraɪt ˈnaʊ]	im Augenblick, gerade	= at the moment
	to search [ˈsɜːtʃ]	suchen, durchsuchen	to search for sth
1C	profile [ˈprəʊfaɪl]	Profil, Beschreibung, Porträt	
	fitness trainer [ˈfɪtnəs treɪnə]	Fitnesstrainer	
	personal trainer [ˌpɜːsnl ˈtreɪnə]	persönlicher Fitnesstrainer	
	exercise machine [ˈeksəsaɪz məʃiːn]	Fitnessgerät	
	diet [ˈdaɪət]	Ernährung; Diät	! Aussprache
	healthy [ˈhelθi]	gesund, gesundheitsfördernd	Fruit and vegetables are healthy.
	lifestyle [ˈlaɪfstaɪl]	Lebensweise	
	inside [ˌɪnˈsaɪd]	drinnen	
	sports centre [ˈspɔːts sentə]	Sportzentrum	
	fit [fɪt]	fit, gesund	I'm fit. Activities don't make me tired.
	to keep fit (kept, kept) [ˌkiːp ˈfɪt, kept, kept]	sich fit halten	What do you do to keep fit? – I go swimming every week.
	outside [ˌaʊtˈsaɪd]	draußen	inside ↔ outside
	stadium [ˈsteɪdiəm]	Stadion	Thousand of fans were in the stadium.
2A	each [iːtʃ]	jede/r/s	T-shirts are £5 each.
	mechanical [mɪˈkænɪkl]	mechanisch	
	plant [plɑːnt]	Pflanze	
	team [tiːm]	Team, Mannschaft, Gruppe	There are eleven people in a football team.
	gardener [ˈgɑːdnə]	Gärtner/in	
	to look after [lʊk ˈɑːftə]	sich kümmern um, pflegen	to look after, to look at, to look forward to
	to cut (cut, cut) [kʌt, kʌt, kʌt]	schneiden	Doppel ‚t' in cutting
	to cut grass [ˌkʌt ˈgrɑːs]	Rasen mähen	
	normally [ˈnɔːmli]	üblicherweise, normalerweise	= usually
	nature [ˈneɪtʃə]	Natur	He's interested in nature.
	to repair [rɪˈpeə]	reparieren	If something is broken, you can try to repair it.
	to service [ˈsɜːvɪs]	warten	You should service your car once a year.
	vehicle [ˈvɪəkl]	Fahrzeug	! Aussprache
	workshop [ˈwɜːkʃɒp]	Werkstatt	
	around [əˈraʊnd]	ungefähr, zirka	= about
	nursery assistant [ˈnɜːsəri əsɪstənt]	Hilfslehrerin im Kindergarten	
	state [steɪt]	staatlich, Staats-	state school ↔ private school
	salon [ˈsælɒn]	(Friseur-, Kosmetik-)Salon	
3A	Turkey Creek [ˈtɜːki kriːk]	fiktiver Name	
	to interview [ˈɪntəvjuː]	interviewen	to interview → an interview
	order [ˈɔːdə]	Reihenfolge	in the right/wrong order
	real [rɪəl]	wirklich, ziemlich; (hier:) sehr	
	top man [ˌtɒp ˈmæn]	Spitzenmann	
	in fact [ɪn ˈfækt]	eigentlich, um genau zu sein	I don't like fish, in fact I hate it!
	postman [ˈpəʊstmən]	Postbote/-botin	
	mail [meɪl]	Post	
	to deliver [dɪˈlɪvə]	(aus)liefern, (Post:) austragen	You order online and they deliver the next day.
	package [ˈpækɪdʒ]	Paket	A package came for you today.
	folks [fəʊks]	Leute	
	truck [trʌk]	(AE:) Lkw	(BE:) lorry

Unitbegleitendes Vocabulary

	busy ['bɪzi]	(viel)beschäftigt	! Aussprache
	to be busy [,bi 'bɪzi]	viel zu tun haben	He has a lot of work, he's very busy.
	barman ['bɑ:mən]	Barkeeper	
	crocodile ['krɒkədaɪl]	Krokodil	
	hunter ['hʌntə]	Jäger	
3B	to hunt [hʌnt]	jagen	Hunters usually hunt in winter.
	to serve [sɜ:v]	(Kunden) bedienen; (Speisen) servieren	They serve steak with chips.
	customer ['kʌstəmə]	Kunde/Kundin	The customer is always right!
	hairdressing salon [,heədresɪŋ 'sælɒn]	Friseursalon	
3D	litre ['li:tə]	Liter	
	newspaper ['nju:speɪpə]	Zeitung	Tim reads a newspaper every morning.
	Here you go. [,hɪə ju 'gəʊ]	Hier, bitte sehr.	
	See you later. [si: jə 'leɪtə]	Bis dann!	
	battery ['bætəri]	Batterie, Akku	Your mobile phone needs a new battery.
	Darwin ['dɑ:wɪn]	*Hauptstadt des Northern Territory*	
	beer [bɪə]	Bier	! Schreibung
	careful ['keəfl]	vorsichtig	She's a good driver. She's very careful.
	to keep still [,ki:p 'stɪl]	ruhig halten	
	to hold (held, held) [həʊld, held, held]	halten, festhalten	Can you hold this package for a moment?
	Watch out! [,wɒtʃ 'aʊt]	Achtung! Vorsicht!	
3F	northern ['nɔ:ðən]	nördlich, Nord-	northern → north
	southern ['sʌðən]	südlich, Süd-	southern → south
	eastern ['i:stən]	östlich, Ost-	eastern → east
	western ['westən]	westlich, West-	western → west
4A	present continuous [,preznt kən'tɪnjuəs]	Verlaufsform des Präsens	
4C	unit ['ju:nɪt]	Lektion	There are 14 units in this book.
	expression [ɪk'spreʃn]	Ausdruck	expression → to express
	category ['kætəgəri]	Kategorie, Klasse	! Betonung
5A	international [,ɪntə'næʃnl]	international	
	to describe [dɪ'skraɪb]	beschreiben	Can you describe the man in the picture?
5B	file [faɪl]	Akte, Ordner	Put it in a file, then I can't lose it.
5C	plural ['plʊərəl]	Plural	'Children' is the plural of 'child'.

Unit 3 Free time

1A	to call [kɔ:l]	rufen, nennen	My name is Michael, but you can call me Mike.
	crazy ['kreɪzi]	verrückt	What a crazy idea!
	Covent Garden [,kɒvnt 'gɑ:dn]	*Stadtteil Londons*	Covent Garden has a lot of shops and restaurants.
1C	nickname ['nɪkneɪm]	Spitzname	
	fact [fækt]	Tatsache	Christmas is on 25th December. That's a fact.
	education [,edjʊ'keɪʃn]	Bildung, Ausbildung	You need a good education for a good job.
	college of further education	berufsbildende Schule	
	full-time ['fʊl taɪm]	Ganztags-, Vollzeit-	I'm at college, so I can't have a full-time job.
	graphic design [,græfɪk dɪ'zaɪn]	Grafikdesign	
	part-time ['pɑ:t taɪm]	Halbtags-, Teilzeit-	
	plenty of ['plenti əv]	reichlich, jede Menge	= a lot of, lots of
	to blog [blɒg]	einen Blog führen	
	of course [,əv 'kɔ:s]	natürlich, selbstverständlich	Can you play football? – Of course I can!
	together [tə'geðə]	zusammen, gemeinsam	The family eats together every day.
2	out of ['aʊt əv]	außerhalb	= outside
2A	notice ['nəʊtɪs]	Notiz, Bekanntmachung	! Betonung
	club [klʌb]	Verein, Klub	
	noticeboard ['nəʊtɪsbɔ:d]	Schwarzes Brett	Look at the noticeboard for more information.
	team sport ['ti:m spɔ:t]	Mannschaftssport(art)	
	exciting [ɪk'saɪtɪŋ]	aufregend, spannend	exciting ↔ boring

Anhang **167**

Unitbegleitendes Vocabulary

	extreme sport [ɪkˈstriːm spɔːt]	Extremsport(art)	
	theatre [ˈθɪətə]	Theater	(AE:) theater
	drama club [ˈdrɑːmə klʌb]	Theaterklub	
	musical [ˈmjuːzɪkl]	Musical	musical → musician
	at lunchtime [ət ˈlʌntʃtaɪm]	mittags	at breakfast time, at dinner time
	adventure [ədˈventʃə]	Abenteuer	Adventure stories are exciting.
	camping [ˈkæmpɪŋ]	Camping	
	rock [rɒk]	Fels	rocks, mountains
	climbing [ˈklaɪmɪŋ]	Klettern	
	kayaking [ˈkaɪækɪŋ]	Kajakfahren	Kayaking and canoeing are popular sports.
	mountain boarding [ˈmaʊntɪn bɔːdɪŋ]	Mountainboarding	
	regular [ˈregjələ]	regelmäßig	He's a regular customer.
	all year [ɔːl ˈjɪə]	das ganze Jahr über	In California you can swim all year.
	leisure [ˈleʒə]	Freizeit	= free time
	session [ˈseʃn]	Stunde, Sitzung	
	training session [ˈtreɪnɪŋ seʃn]	Übungsstunde	
2B	to paint [peɪnt]	malen	Let's paint our faces!
	to be keen on [ˌbi ˈkiːn ɒn]	gern tun, scharf auf etw sein	= to be very interested in
	sporty [ˈspɔːti]	sportlich	
	auto mechanics [ˌɔːtəʊ mɪˈkænɪks]	Kfz-Mechanik	
	stupid [ˈstjuːpɪd]	doof, albern	! Aussprache
	absolutely [ˈæbsəluːtli]	absolut, ganz und gar	
2D	skateboarding [ˈskeɪtbɔːdɪŋ]	Skateboardfahren	
	inline skating [ˈɪnlaɪn skeɪtɪŋ]	Inlineskaten	
	jogging [ˈdʒɒgɪŋ]	Joggen	jogging → to jog
	to chat [tʃæt]	(im Internet) chatten	
	to chill out [tʃɪl]	chillen	
	likes [laɪks]	Vorlieben	
	dislike [dɪsˈlaɪk]	Abneigung	dis- = Gegenteil von (like/**dis**like, agree/**dis**gree)
3A	chips [tʃɪps]	Pommes frites	(AE:) fries
	until [ənˈtɪl]	bis	The shop is open until 7 o'clock.
	owner [ˈəʊnə]	Besitzer/in, Eigentümer/in	owner → to own
	to earn [ɜːn]	verdienen	She has a good job and earns a lot of money.
	joke [dʒəʊk]	Witz	a joke **about** sth
	to laugh [lɑːf]	lachen	to laugh **at** sth
	all day [ˌɔːl ˈdeɪ]	den ganzen Tag lang	all day, all night, all year
	to be free [bi friː]	frei haben	
3B	than [ðæn; ðən]	(nach Komparativ:) als	The weather is better than yesterday.
3C	comparative [kəmˈpærətɪv]	Komparativ	
	superlative [suˈpɜːlətɪv]	Superlativ	
	adjective [ˈædʒəktɪv]	Adjektiv	
	burger [ˈbɜːgə]	Hamburger	
	cheap [tʃiːp]	billig	cheap ↔ expensive
3D	worst [wɜːst]	der/die/das schlechteste	worst ↔ best
4A	to phone [fəʊn]	anrufen, telefonieren	= to call
4C	opposite [ˈɒpəzɪt]	entgegengesetzt, gegenteilig	opposite **of** sth
	meaning [ˈmiːnɪŋ]	Bedeutung	! Nicht mit ‚Meining' verwechseln.
5B	survey [ˈsɜːveɪ]	Umfrage	They had a questionnaire for the survey.
	graph [grɑːf]	Diagramm	
	result [rɪˈzʌlt]	Ergebnis	= answer
	popular [ˈpɒpjələ]	beliebt, populär	popular ↔ unpopular

Unit 4 Products then and now

	product [ˈprɒdʌkt]	Produkt	! Betonung (1. Silbe)
	then [ðen]	einst	
1A	commercial [kəˈmɜːʃl]	kommerziell	commercial → commerce (Handel)
	to produce [prəˈdjuːs]	produzieren, herstellen	! Betonung (2. Silbe)

Unitbegleitendes Vocabulary

	heavy [ˈhevi]	schwer	heavy ↔ light
	gram [græm]	Gramm	
	kilogram [ˈkɪləgræm]	Kilogramm	
1B	web page [ˈweb peɪdʒ]	Webseite	
	phone call [ˈfəʊn kɔːl]	Anruf, Telefongespräch	to make a phone call
	engineer [ˌendʒɪˈnɪə]	Ingenieur	My father builds bridges. He's an engineer.
	corporation [ˌkɔːpəˈreɪʃn]	Konzern	
	to invent [ɪnˈvent]	erfinden	Who invented paper? – The Chinese.
	simple [ˈsɪmpl]	einfach	simple ↔ difficult
	text message [ˈtekst mesɪdʒ]	SMS	
1C	ago [əˈgəʊ]	vor	ago folgt auf ein Substantiv: a month ago
2A	article [ˈɑːtɪkl]	Artikel	! Schreibung und Betonung
	history [ˈhɪstri]	Geschichte	the history of sth
	sneakers [ˈsniːkəz]	Turnschuhe	
	flat [flæt]	flach	Holland is a flat country.
	rubber [ˈrʌbə]	Gummi	
	sole [səʊl]	Sohle	
	canvas [ˈkænvəs]	Segeltuch	
	top [tɒp]	(hier:) Oberteil	
	comfortable [ˈkʌmftəbl]	bequem	comfortable ↔ uncomfortable
	to sneak [sniːk]	schleichen	
	quietly [ˈkwaɪətli]	leise	quietly ↔ loud(ly)
	village [ˈvɪlɪdʒ]	Dorf	village – town – city
	spikes [spaɪks]	Spikes	
	athlete [ˈæθliːt]	Sportler/in, Leichtathlet/in	She's jogging. She's a great athlete.
	Olympic Games [əˌlɪmpɪk ˈgeɪmz]	Olympische Spiele	
	athletics [æθˈletɪks]	Leichtathletik	! Achtung auf die Betonung: athlete – athletics
	actor [ˈæktə]	Schauspieler	An actor acts in a play or a film.
	fashionable [ˈfæʃnəbl]	in Mode	fashion → fashionable
	hi-tech [ˈhaɪ tek]	technologisch fortgeschritten	
	air [eə]	Luft	The air in the mountains is clean.
	pair [peə]	Paar	
2C	irregular [ɪˈregjələ]	unregelmäßig	irregular ↔ regular
2E	simple past [ˌsɪmpl ˈpɑːst]	einfache Vergangenheit	
3A	public relations [ˌpʌblɪk rɪˈleɪʃnz]	PR, Öffentlichkeitsarbeit	
	department [dɪˈpɑːtmənt]	Abteilung	Abkürzung = dept.
	visitor [ˈvɪzɪtə]	Besucher/in	
	original [əˈrɪdʒənl]	ursprünglich, original	Who invented the original mobile?
	to design [dɪˈzaɪn]	entwerfen	
	can [kæn]	Dose	a can of sth
	China [ˈtʃaɪnə]	China	! Aussprache
	lady [ˈleɪdi]	Dame	
	gentleman [ˈdʒentlmən]	Herr	
	pharmacist [ˈfɑːməsɪst]	(AE:) Apotheker	(BE:) chemist
	Atlanta [ətˈlæntə]	Hauptstadt Georgias	
	Georgia [ˈdʒɔːdʒə]	US-Bundesstaat	
	design [dɪˈzaɪn]	Entwurf	
	businessman [ˈbɪznɪsmən]	Geschäftsmann	
	state [steɪt]	Staat, Bundesstaat	California is a state in the USA.
	at first [ət ˈfɜːst]	zunächst, zuerst	I didn't like the DVD at first, but it was really interesting later.
	pharmacy [ˈfɑːməsi]	(AE:) Apotheke	(BE:) chemist
	around the world	auf der ganzen Welt	
	Austria [ˈɒstriə]	Österreich	
5B	to be born [bi ˈbɔːn]	geboren werden/sein	He was born in New York.
	Bavaria [bəˈveərɪə]	Bayern	
	tent [tent]	Zelt	aber ‚zelten' = to camp
	gold miner [ˈgəʊld maɪnə]	Goldgräber	

Anhang **169**

Unitbegleitendes Vocabulary

	cloth [klɒθ]	Tuch, Stoff	This is very warm cloth.
	France [frɑːns]	Frankreich	
	rivet ['rɪvɪt]	Niete	
	to become, became, become [bɪ'kʌm, bɪ'keɪm, bɪ'kʌm]	werden	! *to become* bedeutet nicht ‚bekommen'
P	denim ['denɪm]	Denim (Jeansstoff)	

Unit 5 Do's and don'ts

	do's and don'ts [ˌduːz ən 'dəʊnts]	was man tun und lassen sollte	
1A	chef [ʃef]	Koch/Köchin	! *chef* bedeutet nicht ‚Boss'
	kitchen ['kɪtʃɪn]	Küche	
	construction site [kən'strʌkʃn saɪt]	Baustelle	
	to have to ['hæv tə]	müssen	
	hard hat [ˌhɑːd 'hæt]	Helm	
	clean [kliːn]	sauber	I need a clean shirt for the party.
	at work [ət 'wɜːk]	auf/bei der Arbeit	at work, at play
1C	library ['laɪbrəri]	Bibliothek	You can't buy books in a library.
	sign [saɪn]	Schild	! Aussprache
	rule [ruːl]	Vorschrift, Regel	Can you find a rule for the present continuous?
	cell phone ['sel fəʊn]	(AE:) Handy	(BE:) mobile
	drug [drʌg]	Droge	It is dangerous to take drugs.
	drug free ['drʌg friː]	drogenfrei	
	gun [gʌn]	Schusswaffe, Pistole	
	gun free ['gʌn friː]	schusswaffenfrei	
	zone [zəʊn]	Zone, Bereich	! Aussprache: Englisch ‚z' wie ‚s' in sieben
	mustn't ['mʌsnt]	nicht dürfen	
2A	factory ['fæktri]	Fabrik	They make cars in the factory.
	car park ['kɑː pɑːk]	Parkplatz, Parkhaus	There's a big car park for 100 cars in town.
	something ['sʌmθɪŋ]	etwas	
	smoking ['sməʊkɪŋ]	Rauchen	
	floor [flɔː]	Boden, Fußboden	The girl is sitting on the floor.
	electricity [ɪˌlek'trɪsəti]	Elektrizität, Strom	electricity → electrical → electrician
	lorry ['lɒri]	Lkw	
	driver ['draɪvə]	Fahrer/in	
	bag [bæg]	Tasche, Reisetasche	Where's my bag of shopping?
	fire ['faɪə]	Feuer	
	to transport [træn'spɔːt]	transportieren, befördern	
2C	to smoke [sməʊk]	rauchen	Do they let you smoke at work?
	to leave [liːv]	(hier:) hinterlassen, stehen lassen	Don't leave bags in your hotel room.
	to break (broke, broken) [breɪk, brəʊk, 'brəʊkən]	zerbrechen, kaputtmachen	
	to park [pɑːk]	parken	to park → car park
	to drive (drove, driven) [draɪv, drəʊv, 'drɪvən]	fahren	Aber: to ride a bicycle
	no smoking area	Nichtraucherbereich	
	no parking [ˌnəʊ 'pɑːkɪŋ]	Parken verboten	
	caution [kɔːʃn]	Vorsicht	! Aussprache
	fork-lift truck ['fɔːk lɪft trʌk]	Gabelstapler	
	danger ['deɪndʒə]	Gefahr	If you follow the rules, there is no danger.
	volt [vɒlt]	Volt	
	Keep out! [kiːp 'aʊt]	Betreten verboten!	
	wet [wet]	nass, feucht	Come out of the rain. You're wet.
	case [keɪs]	Fall	
	in case of [ɪn 'keɪs əv]	im Fall von	
	to report to [rɪ'pɔːt tə]	sich melden bei	He has to report to the police every week.
	reception [rɪ'sepʃn]	Rezeption	reception → receptionist
	security [sɪ'kjʊərəti]	Sicherheit	
	property ['prɒpəti]	Eigentum	Houses and flats are property.

Unitbegleitendes Vocabulary

	unattended [ʌnə'tendɪd]	unbeaufsichtigt	Parents should not leave children unattended.
	goggles ['gɒglz]	Schutzbrille	He has goggles for swimming.
	ear protectors [ɪə prə'tektəz]	Gehörschutz	
3	e-zine ['iː ziːn]	E-Zine	
3A	to name [neɪm]	nennen, benennen	I can name a lot of dangerous jobs.
	dangerous ['deɪndʒrəs]	gefährlich	dangerous → danger
	police officer [pə'liːs ɒfɪsə]	Polizeibeamte/r	Man sagt auch: policeman/policewoman.
	firefighter ['faɪəfaɪtə]	Feuerwehrmann	The boys want to be firefighters one day.
	timber ['tɪmbə]	Holz, Bauholz	Their house is made of timber.
	timber cutter ['tɪmbə kʌtəz]	Holzfäller	
	machine [mə'ʃiːn]	Gerät, Maschine	
	to fall (fell, fallen) [fɔːl, fel, 'fɔːlən]	fallen	to fall **on** sb/sth
	fisher [fɪʃə]	(AE:) Fischer/in	Man sagt auch: fisherman/fisherwoman.
	to die [daɪ]	sterben	
	per [pɜː; pə]	pro	
	to catch, caught, caught) [kætʃ, kɔːt, kɔːt]	fangen	
	crab [kræb]	Krebs	Die Krankheit heißt *cancer*.
	land [lænd]	Land, Festland	I felt sick on the boat. I'm better on land.
	storm [stɔːm]	Sturm	wind – rain – snow
	ice [aɪs]	Eis	**!** Schreibung
	to fish [fɪʃ]	fischen	
3B	to build (built, built) [bɪld, bɪlt, bɪlt]	bauen	to build → building → builder
	skyscraper ['skaɪskreɪpə]	Wolkenkratzer, Hochhaus	A skyscraper is a very high building.
	steel [stiːl]	Stahl	China buys a lot of steel.
	steel worker ['stiːl wɜːkə]	Stahlarbeiter	
	safe [seɪf]	sicher	Is your money safe under the bed?
	passenger ['pæsndʒə]	Passagier	The ferry takes 500 passengers.
	passenger plane ['pæsndʒə pleɪn]	Passagierflugzeug	
	cycle courier ['saɪkl kʊrɪə]	Fahrradkurier	
	accident ['æksɪdənt]	Unfall	A lot of people die in car accidents.
3C	crop sprayer ['krɒp spreɪə]	Schädlingsbekämpfungsflugzeug	
	low [ləʊ]	niedrig, tief	low ↔ high
	to kill [kɪl]	töten	They kill too many people in that film.
	finally ['faɪnəli]	schließlich, endlich	first – then – after that – finally
	traffic ['træfɪk]	Verkehr	I'm late. The traffic was terrible.
	thousand ['θaʊznd]	tausend, Tausend	*one/a* thousand
	to fall asleep [ˌfɔːl ə'sliːp]	einschlafen	to fall asleep, to wake up, to get up
	on the road [ˌɒn ðə 'rəʊd]	auf der Straße	
3D	office worker ['ɒfɪs wɜːkə]	Büroangestellte/r	office worker – factory worker
	commuter [kə'mjuːtə]	Pendler/in	commuter → to commute
	boat [bəʊt]	Schiff, Boot	to go **by** boat
4A	suit [suːt]	Anzug	**!** Aussprache
	tie [taɪ]	Krawatte	Must I wear a suit and tie to the party?
	Coney Island [ˌkəʊni 'aɪlənd]	Coney Island	
	to relax [rɪ'læks]	sich ausruhen, sich entspannen	I can't relax until I know the answer.
4B	to go out [gəʊ 'aʊt]	ausgehen	to go out ↔ to stay at home
	smoker ['sməʊkə]	Raucher/in	
4C	dirty ['dɜːti]	schmutzig	dirty ↔ clean
5A	clothes [kləʊðz]	Kleider, Kleidung	Immer im Plural: His clothes **are** nice.
	classroom ['klɑːsrʊm]	Klassenzimmer	
5B	before [bɪ'fɔː]	bevor	before ↔ after
	alcohol ['ælkəhɒl]	Alkohol	
	to close [kləʊz]	schließen, zumachen	to close ↔ to open
	traffic lights ['træfɪk ˌlaɪts]	Ampel	Immer im Plural: The traffic lights **are** green.
	to cross [krɒs]	überqueren	Why did the chicken cross the road?
	on foot [ˌɒn 'fʊt]	zu Fuß	**on** foot, **by** bus/car/boat

Anhang **171**

Unitbegleitendes Vocabulary

	nobody ['nəʊbədi]	niemand	
	everybody ['evrɪˌbɒdi]	jeder, alle	everybody – somebody – nobody
	the States [ðə 'steɪts]	die (Vereinigten) Staaten	I'd love to go to the States.
	automobile [ˌɔːtəməˈbiːl]	(AE:) Auto	(BE:) car
	speed [spiːd]	Geschwindigkeit	What speed are you driving?
	maximum speed	Höchstgeschwindigkeit	
	highway ['haɪweɪ]	(AE:) Autobahn	(BE:) motorway
	cop [kɒp]	(AE:) Polizist/in, Bulle	
	speed cop ['spiːd kɒp]	Polizist/in, der/die Geschwindigkeit kontrolliert	

Unit 6 Success stories

	success [sək'ses]	Erfolg	His first song was a great success.
1A	builder ['bɪldə]	Bauunternehmer/in	
	plumber ['plʌmə]	Klempner/in	‚b' wird nicht ausgesprochen
	Poland ['pəʊlənd]	Polen	
	to move [muːv]	umziehen	They left and moved to a new town.
	own [əʊn]	eigen	! Immer: *my/your/his/…* own
	building firm ['bɪldɪŋ fɜːm]	Bauunternehmen	
	employee [ɪm'plɔɪiː]	Angestellte/r	
	successful [sək'sesfl]	erfolgreich	successful at sth
1B	local ['ləʊkl]	Lokal-, Orts-, örtlich	! Betonung
	diagram ['daɪəɡræm]	Grafik, Schaubild	
	patio ['pætiəʊ]	Terrasse	There's a table outside on the patio.
	to ring sb (rang, rung) [rɪŋ, ræŋ, rʌŋ]	jdn anrufen	= to call sb, to phone sb
	since [sɪns]	seit	
	to stay [steɪ]	bleiben	How long can you stay?
2A	to be no good [ˌbi nəʊ 'ɡʊd]	nichts taugen	good at sth
	top (of the page) [tɒp]	Kopf (der Seite)	top ↔ bottom
	pupil ['pjuːpl]	Schüler/in	
	south-east [ˌsaʊθ'iːst]	Südosten	
	pub [pʌb]	Kneipe	A place where people drink and talk to friends.
	dyslexic [dɪs'leksɪk]	legasthenisch	
	brilliant ['brɪljənt]	genial, glänzend	I like this game. It's brilliant.
	show [ʃəʊ]	Show, (Unterhaltungs-)Sendung	
	unsuccessful [ˌʌnsək'sesfl]	erfolglos	successful ↔ unsuccessful
	normal ['nɔːml]	normal, gewöhnlich	! Betonung
	unemployed [ˌʌnɪm'plɔɪd]	arbeitslos	unemployed → to employ → employee
	to train sb [treɪn]	jdn ausbilden	They trained her to work in a call centre.
	the Netherlands [ðə 'neðələndz]	die Niederlande	
	married ['mærɪd]	verheiratet	married to sb
	to marry ['mæri]	heiraten	he/she marries sb
	present perfect [ˌpreznt 'pɜːfɪkt]	Perfekt	
3A	to organise ['ɔːɡənaɪz]	organisieren	
3B	news [njuːz]	Nachrichten	Immer Singular: The news is …
	cookery ['kʊkəri]	Kochen	cookery → to cook
	cookery course ['kʊkəri kɔːs]	Kochkurs	
3C	everything ['evrɪθɪŋ]	alles	everything ↔ nothing
3D	piece [piːs]	Stück	a piece of (paper)
	clothing ['kləʊðɪŋ]	Kleidung	= clothes
4C	someone ['sʌmwʌn]	jemand	= somebody
5A	buddy ['bʌdi]	Kumpel	
	screen [skriːn]	Bildschirm	
	screen name ['skriːn neɪm]	Benutzername	
	yourself [jɔː'self]	dir/dich/euch (selbst)	Plural: yourselves

Unitbegleitendes Vocabulary

Unit 7 Looking ahead

	to look ahead [ˌlʊk əˈhed]	vorausschauen	Look ahead, don't look behind.
1A	still [stɪl]	noch (immer)	They are still friends.
1C	vacation [vəˈkeɪʃn]	(AE:) Ferien	(BE:) holiday
	to leave home [ˌliːv ˈhəʊm]	von zu Hause ausziehen	
	mom [mɒm]	(AE:) Mama	(BE:) mum
	to look for [ˈlʊk fə]	suchen	to look for, to look at, to look after
2A	elevator [ˈeləveɪtə]	(AE:) Aufzug, Lift	(BE:) lift
	Dallas [ˈdæləs]	Hauptstadt von Texas	
	Texas [ˈteksəs]	US-Bundesstaat	
2C P	cattle [ˈkætl]	Vieh	Immer Plural: The cattle are ...
2D	wages [ˈweɪdʒɪz]	Lohn	They pay good wages.
	nervous [ˈnɜːvəs]	nervös, aufgeregt	! Betonung
3A	houseplant [ˈhaʊsplɑːnt]	Zimmerpflanze	
	candle [ˈkændl]	Kerze	In winter we use lots of candles.
	exercise bike [ˈeksəsaɪz baɪk]	Heimtrainer	
	coffee table [ˈkɒfi teɪbl]	Couchtisch	
	mirror [ˈmɪrə]	Spiegel	He can see himself in the mirror.
	beanbag [ˈbiːnbæg]	Sitzsack	
	tower [ˈtaʊə]	Turm	
	wardrobe [ˈwɔːdrəʊb]	Garderobe	
	bedside cupboard [ˈbedsaɪd kʌbəd]	Nachttisch	bedside cupboard, bedside lamp
	armchair [ˈɑːmtʃeə]	Sessel	
	rug [rʌg]	Teppich, Vorleger	
	computer desk [kəmˌpjuːtə desk]	Computertisch	
	quite [kwaɪt]	ziemlich, recht	She speaks English quite well.
3C	to imagine [ɪˈmædʒɪn]	sich vorstellen	Can you imagine the end of the story?
	useful [ˈjuːsfl]	nützlich	useful ↔ useless
	carpet [ˈkɑːpɪt]	Teppich	
	dining table [ˈdaɪnɪŋ teɪbl]	Esstisch	
	fridge [frɪdʒ]	Kühlschrank	= refrigerator
	music centre [ˈmjuːzɪk sentə]	Stereoanlage	
	entrance [ˈentrəns]	Eingang	entrance → to enter
	sink [sɪŋk]	Spüle	
	cooker [ˈkʊkə]	Herd	cooker → to cook → cookery
	washbasin [ˈwɒʃbeɪsn]	Waschbecken	There are two washbasins in the bathrooom.
	shower [ˈʃaʊə]	Dusche	Did you have a bath or a shower?
	toilet [ˈtɔɪlət]	Toilette	
4B	car mechanic [ˈkɑː mɪkænɪk]	Automechaniker/in	
4C	downtown [ˈdaʊntaʊn]	(AE:) Innenstadt	
	gas [gæs]	(AE:) Benzin	
	store [stɔː]	(AE:) Laden, Geschäft	The stores open until 10 p.m.
	cookie [ˈkʊki]	(AE:) Keks	
	cab [kæb]	(AE:) Taxi	
	underground [ˈʌndəgraʊnd]	(BE:) U-Bahn	A lot of cities have got an underground.
	taxi [ˈtæksi]	(BE:) Taxi	
	biscuit [ˈbɪskɪt]	(BE:) Keks	
	lift [lɪft]	(BE:) Aufzug, Lift	
	petrol [ˈpetrəl]	(BE:) Benzin	Petrol is very expensive these days!
	flat [flæt]	(BE:) Wohnung	

Unit 8 A month in New Zealand

1A	apprentice [əˈprentɪs]	Azubi	He was an apprentice for two years.
	car company [ˈkɑː kʌmpəni]	Autofirma	
	island [ˈaɪlənd]	Insel	! Die erste Silbe wird wie *eye* ausgesprochen.
	barbecue [ˈbɑːbɪkjuː]	Grillparty	
1B	Kiwi [ˈkiːwi]	Neuseeländer/in; Kiwi	A Kiwi is a bird and a fruit

Anhang **173**

Unitbegleitendes Vocabulary

	delicious [dɪˈlɪʃəs]	köstlich	Mmm! This cake is delicious.
	horrible [ˈhɒrəbl]	scheußlich, grässlich	horrible, terrible
	to taste [teɪst]	schmecken	The coffee tastes very strong.
	to be fed up (with sth) [ˌfed ˈʌp]	die Nase voll haben	I'm fed up with Kevin. He never helps me.
	to be full up [ˌful ˈʌp]	satt sein	
1C	to survive [səˈvaɪv]	überleben	He survived for days in a small boat.
2A	heading [ˈhedɪŋ]	Überschrift	
	paragraph [ˈpærəgrɑːf]	Absatz	word – phrase – sentence – paragraph
	kind [kaɪnd]	Art, Sorte	a kind **of**
	New Zealander [njuːˈziːləndə]	Neuseeländer/in	
	themselves [ðemˈselvz]	selbst	Some people talk to themselves.
	lake [leɪk]	See	lake, mountain, river
	forest [ˈfɒrɪst]	Wald	
	director [dəˈrektə]	Regisseur/in	The director of the film is famous.
	Lord Of The Rings [ˌlɔːd, ˈrɪŋz]	Herr der Ringe *(Buch- u. Filmtitel)*	
	per cent [pəˈsent]	Prozent	
	European [jʊərəˈpiːən]	europäisch; Europäer/in	Germany and Britain are European countries.
	captain [ˈkæptɪn]	Kapitän	She's captain of the sports team.
	that's why [ˌðæts ˈwaɪ]	deshalb, darum	I went to bed at two. That's why I'm tired.
	skiing [ˈskiːɪŋ]	Skifahren	
	match [mætʃ]	Spiel, Partie	match, game
	war [wɔː]	Krieg	The war was terrible.
	frightening [ˈfraɪtnɪŋ]	schrecklich, erschreckend	That was a frightening film.
	Auckland [ˈɔːklənd]	*größte Stadt in Neuseeland*	
	capital [ˈkæpɪtl]	Hauptstadt	London is the capital of England.
	Wellington [ˈwelɪŋtən]	*Hauptstadt Neuseelands*	
	accent [ˈæksnt]	Akzent	The kids laughed at Susan's Scottish accent.
	jandals [ˈdʒændlz]	*(NewZE:)* Flip-Flops	*(BE:)* flip-flops
	barbie [ˈbɑːbi]	*(NewZE:)* Grillparty	*(BE:)* barbecue
3	polite [pəˈlaɪt]	höflich	polite ↔ impolite
3B	pancake [ˈpænkeɪk]	Pfannkuchen	
	Here you are. [ˌhɪə ju ˈɑː]	(Hier,) bitte sehr.	Could you give me some milk? – Here you are.
	fantastic [fænˈtæstɪk]	fantastisch	Surfing is fantastic.
	I'm afraid … [ˌaɪm əˈfreɪd]	leider	I'm afraid I can't come to the party.
	orange juice [ˈɒrɪndʒ dʒuːs]	Orangensaft	
	at night [ət ˈnaɪt]	abends, nachts	**at** night; **in the** morning/afternoon/evening
	blanket [ˈblæŋkɪt]	Decke	Our dog's bed is a box with a blanket in it.
	How are you? [ˌhaʊ ˈɑː jə]	Wie geht es dir/Ihnen?	
	togs [tɒgz]	*(NewZE:)* Badeanzug	
	pardon [ˈpɑːdn]	Entschuldigung, Verzeihung	My name is Mickey Mouse. – Pardon?
	swimsuit [ˈswɪmsuːt]	Badeanzug	
3F	soup [suːp]	Suppe	Hot soup is good on a cold day.
	dessert [dɪˈzɜːt]	Nachtisch	**!** Betonung
	to borrow [ˈbɒrəʊ]	leihen, ausleihen, borgen	Can I borrow your bike for an hour?
	flightless [ˈflaɪtləs]	flugunfähig	
5A	penfriend [ˈpenfrend]	Brieffreund/in	
5C	glad [glæd]	froh	glad, happy, pleased
	exam [ɪgˈzæm]	Prüfung, Examen	= **exam**ination
	flight [flaɪt]	Flug	flight → to fly
	jump [dʒʌmp]	Sprung	
	to end [end]	enden, zu Ende gehen	How does the film end?

Unit 9 Travel

1A	tram [træm]	Straßenbahn, Tram	
	hardly ever [ˌhɑːdli ˈevə]	kaum jemals	I hardly ever get up at 5 a.m.
1B	meeting [ˈmiːtɪŋ]	Sitzung, Besprechung, Treffen	to meet → meeting
	business trip [ˈbɪznəs trɪp]	Geschäftsreise	
	to check in [tʃek ˈɪn]	einchecken	Check in two hours before the plane leaves.

Unitbegleitendes Vocabulary

	check-in ['tʃekɪn]	Abfertigung	
	check-in desk ['tʃekɪn desk]	Abfertigungsschalter	
	clerk [klɑːk; klɜːrk]	Angestellte/r	Sb in an office or at an information desk.
	boarding card ['bɔːdɪŋ kɑːd]	Bordkarte	
2A	seat [siːt]	Sitz	
	gate [geɪt]	Flugsteig, Gate	Which gate does your plane leave from?
	departure [dɪˈpɑːtʃə]	Abflug, Abfahrt	Abkürzung = dep.
	departures [dɪˈpɑːtʃəz]	Abflughalle, Terminal	
	to depart [dɪˈpɑːt]	abfliegen, abfahren	to arrive ↔ to depart
	security check [sɪˈkjʊərəti ˌtʃek]	Sicherheitskontrolle	
	passport check ['pɑːspɔːt tʃek]	Passkontrolle	
	through [θruː]	durch (… hindurch)	! Aussprache: -ough wie -o in do
	baggage ['bægɪdʒ]	Gepäck	! baggage ist Singular: The baggage is …
	hand baggage ['hænd bægɪdʒ]	Handgepäck	
	passport ['pɑːspɔːt]	Pass, Reisepass	You need a passport to go to Russia.
	passport officer ['pɑːspɔːt ɒfɪsə]	Passbeamte/r	
	on board [ɒn 'bɔːd]	an Bord	on board a ship / a plane
	to get on board [ˌget ɒn 'bɔːd]	an Bord gehen	
	to take off [teɪk 'ɒf]	(Flugzeug:) starten, abheben	The plane is leaving the airport. It is taking off.
	baggage reclaim ['riːkleɪm]	Gepäckausgabe	
	customs ['kʌstəmz]	Zoll	They check your bags at customs.
	customs check ['kʌstəmz tʃek]	Zollkontrolle	
	customs officer ['kʌstəmz ɒfɪsə]	Zollbeamter	
2B	twice [twaɪs]	zweimal	! Nicht: two times
	cup [kʌp]	Tasse	Would you like a cup of tea?
2C	definition [ˌdefɪˈnɪʃn]	Definition	
	boarding pass ['bɔːdɪŋ pɑːs]	Bordkarte	You get your boarding pass from a machine.
2D	to explain [ɪkˈspleɪn]	erklären, erläutern	Can you explain the rules of ice hockey to me?
3A	roller coaster [ˈrəʊləkəʊstə]	Achterbahn	
	theme park [ˈθiːm ˌpɑːk]	Vergnügungs-, Themenpark	Theme parks are popular with children.
	fair [feə]	Jahrmarkt	
	electrical technician	Elektriker/in	
	equipment [ɪˈkwɪpmənt]	Geräte, Ausrüstung, Ausstattung	The equipment they have is very old.
	quiet [ˈkwaɪət]	ruhig	quiet ↔ loud
	ideal [aɪˈdɪəl]	ideal	! Betonung
	adult [ˈædʌlt]	Erwachsene/r	child ↔ adult
	children's playground	Kinderspielplatz	
	Wi-Fi [ˌwaɪ ˈfaɪ]	drahtlos, wireless	
	connection [kəˈnekʃn]	Verbindung	Substantive mit –tion: direc**tion**, conversa**tion**
	to note sth [nəʊt]	(etw:) beachten	
	non-smoking [ˌnɒn ˈsməʊkɪŋ]	Nichtraucher-	
	total [ˈtəʊtl]	Gesamtanzahl	If you add 3 and 6, it comes to a total of 9.
3B	key [kiː]	Schlüssel	
	registration form [ˌredʒɪˈstreɪʃn]	Anmeldeformular	
	to fill in [fɪl ˈɪn]	ausfüllen	
	to enjoy sth [ɪnˈdʒɔɪ]	etw genießen	I enjoyed the party a lot.
	stay [steɪ]	Aufenthalt	stay → to stay
3C	to change [tʃeɪndʒ]	austauschen	She changes her car every year!
5A	postcard [ˈpəʊstˌkɑːd]	Postkarte	
5B	role-play [ˈrəʊlˌpleɪ]	Rollenspiel	
	situation [ˌsɪtjuˈeɪʃn]	Situation, Lage	
	to role-play [ˈrəʊlˌpleɪ]	in einem Rollenspiel darstellen	

Go for it!

L	Go for it! [ˈgəʊ fər ɪt]	Los!	
	cover [ˈkʌvə]	Titelseite	I bought the CD because I liked the cover.
	title [ˈtaɪtl]	Titel	*Kickoff* is the title of this book.
	to come out [ˌkʌm ˈaʊt]	herauskommen	
	issue [ˈɪʃuː]	(Zeitschrift:) Ausgabe	There are 12 issues a year.

Unitbegleitendes Vocabulary

	competition [ˌkɒmpəˈtɪʃn]	Wettbewerb	He wants to win the competition.
	to panic [ˈpænɪk]	in Panik geraten	
	to vote for sth [ˈvəʊt fə]	für etw stimmen	to vote **for** ↔ to vote **against**
	official [əˈfɪʃl]	offiziell, Amts-	
R	billion [ˈbɪljən]	Milliarde	= a thousand million
	sort [sɔːt]	Sorte, Art	sort *of* (fruit) = kind *of* (fruit)
	colony [ˈkɒləni]	Kolonie	India was a British colony.
	Quebec [kwɪˈbek]	Québec	
	region [ˈriːdʒn]	Region, Gebiet	A region is a large part of a country.
	French [frentʃ]	französisch, Französisch	Many people speak French in Canada.
	India [ˈɪndɪə]	Indien	
	to find out [ˌfaɪnd ˈaʊt]	(etw:) herausfinden	Sorry, I don't know, but I'll find out for you.

Unit 10 A visit to a company

	visit [ˈvɪzɪt]	Besuch	visit → to visit
1A	chemicals [ˈkemɪklz]	Chemikalien	
	laboratory [ləˈbɒrətəri]	Labor	! Betonung
	to spend (spent, spent) [spend, spent, spent]	(Zeit:) verbringen	zwei Bedeutungen: *to spend time* und *to spend money*
	paint [peɪnt]	Farbe	
	PLC [ˌpiː elˈ siː]	Aktiengesellschaft	
	appointment [əˈpɔɪntmənt]	Termin	I have an appointment at the doctor.
1B	slowly [ˈsləʊli]	langsam	Not so fast! Can you speak slowly, please?
1C	punctually [ˈpʌŋktʃuəli]	pünktlich	
	badly [ˈbædli]	schlecht	badly ↔ well
2A	to grow (grew, grown) [grəʊ, gruː, grəʊn]	wachsen	Some plants grow very fast.
	main [meɪn]	Haupt-	My main hobby is my car.
	process [ˈprəʊses]	Prozess, Vorgang, Verfahren	
	manufacturer [ˌmænjəˈfæktʃərə]	Hersteller, Fabrikant	
	head office [ˌhed ˈɒfɪs]	Zentrale	
	Russia [ˈrʌʃə]	Russland	
	automatically [ˌɔːtəˌmætɪkli]	automatisch	The light goes out automatically at night.
	robot [ˈrəʊbɒt]	Roboter	
	home [həʊm]	Zuhause	He works in London but his home is Manchester.
	tractor [ˈtræktə]	Traktor	Farmers use tractors.
	bridge [brɪdʒ]	Brücke	A bridge goes over a river.
	DIY (Do-it-yourself) [ˌdiː aɪ ˈwaɪ]	Heimwerken	
	DIY shop [ˌdiː aɪ ˈwaɪ ʃɒp]	Baumarkt	
	exactly [ɪgˈzæktli]	genau	Exactly! That's what I think, too.
	to be happy [bɪ ˈhæpi]	sich freuen	to be happy ↔ to be sad
	automatic [ˌɔːtəˈmætɪk]	automatisch	
	exact [ɪgˈzækt]	genau	Nobody knows the exact numbers.
	to travel [ˈtrævl]	fahren	
2B	to introduce sb [ˌɪntrəˈdjuːs]	jdn vorstellen	to introduce a person **to** sb
	How do you do? [haʊ ˌdə juː ˈduː]	Angenehm!	
	Nice to meet you. [ˌnaɪs tə ˈmiːt juː]	Schön, Sie kennenzulernen.	
	to look round [ˌlʊk ˈraʊnd]	sich umsehen	Would you like to look round the house?
	this way [ˌðɪs ˈweɪ]	hier entlang	
	to act [ækt]	spielen, schauspielern	to act → actor → actress
3	tour [tʊə]	Rundgang, Tour	How long is the tour of the town?
3A	raw materials [ˌrɔː məˈtɪəriəlz]	Rohstoffe	
	production [prəˈdʌkʃn]	Produktion	production → produce → product
	quality control [ˈkwɒləti kənˌtrəʊl]	Qualitätssicherung	
	warehouse [ˈweəhaʊs]	Lager	
	dispatch [dɪˈspætʃ]	Versand	= to send
3B	powder [ˈpaʊdə]	Pulver	You can buy it as powder or in bottles.
	oil [ɔɪl]	Öl	

Unitbegleitendes Vocabulary

	to store [stɔː]	lagern	If you store sth, you keep it and use it later.
	tank [tæŋk]	Tank	
	up there [ˌʌp 'ðeə]	da oben	up there ↔ down there
	to mix [mɪks]	mischen	Don't mix salt and sugar!
	at the moment [ət ðə 'məʊmənt]	im Augenblick	= now
	carefully ['keəfli]	sorgfältig	Listen carefully to Ms Roberts.
	quality ['kwɒləti]	Qualität	
	to load [ləʊd]	laden, verladen	to load ↔ to unload
	onto ['ɒntə]	auf	on + to = onto
	research and development [rɪˌsɜːtʃ ən dɪ'veləpmənt]	Forschungs- und Entwicklungsabteilung	
	administrative [əd'mɪnɪstrətɪv]	Verwaltungs-	administrative → administration
3C	to compare [kəm'peə]	vergleichen	You can't compare black and white.
4A	punctual ['pʌŋktʃʊəl]	pünktlich	= on time
5B	report [rɪ'pɔːt]	Bericht	
	to include [ɪn'kluːd]	einbeziehen, einschließen	The tour included a visit to the shops.
	(the) following ['fɒləʊɪŋ]	der/die/das folgende	
	description [dɪ'skrɪpʃn]	Beschreibung	description → to describe
5C	Japan [dʒə'pæn]	Japan	! Aussprache, Betonung
	location [ləʊ'keɪʃn]	Ort, Standort	The hotel was in a good location.
Go for it!			
L	according to [ə'kɔːdɪŋ tə]	gemäß, zufolge, nach	According to the newspaper, …
	colleague ['kɒliːg]	Kollege/Kollegin	
	to brainstorm ['breɪnstɔːm]	(Ideen) sammeln	
	opinion [ə'pɪnjən]	Meinung	! Nicht verwechseln mit *meaning*.
	to agree with sb [ə'griː wɪð]	mit jdm übereinstimmen	I don't agree with your opinion.
R	to guess [ges]	meinen	Guess how old I am!
	to work long hours	lange Arbeitszeiten haben	
	Japanese [ˌdʒæpn'iːz]	japanisch, Japaner/in	
	Tokyo ['təʊkɪəʊ]	Tokio	
	to commute [kə'mjuːt]	(zur Arbeit) pendeln	to commute **to** work
	workaholic [wɜːkə'hɒlɪk]	Arbeitssüchtige/r	

Unit 11 Future technology

	future ['fjuːtʃə]	Zukunft	past – present – future
	technology [tek'nɒlədʒi]	Technologie	
1A	self-aware [self e'weə]	sich seiner selbst bewusst	
	to take over [ˌteɪk 'əʊvə]	übernehmen	She is going to take over my job.
	sci-fi [ˌsaɪ 'faɪ]	Sciencefiction	
	alien ['eɪlɪən]	Außerirdische/r	
	planet ['plænɪt]	Planet	! Betonung
	high-tech ['haɪtek]	hoch technisiert, Hightech-	
1B	science fiction [ˌsaɪəns 'fɪkʃn]	Sciencefiction	
2	… years from now	in … Jahren	
2A	textiles ['tekstaɪlz]	Textilien	
	jacket ['dʒækɪt]	Jacke, Jackett	In hot weather you don't need a jacket.
	to change [tʃeɪndʒ]	ändern, sich verändern	You've changed since we last met.
	warm [wɔːm]	warm	hot – warm – cold
	shirt [ʃɜːt]	Hemd	shirt, jacket, tie
	earring ['ɪərɪŋ]	Ohrring	She wears gold earrings.
	energy ['enədʒi]	Energie, Energiequelle	
	message ['mesɪdʒ]	Nachricht, Mitteilung	There's a message for you on the phone.
	virtual reality [ˌvɜːtʃuəl ri'æləti]	virtuelle Realität	
	showroom ['ʃəʊruːm]	Ausstellungsraum	You can see the new car in the showroom.
	trolley ['trɒli]	Einkaufswagen	
	fruit juice ['fruːt dʒuːs]	Fruchtsaft	
2B	yoghurt ['jɒgət]	Joghurt	

Unitbegleitendes Vocabulary

3	climate ['klaɪmət]	Klima	a cold/hot climate	
	climate change ['klaɪmət tʃeɪndʒ]	Klimawandel		
3A	CO_2 [ˌsiː əʊ 'tuː]	CO_2		
	earth [ɜːθ]	Erde	The earth is round.	
	atmosphere ['ætməsfɪə]	Atmosphäre		
	global warming [ˌgləʊbl 'wɔːmɪŋ]	Erderwärmung		
	fossil fuel ['fɒsl ˌfjuːəl]	fossiler Brennstoff		
	desert ['dezət]	Wüste	! Nicht mit d*ess*ert verwecheln.	
	others ['ʌðəz]	andere	If I don't do it, others will do it.	
	solar power ['səʊlə 'paʊə]	solar, Sonnen-		
	satellite ['sætlaɪt]	Satellit		
	flood [flʌd]	Flut	! Aussprache	
	extra ['ekstrə]	besonders	an extra strong coffee	
	disaster [dɪ'zɑːstə]	Katastrophe		
	basically ['beɪsɪkli]	grundsätzlich, im Prinzip	Basically, I agree but …	
	coal [kəʊl]	Kohle	In the past people burnt more coal.	
	industry ['ɪndəstri]	Industrie, Branche		
	to warm [wɔːm]	erwärmen, sich erwärmen		
	roughly ['rʌfli]	ungefähr	It's roughly two hours from London to Paris.	
	enormous [ɪ'nɔːməs]	riesig, ungeheuer	My girlfriend wears enormous earrings.	
	to save [seɪv]	sparen	She saves £10 a month.	
	to damage ['dæmɪdʒ]	(einer Sache) schaden		
	monorail ['mɒnəʊreɪl]	Einschienenbahn		
	microwave ['maɪkrəʊweɪv]	Mikrowelle		
5A	diary ['daɪəri]	Tagebuch, Terminkalender	A blog is like a diary.	
5B	Belgium ['beldʒəm]	Belgien		
	Sweden ['swiːdn]	Schweden		
5C	radio programme	Radiosendung		
	topic ['tɒpɪk]	Thema	What is the topic of this unit?	
	everyday ['evrɪdeɪ]	alltäglich, Alltags-		
	interviewer ['ɪntəvjuːə]	Interviewer/in	interviewer → an interview → to interview	

Go for it!

L	character ['kærəktə]	(Film-, Roman-)Figur	A character is a person in a book or story.	
	to be set in [bi 'set ɪn]	(Film, Roman:) spielen in		
	trilogy ['trɪlədʒi]	Trilogie		
	review [rɪ'vjuː]	Kritik, Rezension	Have you read the review of the film?	
	of all time [ˌəv ɔːl 'taɪm]	aller Zeiten		
	funny ['fʌni]	komisch, lustig	Comics can be funny.	
	action movie ['ækʃn]	Actionfilm		
	horror movie ['hɒrə]	Horrorfilm	.	
	romantic movie [rəʊ'mæntɪk]	Liebesfilm		
	comedy ['kɒmədi]	Komödie		
	special effects [ˌspeʃl ɪ'fekts]	Spezialeffekte		
	sound track ['saʊndtræk]	Tonspur, Soundtrack		
	amazing [ə'meɪzɪŋ]	erstaunlich	Your new mobile is amazing!	
R	to reload [ˌriː'ləʊd]	neu laden		
	revolution [ˌrevə'luːʃn]	Revolution; Umdrehung		
	hacker ['hækə]	Hacker/in, Computerfreak		
	organisation [ˌɔːgənaɪ'zeɪʃn]	Organisation	organisation → organise	
	head [hed]	Chef/in	head of a company	
	secret ['siːkrət]	Geheimnis	Don't tell people. It's a secret.	
	to fight [faɪt]	kämpfen		
	videophone ['vɪdɪəʊfəʊn]	Bildtelefon		
	landscape ['lændskeɪp]	Landschaft		
	to hurt (hurt, hurt) [hɜːt, hɜːt, hɜːt]	verletzen, sich verletzen	I hurt my leg when I played football.	
	brain [breɪn]	Gehirn		
	scientist ['saɪəntɪst]	Wissenschaftler/in	Scientists are studying the sun.	

Unit 12 Job hunting

1A	to apply for [əˈplaɪ fə]	sich bewerben um	I applied for a part-time job.	
	fully-qualified [ˌfʊli ˈkwɒlɪfaɪd]	ausgebildet, qualifiziert		
	assistant [əˈsɪstnt]	Helfer/in	That's the boss's assistant.	
	advertisement [ədˈvɜːtɪsmənt]	Anzeige	Advertisements tell you to buy things.	
	job ad(vertisement)	Stellenanzeige		
1B	currently [ˈkʌrəntli]	derzeit, zurzeit, momentan	= at the moment, now	
	aged [eɪdʒd]	im Alter von		
	further [ˈfɜːðə]	weitere/r/s	I have no further questions.	
	step [step]	Schritt		
	to seek [siːk]	suchen		
	applicant [ˈæplɪkənt]	Bewerber/in	applicant → to apply → application	
	at least [ət ˈliːst]	mindestens		
	experience [ɪkˈspɪəriəns]	Erfahrung	! Immer im Singular	
	to suit sb [sjuːt]	für jdn geeignet sein	I have a child, so a part-time job suits me.	
	qualification [ˌkwɒlɪfɪˈkeɪʃn]	Ausbildung, Qualifikation	qualification → qualified	
1D	half, halves [hɑːf, hɑːvz]	Hälfte, Hälften	half – quarter	
2A	sales assistant [ˈseɪlz əsɪstənt]	Verkäufer/in		
	retailer [ˈriːteɪlə]	Einzelhändler		
	retail [ˈriːteɪl]	Einzelhandel	! Betonung	
	salary [ˈsæləri]	Lohn, Gehalt	*Salary* für Angestellte, *wages* für Arbeiter	
P	telecommunications industry [ˌtelɪkəmjuːnɪˈkeɪʃnz]	Telekommunikationsbranche		
P	excellent [ˈeksələnt]	hervorragend	Her English is excellent.	
P	skill [skɪl]	Fähigkeit		
P	correspondence [ˌkɒrɪˈspɒndəns]	Korrespondenz	A lot of correspondence is emails these days.	
P	to telephone [ˈtelɪfəʊn]	telefonieren		
	knowledge [ˈnɒlɪdʒ]	Wissen, Kenntnis(se)	! Immer im Singular	
2C	necessary [ˈnesəsri]	nötig, notwendig	Don't bring flowers. It's not necessary.	
3	job interview [ˈdʒɒb ɪntəvjuː]	Vorstellungsgespräch		
3A	traineeship [ˌtreɪˈniːʃɪp]	Ausbildung(splatz)	→ trainee → trainer → training → to train	
	flight attendant [flaɪt əˈtendənt]	Flugbegleiter/in		
	CV = curriculum vitae [ˌsiː ˈviː]	Lebenslauf		
	sales [seɪlz]	Verkauf, Vertrieb		
	personnel [ˌpɜːsənˈel]	Personal		
	primary school [ˈpraɪməri ˌskuːl]	Grundschule		
	secondary school [ˈsekəndri ˌskuːl]	weiterführende Schule		
	end [end]	Ende, Schluss	December is at the end of the year.	
	program [ˈprəʊɡræm]	Programm	! Geschrieben *program* (nicht *programme*) in der Bedeutung ‚Software'.	
	Turkish [ˈtɜːkɪʃ]	türkisch, Türkisch		
	personal [ˈpɜːsənl]	persönlich	! Betonung: **per**sonal – person**nel**	
	date of birth [ˌdeɪt əv ˈbɜːθ]	Geburtsdatum		
	tourism [ˈtʊərɪzm]	Tourismus		
	work experience	Berufserfahrung	He never worked. He has no work experience.	
	travel agent [ˈtrævl ˌeɪdʒənt]	Reisekaufmann/-frau; Reisebüro	! *travel agent* für die Person *und* das Geschäft	
	fluent [ˈfluːənt]	fließend	a fluent speaker of English	
	mother tongue [ˌmʌðə ˈtʌŋ]	Muttersprache		
	interest [ˈɪntrəst]	Interesse	She's got many interests and hobbies.	
3B	Turkey [ˈtɜːki]	Türkei	! ohne Artikel: ~~The~~ Turkey is a large country.	
	singing group [ˈsɪŋɪŋ ɡruːp]	Gesangsensemble		
	concert [ˈkɒnsət]	Konzert	They play in six concerts a year.	
	city hall [ˌsɪti ˈhɔːl]	Stadthalle		
	training [ˈtreɪnɪŋ]	Ausbildung		
	training centre [ˈtreɪnɪŋ ˌsentə]	Ausbildungszentrum		
4A	Brandenburg Gate	das Brandenburger Tor		
	Beware of the dog! [bɪˌweər]	Warnung vor dem Hund!		
5A	cartoon [kɑːˈtuːn]	Illustration, Karikatur		

Unitbegleitendes Vocabulary

5C	possible ['pɒsəbl]	möglich	possible ↔ impossible
	to print [prɪnt]	drucken, ausdrucken	
Go for it!			
L	perfect ['pɜːfɪkt]	perfekt	perfect ↔ imperfect
	to disagree with sb/sth [ˌdɪsəˈgriː]	jdm/einer Sache nicht zustimmen	to disagree ↔ to agree
R	spot [spɒt]	Punkt, Fleck	
	genius ['dʒiːniəs]	Genie	Einstein was a genius.
	cap [kæp]	Mütze	
	probably ['prɒbəbli]	wahrscheinlich	We'll probably come home after dinner.
	to be late [bi 'leɪt]	sich verspäten, zu spät kommen	I'm cooking a special meal, so don't be late!
	to go wrong with sth	etw verkehrt machen	
	to plan [plæn]	sich vornehmen	
	fashion model ['fæʃn ˌmɒdl]	Fotomodell, Mannequin	
	smart [smɑːt]	schick	He always wears smart clothes.
	to shake hands (shook, shaken) [ʃeɪk, ʃʊk, 'ʃeɪkən]	(sich) die Hand geben, die Hände schütteln	
	to smile [smaɪl]	lächeln	I like people who always smile.
	positive ['pɒzətɪv]	positiv	
	upright ['ʌpraɪt]	aufrecht, gerade	
	eye contact ['aɪ kɒntækt]	Augenkontakt	
	clearly ['klɪəli]	deutlich, klar	I can't hear. Speak more clearly!
	truth [truːθ]	Wahrheit	**to tell** the truth
	to say so ['seɪ səʊ]	es sagen	
	to thank sb [θæŋk]	jdm danken	to thank a person **for** sth

Unit 13 Global business

1	goods [gʊdz]	Güter, Waren	They store the goods in the warehouse.
1A	delivery [dɪˈlɪvəri]	Lieferung	delivery → to deliver
	bakery ['beɪkəri]	Bäckerei	bakery → to bake
1B	on sale [ˌɒn 'seɪl]	erhältlich	Tickets are on sale at the cinema.
	cheese [tʃiːz]	Käse	
	pepperoni [ˌpepəˈrəʊni]	Peperoni	
	sausage ['sɒsɪdʒ]	Wurst	
	chocolate ['tʃɒklət]	Schokolade	**!** chocolate**s** = Pralinen
2B	mouse, mice [maʊs, maɪs]	Maus, Mäuse	
	keyboard ['kiːbɔːd]	Tastatur	
	to manufacture [ˌmænjʊˈfæktʃə]	herstellen	
	hard drive [ˌhɑːd 'draɪv]	Festplatte	
	mother board ['mʌðə bɔːd]	Hauptplatine	
	CPU [ˌsiː piː 'juː]	CPU	
	central ['sentrəl]	zentral	
	to process ['prəʊses]	verarbeiten	**!** Betonung
	to assemble [əˈsembl]	montieren, zusammenbauen	
2C	Ireland ['aɪələnd]	Irland	**!** Schreibung
	assembly [əˈsembli]	Montage	
	Czech Republic [ˌtʃek rɪˈpʌblɪk]	Tschechische Republik	
	Singapore [ˌsɪŋəˈpɔː]	Singapur	
3	globalisation [ˌgləʊbəlaɪˈzeɪʃn]	Globalisierung	
3A	farm [fɑːm]	Farm, Bauernhof	
	to grow [grəʊ]	(Pflanze:) anbauen	We grow vegetables in our garden.
	farmer ['fɑːmə]	Farmer/in, Bauer/Bäuerin	
	grower ['grəʊə]	Bauer/Bäuerin, Pflanzer/in	
	market ['mɑːkɪt]	Markt	
	to import [ɪmˈpɔːt]	importieren	Europe also imports food from America.
	Silicon Valley [ˌsɪlɪkən 'væli]	*Computerzentrum in Kalifornien*	
	telephone ['telɪfəʊn]	Telefon	Abkürzung = phone
	on the telephone [ˌɒn ðə 'telɪfəʊn]	am Telefon	

Unitbegleitendes Vocabulary

	helpline	[ˈhelplaɪn]	Hotline	
	poor	[pɔː; pʊə]	arm	The farmers are very poor.
	mine	[maɪn]	Bergwerk	It's dangerous to work in mines.
	cheaply	[ˈtʃiːpli]	billig	You can buy them cheaply in Poland.
3C	on the one hand		einerseits	
	on the other hand		andererseits	
	reason	[ˈriːzn]	Grund, Begründung	Why did you do it? Give me a reason.
	on the whole	[ˌɒn ðə ˈhəʊl]	im Großen und Ganzen	On the whole, it was a good interview.
4A	passive	[ˈpæsɪv]	(Grammatik:) Passiv	
4B	active	[ˈæktɪv]	(Grammatik:) Aktiv	
	Chinese	[tʃaɪˈniːz]	chinesisch, Chinese/Chinesin	
5A	overseas	[ˌəʊvəˈsiːz]	(in/nach) Übersee	China and India are overseas markets.
5B	Indian	[ˈɪndiən]	indisch	
	boomtown	[ˈbuːmtaʊn]	Stadt in rapidem Aufschwung	
	headquarters	[ˌhedˈkwɔːtəz]	Zentrale	= head office
	golf course	[ˈɡɒlf kɔːs]	Golfplatz	There are a lot of golf courses in Scotland.
	contrast	[ˈkɒntrɑːst]	Kontrast	
5C	toothpaste	[ˈtuːθpeɪst]	Zahncreme	
	complicated	[ˈkɒmplɪkeɪtɪd]	kompliziert	This computer program is very complicated.
Go for it!				
L	traditional	[trəˈdɪʃənl]	traditionell	! Nur ein 'l': tradition**al**, punctu**al**, personn**el**
	greeting	[ˈɡriːtɪŋ]	Begrüßung	greeting → to greet
	hospitality	[hɒspɪˈtæləti]	Gastfreundschaft	Nicht mit *hospital* verwechseln!
	boss	[bɒs]	Chef	A *chef* works in a restaurant in English!
	impolite	[ˌɪmpəˈlaɪt]	unhöflich	impolite ↔ polite
	plate	[pleɪt]	Teller	The plate for a pizza must be big.
	rude	[ruːd]	unhöflich, unverschämt	
	presentation	[ˌpreznˈteɪʃn]	Präsentation	presentation → to present
	visual aids	[ˌvɪʒuəl ˈeɪdz]	visuelle Hilfen	
R	action	[ˈækʃn]	Handlung	There was a lot of action in the film.
	to invite	[ɪnˈvaɪt]	einladen	
	present	[ˈpreznt]	Geschenk	! Betonung: **pre**sent und to pres**ent**
	bad luck	[ˌbæd ˈlʌk]	Unglück	
	tradition	[trəˈdɪʃn]	Tradition	tradition → traditional
	custom	[ˈkʌstəm]	Sitte, Brauch	It's a custom to wear funny costumes at Halloween.
	respect	[rɪˈspekt]	Respekt, Achtung	respect **for** your teacher
	to keep face	[ˌkiːp ˈfeɪs]	das Gesicht wahren	
	host	[həʊst]	Gastgeber/in	The host says 'welcome' to the guests..
	to drop sth	[drɒp]	etw fallenlassen	! dro**pp**ed
	chopsticks	[ˈtʃɒpstɪks]	(Ess-)Stäbchen	
	queue	[kjuː]	(Menschen-)Schlange	*queue* reimt sich mit *new*
	say	[seɪ]	zum Beispiel	

Unit 14 Why do we work?

	satisfaction	[ˌsætɪsˈfækʃn]	Zufriedenheit	'I can't get no satisfaction.' (*Lied*)
1A	to crash into sth	[ˈkræʃ ɪntə]	(*hier:*) in etw hineinfliegen	
	fire department	[ˈfaɪə dɪpɑːtmənt]	Feuerwehr	
	such a	[ˈsʌtʃ ə]	so ein/e/r/s	I can't remember. It's such a long time ago.
2A	trouble	[ˈtrʌbl]	Schwierigkeiten, Probleme	
	homeless	[ˈhəʊmləs]	obdachlos	home → homeless
	to be good with sb		mit jdm gut umgehen können	He's very good with animals.
	youth worker	[ˈjuːθ wɜːkə]	Sozialarbeiter für Jugendliche	
	alcoholic	[ˌælkəˈhɒlɪk]	Alkoholiker/in	
	notice	[ˈnəʊtɪs]	Bekanntmachung, Aushang	It's closed. There's a notice on the door.
	railway	[ˈreɪlweɪ]	Eisenbahn	There's a fast railway to London.
	coast	[kəʊst]	Küste	Dover is on the south coast of England.

Anhang **181**

Unitbegleitendes Vocabulary

	east coast [ˌiːst ˈkəʊst]	Ostküste	
	west coast [ˌwest ˈkəʊst]	Westküste	
	nearly [ˈnɪəli]	fast, beinah	Are you OK? You nearly fell.
	track worker [ˈtræk wɜːkə]	Gleisarbeiter	
	railway tracks [ˈreɪlweɪ træks]	Bahngleise	
	dead tired [ˌded ˈtaɪəd]	todmüde	
	to give up [ˌɡɪv ˈʌp]	aufgeben	They didn't win, but they didn't give up.
3A	statistics [stəˈtɪstɪks]	Statistik	
	electrician [ɪˌlekˈtrɪʃn]	Elektriker/in	
	industrial clerk [ɪnˈdʌstrɪəl ˌklɑːk]	Industriekaufmann/-frau	
3C	presenter [prɪˈsentə]	Moderator/in	
	both [bəʊθ]	beide/s	They both found a new job.
	series [ˈsɪəriːz]	Serie	
	carpenter [ˈkɑːpəntə]	Zimmermann	A carpenter works with wood.
	toy [tɔɪ]	Spielzeug	Children play with toys.
	apprenticeship [əˈprentɪʃɪp]	Lehre, Lehrstelle	You do an apprenticeship for three years.
	surprised [səˈpraɪzd]	überrascht, erstaunt	He came late. We were surprised to see him.
	fashion designer [ˈfæʃn dɪˌzaɪnə]	Modedesigner/in	
	care worker [ˈkeə wɜːkə]	Pfleger/in	
	disabled [dɪsˈeɪbld]	behindert	
	bricklayer [ˈbrɪkleɪə]	Maurer/in	
3D	in our opinion [ɪn aʊər əˈpɪnjən]	unserer Meinung nach	It's just our opinion. You have to decide.
4A	past perfect [ˌpɑːst ˈpɜːfɪkt]	(Grammatik:) Plusquamperfekt	
	to change one's clothes	sich umziehen	
	to download [ˈdaʊnləʊd]	herunterladen	
4B	ill [ɪl]	krank	If you're ill, it's best to go to bed.
	angry [ˈæŋɡri]	böse, wütend	She was angry when you arrived late.
4D	odd word out [ˌɒd wɜːd ˈaʊt]	das Wort, das nicht dazu passt	
	university [ˌjuːnɪˈvɜːsəti]	Universität	
5B	communication [kəˌmjuːnɪˈkeɪʃn]	Kommunikation	
P	to enjoy doing sth [ɪnˈdʒɔɪ duɪŋ]	etw gern tun	He enjoys relaxing after work.
P	social studies [ˌsəʊʃl ˈstʌdiz]	Sozialkunde	
P	social worker [ˈsəʊʃl ˌwɜːkə]	Sozialarbeiter/in	

Go for it!

L	special [ˈspeʃl]	(Magazin:) Sonderausgabe	
	task [tɑːsk]	Aufgabe	The interviewer gave me a task to do.
	board [bɔːd]	Tafel	to write **on** the board
R	grade [ɡreɪd]	Note	
	to follow [ˈfɒləʊ]	folgen	
	pencil [ˈpensl]	Bleistift	pencil – pen – rubber – biro – felt-tip pen
	checklist [ˈtʃeklɪst]	Checkliste	
	to sound [saʊnd]	klingen	I like your music – it sounds good.
	mark [mɑːk]	Note, Punkt(zahl)	100 marks gives you grade A.
	to lose (lost, lost) [luːz, lɒst, lɒst]	verlieren	Here's a new pencil. Don't lose it!
	correctly [kəˈrektli]	richtig, korrekt	
	once [wʌns]	einmal	Once, twice, three times, four times …
	Keep it short and simple!	Fasse dich kurz und drücke dich einfach aus!	
	clear [klɪə]	klar, deutlich	Do you understand? – Yes, that's very clear.
	Good luck! [ˌɡʊd ˈlʌk]	Viel Glück!	good luck ↔ bad luck

Anhang

Vocabulary

Alphabetisches Vocabulary

A
above 18 oben(stehend)
absolutely 37 absolut, ganz und gar
accent 77 Akzent
access 11 Zugang
accident 54 Unfall
according to 104 gemäß, zufolge, nach
to act 99 spielen, schauspielern
action 135 Handlung
action movie 114 Actionfilm
active 132 *(Grammatik:)* Aktiv
actor 44 Schauspieler
adjective 39 Adjektiv
administration 23 Verwaltung
administrative 100 Verwaltungs-
adult 90 Erwachsene/r
adventure 36 Abenteuer
advertisement 116 Anzeige
aged 117 im Alter von
ago 43 vor
to agree with sb 104 mit jdm übereinstimmen
air 44 Luft
album 13 Album, CD, Schallplatte
alcohol 57 Alkohol
alcoholic 138 Alkoholiker/in
alien 106 Außerirdische/r
all day 38 den ganzen Tag lang
All the best, 25 *(Brief:)* Alles Gute,
all year 36 das ganze Jahr über
almost 22 fast, beinah
amazing 114 erstaunlich
angry 142 böse, wütend
apartment 14 *(AE:)* Wohnung
applicant 117 Bewerber/in
to apply for 116 sich bewerben um
appointment 96 Termin
apprentice 74 Azubi
apprenticeship 141 Lehre, Lehrstelle
area 23 Gebiet
armchair 70 Sessel
around 28 ungefähr, zirka
around the world 46 auf der ganzen Welt
art 23 Kunst, Grafik
article 44 Artikel
to assemble 128 montieren, zusammenbauen
assembly 129 Montage
assistant 116 Helfer/in
at first 46 zunächst, zuerst
at least 117 mindestens
at lunchtime 36 mittags
at night 78 abends, nachts
at the moment 100 im Augenblick
at work 50 auf/bei der Arbeit
athlete 44 Sportler/in, Leichtathlet/in
athletics 44 Leichtathletik
atmosphere 110 Atmosphäre
Australia 8 Australien
Austria 46 Österreich
auto mechanics 37 Kfz-Mechanik
automatic 98 automatisch
automatically 98 automatisch
automobile 57 *(AE:)* Auto
automotive mechanics 23 Kraftfahrzeugmechanik

B
backpacker 16 Rucksacktourist/in
bad luck 135 Unglück
badly 97 schlecht
bag 52 Tasche, Reisetasche
baggage 88 Gepäck
baggage reclaim 88 Gepäckausgabe
bakery 126 Bäckerei
band 6 (Musik-)Band
barbecue 74 Grillparty
barbie 77 *(NewZE:)* Grillparty
barman 30 Barkeeper
basically 111 grundsätzlich, im Prinzip
battery 31 Batterie, Akku
Bavaria 49 Bayern
to be born 49 geboren werden/sein
to be busy 30 viel zu tun haben
to be fed up (with sth) 75 die Nase voll haben
to be free 38 frei haben
to be full up 75 satt sein
to be good with sb 138 mit jdm gut umgehen können
to be happy 98 sich freuen
to be keen on 37 etw gern tun, scharf auf etw sein
to be late 125 sich verspäten, zu spät kommen
to be no good 60 nichts taugen
to be set in 114 *(Film, Roman:)* spielen in
bean 16 Bohne
beanbag 70 Sitzsack
beauty 23 Schönheit, Kosmetik
to become (became, become) 49 werden
bedside cupboard 70 Nachttisch
beer 31 Bier
before 57 bevor
Belgium 113 Belgien
Best wishes, 25 *(Brief:)* Alles Gute

between 23 zwischen
Beware of the dog! 122 Warnung vor dem Hund!
billion 95 Milliarde
biscuit 72 *(BE:)* Keks
blanket 78 Decke
board 144 Tafel
boarding card 87 Bordkarte
boarding pass 88 Bordkarte
boat 55 Schiff, Boot
to book 16 reservieren, buchen
boomtown 133 *Stadt in rapidem Aufschwung*
to borrow 79 leihen, ausleihen, borgen
boss 134 Chef
both 141 beide/s
bottom 25 Ende, *(Seite:)* Fuß
brain 115 Gehirn
to brainstorm 104 (Ideen) sammeln
break 20 Pause
to break (broke, broken) 52 zerbrechen, kaputtmachen
bricklayer 141 Maurer/in
bridge 98 Brücke
brilliant 60 genial, glänzend
brochure 10 Prospekt, Broschüre
buddy 65 Kumpel
to build (built, built) 54 bauen
builder 58 Bauunternehmer/in
building firm 58 Bauunternehmen
burger 39 Hamburger
bus driver 16 Busfahrer/in
business administration 23 Betriebswirtschaftslehre
business course 19 Betriebswirtschaftslehrgang
business trip 87 Geschäftsreise
businessman 46 Geschäftsmann
busy 30 (viel)beschäftigt
bye 10 tschüs

C
cab 72 *(AE:)* Taxi
cafeteria 20 Cafeteria, Kantine
California 18 Kalifornien
to call 16 anrufen
to call 34 rufen, nennen
camping 36 Camping
can 46 Dose
candle 70 Kerze
canoeing 10 Kanufahren
canvas 44 Segeltuch
cap 125 Mütze
capital 77 Hauptstadt
capital letter 25 Großbuchstabe

Anhang **183**

Alphabetisches Vocabulary

captain 76 Kapitän
car company 74 Autofirma
car mechanic 72 Automechaniker/in
car park 52 Parkplatz, Parkhaus
care worker 141 Pfleger/in
career 26 Beruf, Laufbahn, Karriere
careful 31 vorsichtig
carefully 100 sorgfältig
carpenter 141 Zimmermann
carpet 71 Teppich
carrot 16 Karotte, Möhre
cartoon 123 Illustration, Karikatur
case 53 Fall
to catch (caught, caught) 54 fangen
category 32 Kategorie, Klasse
cattle 68 Vieh
caution 53 Vorsicht
cell phone 51 *(AE:)* Handy
central 128 zentral
certainly 16 gewiss, sicherlich
to change 91 austauschen
to change 108 ändern, sich verändern
to change one's clothes 142 sich umziehen
character 114 (Film-, Roman-)Figur
to chat 37 (im Internet) chatten
cheap 39 billig
cheaply 131 billig
to check 10 überprüfen, kontrollieren
to check in 87 einchecken
check-in 87 Abfertigung
check-in desk 87 Abfertigungsschalter
cheese 127 Käse
chef 50 Koch/Köchin
chemicals 96 Chemikalien
child care 23 Kinderbetreuung
children's playground 90 Kinderspielplatz
to chill out 37 chillen
Chinese 132 chinesisch, Chinese/Chinesin
chips 38 *(BE:)* Pommes frites
chocolate 127 Schokolade
to choose (chose, chosen) 17 wählen, auswählen, aussuchen
chopsticks 135 (Ess-)Stäbchen
city hall 121 Stadthalle
classroom 57 Klassenzimmer
clean 50 sauber
clear 145 klar, deutlich
clearly 125 deutlich, klar
clerk 87 Angestellte/r
climate 110 Klima
climate change 110 Klimawandel
climbing 36 Klettern
to close 57 schließen, zumachen
cloth 49 Tuch, Stoff
clothes 57 Kleider, Kleidung
clothing 63 Kleidung
coal 111 Kohle

coast 139 Küste
coffee table 70 Couchtisch
colleague 104 Kollege/Kollegin
college 18 Hochschule, Berufsbildende Schule, Universität
college of further education 35 berufsbildende Schule
Cologne 6 Köln
colony 95 Kolonie
to come out 94 herauskommen
comedy 114 Komödie
comfortable 44 bequem
commercial 42 kommerziell
community 19 Gemeinde
to commute 105 pendeln
commuter 55 Pendler/in
company 14 Unternehmen, Firma
comparative 39 Komparativ
to compare 100 vergleichen
competition 94 Wettbewerb
to complete 10 vervollständigen
complicated 133 kompliziert
computer desk 70 Computertisch
concert 121 Konzert
connection 90 Verbindung
construction 23 Baugewerbe
construction site 50 Baustelle
construction worker 8 Bauarbeiter/in
to contact 11 sich in Verbindung setzen mit
contrast 133 Kontrast
conversation 16 Gespräch, Unterhaltung
cooker 71 Herd
cookery 62 Kochen
cookery course 62 Kochkurs
cookie 72 *(AE:)* Keks
cool 19 kühl, cool
cop 57 *(AE:)* Polizist/in, Bulle
corporation 43 Konzern
correctly 145 richtig, korrekt
correspondence 118 Korrespondenz
course 19 Kurs, Lehrgang
cover 94 Titelseite
crab 54 Krebs
to crash into sth 136 in etw hineinfliegen
crazy 34 verrückt
credit 23 *(etw.:)* Leistungspunkte
credit card 16 Kreditkarte
crocodile 30 Krokodil
crop sprayer 55 Schädlingsbekämpfungsflugzeug
to cross 57 überqueren
cup 88 Tasse
currently 117 derzeit, zurzeit, momentan
CV = curriculum vitae 120 Lebenslauf
custom 135 Sitte, Brauch
customer 31 Kunde/Kundin
customs 88 Zoll
customs check 88 Zollkontrolle
customs officer 88 Zollbeamter

to cut (cut, cut) 28 schneiden
to cut grass 28 Rasen mähen
cycle courier 54 Fahrradkurier
cycling 10 Fahrradfahren
Czech Republic 129 Tschechische Republik

D

to damage 111 (einer Sache) schaden
danger 53 Gefahr
dangerous 54 gefährlich
date of birth 120 Geburtsdatum
dead tired 139 todmüde
Dear ..., 25 *(Brief:)* Liebe/r ...,
decorator 9 Maler/in, Tapezierer/in
delicious 75 köstlich
to deliver 30 (aus)liefern, *(Post:)* austragen
delivery 126 Lieferung
to depart 88 abfliegen, abfahren
department 46 Abteilung
departure 88 Abflug, Abfahrt
departures 88 Abflughalle, Terminal
to describe 33 beschreiben
description 103 Beschreibung
desert 110 Wüste
design 23 Gestaltung, Design
to design 46 entwerfen
design 46 Entwurf
dessert 79 Nachtisch
details 23 Einzelheiten, Angaben
diagram 59 Grafik, Schaubild
diary 113 Tagebuch, Terminkalender
to die 54 sterben
diet 27 Ernährung; Diät
dining room 10 Esszimmer, Speisesaal
dining table 71 Esstisch
director 76 Regisseur/in
dirty 56 schmutzig
disabled 141 behindert
to disagree with sb/sth 124 jdm/ einer Sache nicht zustimmen
disaster 111 Katastrophe
dislike 37 Abneigung
dispatch 100 Versand
DIY (Do-it-yourself) 98 Heimwerken
DIY shop 98 Baumarkt
do's and don'ts 50 was man tun und lassen sollte
doctor 9 Arzt, Ärztin
doctor's receptionist 9 Sprechstundenhilfe
double room 16 Doppelzimmer
to download 142 herunterladen
downtown 72 *(AE:)* Innenstadt
drama club 36 Theaterklub
to drive (drove, driven) 52 fahren
driver 52 Fahrer/in
to drop sth 135 etw fallenlassen
drug 51 Droge
drug free 51 drogenfrei
dyslexic 60 legasthenisch

Alphabetisches Vocabulary

E

each 28 jede/r/s
ear protectors 53 Gehörschutz
to earn 38 verdienen
earring 108 Ohrring
earth 110 Erde
east coast 139 Ostküste
eastern 31 östlich, Ost-
education 35 Bildung, Ausbildung
electrical 16 elektrisch
electrical technician 90 Elektriker/in
electrician 140 Elektriker/in
electricity 52 Elektrizität, Strom
electronics 23 Elektronik
elevator 68 *(AE:)* Aufzug, Lift
employee 58 Angestellte/r
to end 81 enden, zu Ende gehen
end 120 Ende, Schluss
energy 108 Energie, Energiequelle
engine 16 Motor
engineer 43 Ingenieur
English-speaking 12 englischsprachig
to enjoy doing sth 143 etw gern tun
to enjoy sth 91 etw genießen
enormous 111 riesig, ungeheuer
enough 23 genug, genügend
entrance 71 Eingang
entry 6 Zugang, Aufnahme
equipment 90 Geräte, Ausrüstung, Ausstattung
European 76 europäisch; Europäer/in
even 23 sogar, noch
everybody 57 jeder, alle
everyday 113 alltäglich, Alltags-
everyone 23 jeder, alle
everything 63 alles
exact 98 genau
exactly 98 genau
exam 81 Prüfung, Examen
excellent 118 hervorragend
exciting 36 aufregend, spannend
exercise bike 70 Heimtrainer
exercise machine 27 Fitnessgerät
experience 117 Erfahrung
to explain 89 erklären, erläutern
expression 32 Ausdruck
extra 111 besonders
extreme sport 36 Extremsport(art)
eye contact 125 Augenkontakt

F

face 12 Gesicht
facilities 10 Einrichtungen
fact 35 Tatsache
factory 52 Fabrik
fair 90 Jahrmarkt
to fall (fell, fallen) 54 fallen
to fall asleep 55 einschlafen
fantastic 78 fantastisch
farm 130 Farm, Bauernhof
farmer 130 Farmer/in, Bauer/Bäuerin

fashion 14 Mode
fashion designer 141 Modedesigner/in
fashion model 125 Fotomodell, Mannequin
fashionable 44 in Mode
festival 6 Festival
to fight 115 kämpfen
file 33 Akte, Ordner
to fill in 91 ausfüllen
finally 55 schließlich, endlich
to find out 95 *(etw)* herausfinden
fire 52 Feuer
fire department 136 Feuerwehr
firefighter 54 Feuerwehrmann
to fish 54 fischen
fisher 54 *(AE:)* Fischer/in
fit 27 fit, gesund
fitness club 15 Fitnessklub
fitness trainer 27 Fitnesstrainer
flat 44 flach
flat 72 *(BE:)* Wohnung
flight 81 Flug
flight attendant 120 Flugbegleiter/in
flightless 79 flugunfähig
flood 111 Flut
floor 52 Boden, Fußboden
fluent 120 fließend
folks 30 Leute
to follow 145 folgen
(the) following 103 der/die/das folgende
forest 76 Wald
fork-lift truck 53 Gabelstapler
fossil fuel 110 fossiler Brennstoff
France 49 Frankreich
French 95 französisch, Französisch
fridge 71 Kühlschrank
fries 16 *(AE:)* Pommes
frightening 76 schrecklich, erschreckend
fruit juice 109 Fruchtsaft
full-time 35 Ganztags-, Vollzeit-
fully-qualified 116 ausgebildet, qualifiziert
funny 114 komisch, lustig
further 117 weitere/r/s
future 106 Zukunft

G

G'day 8 *(AustrE:)* Guten Tag!
gardener 28 Gärtner/in
gas 72 *(AE:)* Benzin
gate 88 Flugsteig, Gate
genius 125 Genie
gentleman 46 Herr
to get on board 88 an Bord gehen
to give up 139 aufgeben
glad 81 froh
global warming 110 Erderwärmung
globalisation 130 Globalisierung
Go for it! 94 Los!
to go off 16 losgehen

to go on holiday (to) 10 Urlaub machen (in)
to go out 56 ausgehen
to go wrong with sth 125 etw verkehrt machen
goggles 53 Schutzbrille
gold miner 49 Goldgräber
golf course 133 Golfplatz
Good luck! 145 Viel Glück!
goods 126 Güter, Waren
grade 145 Note
gram 42 Gramm
graph 41 Diagramm
graphic design 35 Grafikdesign
greeting 134 Begrüßung
group 25 Gruppe
to grow (grew, grown) 98 wachsen
to grow 130 *(Pflanze:)* anbauen
grower 130 Bauer/Bäuerin, Pflanzer/in
to guess 105 meinen
gun 51 Schusswaffe, Pistole
gun free 51 schusswaffenfrei

H

hairdresser 23 Friseur/in
hairdressing salon 31 Friseursalon
half, halves 117 Hälfte, Hälften
hand baggage 88 Handgepäck
to hang out with 20 sich mit jdm rumtreiben
hard drive 128 Festplatte
hard hat 50 Helm
hardly ever 86 kaum jemals
to have to 50 müssen
head 115 Chef/in
head office 98 Zentrale
heading 76 Überschrift
headquarters 133 Zentrale
health 23 Gesundheit
healthy 27 gesund, gesundheitsfördernd
heavy 42 schwer
helpline 130 Hotline
Here you are. 78 (Hier,) bitte sehr.
Here you go. 31 Hier, bitte sehr.
high school 22 Oberschule
highway 57 *(AE:)* Autobahn
history 44 Geschichte
hi-tech 44 technologisch fortgeschritten
to hold (held, held) 31 halten, festhalten
home 98 Zuhause
homeless 138 obdachlos
to hope 19 hoffen
horrible 75 scheußlich, grässlich
horror movie 114 Horrorfilm
hospitality 134 Gastfreundschaft
host 135 Gastgeber/in
hostel 10 Herberge
houseplant 70 Zimmerpflanze

Alphabetisches Vocabulary

How are you? 78 Wie geht es dir/Ihnen?
How do you do? 99 Angenehm!
to hunt 31 jagen
hunter 30 Jäger
to hurt (hurt, hurt) 115 verletzen, sich verletzen

I

I'm afraid … 78 leider
ice 54 Eis
ideal 90 ideal
ill 142 krank
to imagine 71 sich vorstellen
impolite 134 unhöflich
to import 130 importieren
in case of 53 im Fall von
in fact 30 eigentlich, um genau zu sein
in our opinion 141 unserer Meinung nach
to include 103 einbeziehen, einschließen
India 95 Indien
Indian 133 indisch
industrial clerk 140 Industriekaufmann/-frau
industry 111 Industrie, Branche
information 25 Auskunft, Information(en)
information technology 23 Informationstechnologie
inline skating 37 Inlineskaten
inside 27 drinnen
interest 120 Interesse
to interview 30 interviewen
interviewer 113 Interviewer/in
to introduce sb 99 jdn vorstellen
to invent 43 erfinden
to invite 135 einladen
Ireland 128 Irland
irregular 45 unregelmäßig
island 74 Insel
issue 94 *(Zeitschrift:)* Ausgabe
Italy 12 Italien

J

jacket 108 Jacke, Jackett
jandals 77 *(NewZE:)* Flip-Flops
Japan 103 Japan
Japanese 105 japanisch, Japaner/in
job ad(vertisement) 116 Stellenanzeige
job interview 120 Vorstellungsgespräch
to jog 14 joggen
jogging 37 Joggen
joke 38 Witz
jump 81 Sprung
Just a minute! 16 Einen Moment!

K

kayaking 36 Kajakfahren
to keep (kept, kept) face 135 das Gesicht wahren
to keep fit 27 sich fit halten
Keep out! 53 Betreten verboten!
to keep still 31 ruhig halten
key 91 Schlüssel
keyboard 128 Tastatur
to kill 55 töten
kilogram 42 Kilogramm
kind 76 Art, Sorte
kitchen 50 Küche
Kiwi 75 Neuseeländer/in; Kiwi
knowledge 118 Wissen, Kenntnis(se)

L

LA 13 Los Angeles
laboratory 96 Labor
lady 46 Dame
lake 76 See
land 54 Land, Festland
landscape 115 Landschaft
to last 22 dauern
to laugh 38 lachen
to leave (left, left) 22 weggehen, verlassen
to leave 52 hinterlassen, stehen lassen
to leave home 67 von zu Hause ausziehen
leisure 36 Freizeit
library 51 Bibliothek
lifestyle 27 Lebensweise
lift 72 *(BE:)* Aufzug, Lift
likes 37 Vorlieben
litre 31 Liter
to load 100 laden, verladen
local 59 Lokal-, Orts-, örtlich
location 103 Ort, Standort
to look after 28 sich kümmern um, pflegen
to look ahead 66 vorausschauen
to look for 67 suchen
to look forward to doing sth 16 sich auf etw freuen
to look round 99 sich umsehen
lorry 52 Lkw
to lose (lost, lost) 145 verlieren
low 55 niedrig, tief
lunch break 20 Mittagspause

M

machine 54 Gerät, Maschine
mail 30 Post
main 98 Haupt-
to manufacture 128 herstellen
manufacturer 98 Hersteller, Fabrikant
mark 145 Note, Punkt(zahl)
market 130 Markt
marketing company 20 Vertriebsgesellschaft
married 60 verheiratet
to marry 60 heiraten
to match 14 zuordnen
match 76 Spiel, Partie
maximum speed 57 Höchstgeschwindigkeit
maybe 16 vielleicht
meaning 40 Bedeutung
mechanic 16 Mechaniker/in
mechanical 28 mechanisch
media 23 Medien
medium rare 16 *(Steak:)* medium
meeting 87 Sitzung, Besprechung, Treffen
menu 16 Speisekarte
message 108 Nachricht, Mitteilung
microwave 111 Mikrowelle
million 12 Million
mine 131 Bergwerk
mirror 70 Spiegel
missing 14 fehlend
to mix 100 mischen
mobile phone 13 Handy
mom 67 *(AE:)* Mama
monorail 111 Einschienenbahn
most of the time 16 meistens
mother board 128 Hauptplatine
mother tongue 120 Muttersprache
motor bike 13 Motorrad
mountain 10 Berg
mountain boarding 36 Mountainboarding
mouse, mice 128 Maus, Mäuse
to move 58 umziehen
movie theater 11 *(AE:)* Kino
much 10 viel
music centre 71 Stereoanlage
musical 36 Musical
musical instrument 13 Musikinstrument
musician 12 Musiker/in
mustn't 51 nicht dürfen

N

to name 54 nennen, benennen
native speaker 8 Muttersprachler/in
nature 28 Natur
nearly 139 fast, beinah
necessary 119 nötig, notwendig
to need 23 brauchen, benötigen
nervous 69 nervös, aufgeregt
New Zealand 8 Neuseeland
New Zealander 76 Neuseeländer/in
news 62 Nachrichten
newspaper 31 Zeitung
Nice to meet you. 99 Schön, Sie kennenzulernen.
nickname 35 Spitzname
no parking 53 Parken verboten
no smoking area 53 Nichtraucherbereich
nobody 57 niemand

Alphabetisches Vocabulary

non-smoking 90 Nichtraucher-
normal 60 normal, gewöhnlich
normally 28 üblicherweise, normalerweise
northern 31 nördlich, Nord-
to note down 12 notieren, aufschreiben
to note sth 90 beachten
notice 36 Notiz, Bekanntmachung
notice 138 Bekanntmachung, Aushang
noticeboard 36 Schwarzes Brett
nurse 8 Krankenschwester, Krankenpfleger
nursery assistant 29 Hilfslehrerin im Kindergarten

O

ocean 19 Ozean
odd word out 142 das Wort, das nicht dazu passt
of all time 114 aller Zeiten
of course 35 natürlich, selbstverständlich
to offer 22 bieten, anbieten
office worker 55 Büroangestellte/r
official 94 offiziell, Amts-
oil 100 Öl
Olympic Games 44 Olympische Spiele
on board 88 an Bord
on foot 57 zu Fuß
on sale 127 erhältlich
on the one hand 131 einerseits
on the other hand 131 andererseits
on the phone 10 am Telefon
on the road 55 auf der Straße
on the telephone 130 am Telefon
on the whole 131 im Großen und Ganzen
on TV 12 im Fernsehen
once 145 einmal
one day 22 eines Tages
onto 100 auf
opinion 104 Meinung
opposite 40 entgegengesetzt, gegenteilig
orange juice 78 Orangensaft
to order 16 bestellen
order 30 Reihenfolge
to organise 62 organisieren
original 46 ursprünglich, original
others 110 andere
out of 36 außerhalb
outside 27 draußen
over 23 über
overseas 133 (in/nach) Übersee
own 58 eigen
owner 38 Besitzer/in, Eigentümer/in

P

package 30 Paket
to paint 37 malen
paint 96 Farbe
painter 9 Maler/in, Anstreicher/in
pair 44 Paar
pancake 78 Pfannkuchen
to panic 94 in Panik geraten
paragraph 76 Absatz
pardon 78 Entschuldigung, Verzeihung
to park 52 parken
part-time 35 Halbtags-, Teilzeit-
passenger 54 Passagier
passenger plane 54 Passagierflugzeug
passive 132 (Grammatik:) Passiv
passport 88 Pass, Reisepass
passport check 88 Passkontrolle
passport officer 88 Passbeamte/r
past 14 (Uhrzeit:) nach
past perfect 142 (Grammatik:) Plusquamperfekt
patio 59 Terrasse
pea 16 Erbse
pencil 145 Bleistift
penfriend 81 Brieffreund/in
pepperoni 127 Peperoni
per 54 pro
per cent 76 Prozent
perfect 124 perfekt
personal 120 persönlich
personal trainer 27 persönlicher Fitnesstrainer
personnel 120 Personal
petrol 72 (BE:) Benzin
pharmacist 46 (AE:) Apotheker
pharmacy 46 (AE:) Apotheke
to phone 40 anrufen, telefonieren
phone call 43 Anruf, Telefongespräch
phrase 19 Wendung, Ausdruck
piece 63 Stück
pilot 12 Pilot/in
to plan 125 sich vornehmen
planet 106 Planet
plant 28 Pflanze
plate 134 Teller
PLC 96 Aktiengesellschaft
plenty of 35 reichlich, jede Menge
plumber 58 Klempner/in
to point to 14 auf etw zeigen
Poland 58 Polen
police officer 54 Polizeibeamte/r
polite 78 höflich
poor 131 arm
popular 41 beliebt, populär
posh 12 piekfein, todschick
possible 123 möglich
postcard 93 Postkarte
poster 12 Plakat
postman 30 Postbote/-botin
powder 100 Pulver
practice 24 Praxis, Übung
present 135 Geschenk
present continuous 32 Verlaufsform des Präsens
present perfect 61 Perfekt
presentation 134 Präsentation
presenter 141 Moderator/in
primary school 120 Grundschule
to print 123 drucken, ausdrucken
private 12 privat
probably 125 wahrscheinlich
process 98 Prozess, Vorgang, Verfahren
to process 128 verarbeiten
to produce 42 produzieren, herstellen
product 42 Produkt
production 100 Produktion
profile 27 Profil, Beschreibung, Porträt
program 120 Programm
property 53 Eigentum
pub 60 Kneipe
public relations 46 PR, Öffentlichkeitsarbeit
punctual 102 pünktlich
punctually 97 pünktlich
pupil 60 Schüler/in

Q

qualification 117 Ausbildung, Qualifikation
quality 100 Qualität
quality control 100 Qualitätssicherung
a quarter to 14 (Uhrzeit:) Viertel vor
questionnaire 13 Fragebogen
queue 135 (Menschen-)Schlange
quiet 90 ruhig
quietly 44 leise
quite 70 ziemlich, recht

R

radio programme 113 Radiosendung
railway 139 Eisenbahn
railway tracks 139 Bahngleise
raw materials 100 Rohstoffe
ready 16 bereit, fertig
real 30 wirklich, ziemlich; sehr
reason 131 Grund, Begründung
reception 53 Rezeption
receptionist 9 Empfangsdame, -mitarbeiter
region 95 Region, Gebiet
registration form 91 Anmeldeformular
regular 36 regelmäßig
to relax 56 sich ausruhen, sich entspannen
to reload 115 neu laden
to repair 28 reparieren
report 103 Bericht
to report to 53 sich melden bei
research and development 100 Forschungs- und Entwicklungsabteilung

Alphabetisches Vocabulary

to reserve 16 reservieren
respect 135 Respekt, Achtung
result 41 Ergebnis
retail 118 Einzelhandel
retail services 23 Einzelhandel
retailer 118 Einzelhändler
review 114 Kritik, Rezension
revision 25 Wiederholen (von Lehrstoffen)
revolution 115 Revolution; Umdrehung
right now 26 im Augenblick, gerade
to ring sb (rang, rung) 59 jdn anrufen
rivet 49 Niete
robot 98 Roboter
rock 36 Fels
role-play 93 Rollenspiel
to role-play 93 in einem Rollenspiel darstellen
roller coaster 90 Achterbahn
romantic movie 114 Liebesfilm
roughly 111 ungefähr
rubber 44 Gummi
rude 134 unhöflich, unverschämt
rug 70 Teppich, Vorleger
rule 51 Vorschrift, Regel
Russia 98 Russland

S

safe 54 sicher
salary 118 Lohn, Gehalt
sales 120 Verkauf, Vertrieb
sales assistant 118 Verkäufer/in
salon 29 (Friseur-, Kosmetik-)Salon
satellite 110 Satellit
satisfaction 136 Zufriedenheit
sausage 127 Wurst
to save 111 sparen
say 135 zum Beispiel
to say hello to sb 14 jdn begrüßen
to say so 125 es sagen
scientist 115 Wissenschaftler/in
sci-fi 106 Sciencefiction
scooter 13 Motorroller
screen 65 Bildschirm
screen name 65 Benutzername
to search 26 suchen, durchsuchen
seat 88 Sitz
secondary school 120 weiterführende Schule
secret 115 Geheimnis
security 53 Sicherheit
security check 88 Sicherheitskontrolle
See you later. 31 Bis dann!
to seek 117 suchen
self-aware 106 sich seiner selbst bewusst
series 141 Serie
to serve 31 *(Kunden)* bedienen; *(Speisen)* servieren
to service 28 warten

session 36 Stunde, Sitzung
to shake hands (shook, shaken) 125 (sich) die Hand geben, die Hände schütteln
shirt 108 Hemd
shoe shop 16 Schuhgeschäft
shop assistant 16 Verkäufer/in
should 16 sollte/n
show 60 Show, (Unterhaltungs-)Sendung
shower 71 Dusche
showroom 109 Ausstellungsraum
sign 51 Schild
simple 43 einfach
simple past 45 einfache Vergangenheit
simple present 24 einfaches Präsens
since 59 seit
singer 12 Sänger/in
singing group 121 Gesangsensemble
single room 16 Einzelzimmer
sink 71 Spüle
sir 16 (mein) Herr
to sit down 16 sich (hin)setzen
situation 93 Situation, Lage
size 16 Größe
skateboarding 37 Skateboardfahren
skiing 76 Skifahren
skill 118 Fähigkeit
skyscraper 54 Wolkenkratzer, Hochhaus
slowly 97 langsam
smart 125 schick
to smile 125 lächeln
to smoke 52 rauchen
smoker 56 Raucher/in
smoking 52 Rauchen
to sneak 44 schleichen
sneakers 44 Turnschuhe
social studies 143 Sozialkunde
social work 23 Sozialarbeit
social worker 143 Sozialarbeiter/in
solar power 110 solar, Sonnen-
sole 44 Sohle
someone 64 jemand
something 52 etwas
sort 95 Sorte, Art
to sound 145 klingen
sound track 114 Tonspur, Soundtrack
soup 79 Suppe
south-east 60 Südosten
southern 31 südlich, Süd-
speaking 10 am Apparat
special 144 *(Magazin:)* Sonderausgabe
special effects 114 Spezialeffekte
speed 57 Geschwindigkeit
to spend (spent, spent) 96 *(Zeit:)* verbringen
spikes 44 Spikes
sports centre 27 Sportzentrum
sporty 37 sportlich
spot 125 Punkt, Fleck

stadium 27 Stadion
star 12 Star
to start 16 starten
state 29 staatlich, Staats-
state 46 Staat, Bundesstaat
statistics 140 Statistik
to stay 59 bleiben
stay 91 Aufenthalt
steak 16 Steak
steel 54 Stahl
steel worker 54 Stahlarbeiter
step 117 Schritt
still 66 noch (immer)
to stop 16 anhalten, stehen bleiben; *(Motor:)* ausgehen
store 72 *(AE:)* Laden, Geschäft
to store 100 lagern
storm 54 Sturm
straight away 21 sogleich, unverzüglich
stupid 37 doof, albern
subject 23 Fach; Thema
subject 25 *(Brief:)* Betreff
subject area 23 Fachgebiet
subway 14 *(AE:)* U-Bahn
success 58 Erfolg
successful 58 erfolgreich
such a 136 so ein/e/r/s
suit 56 Anzug
to suit sb 117 für jdn geeignet sein
superlative 39 Superlativ
supper 14 Abendessen
to surf 15 surfen
surprised 141 überrascht, erstaunt
survey 41 Umfrage
to survive 75 überleben
Sweden 113 Schweden
swimming pool 11 Schwimmbad
swimsuit 78 Badeanzug

T

to take it in turns 7 sich abwechseln
to take off 88 *(Flugzeug:)* starten, abheben
to take over 106 übernehmen
task 144 Aufgabe
to taste 75 schmecken
tattoo 12 Tätowierung
team sport 36 Mannschaftssport(art)
technician 8 Techniker/in
technology 106 Technologie
telecommunications industry 118 Telekommunikationsbranche
to telephone 118 telefonieren
telephone 130 Telefon
tent 49 Zelt
terrible 13 furchtbar, fürchterlich
to test 16 testen, ausprobieren
text message 43 SMS
textiles 108 Textilien
than 39 *(nach Komparativ:)* als
to thank sb 125 jdm danken
thanks a lot 16 vielen Dank

Alphabetisches Vocabulary

thanks very much 10 vielen Dank
that's why 76 deshalb, darum
the Netherlands 60 die Niederlande
the States 57 die Staaten
theatre 36 Theater
theme park 90 Vergnügungs-, Themenpark
themselves 76 selbst
then 42 einst
this way 99 hier entlang
thousand 55 tausend, Tausend
through 88 durch (… hindurch)
ticket 16 Fahrschein
tie 56 Krawatte
timber 54 Holz, Bauholz
timber cutter 54 Holzfäller
tip 15 Tipp, Hinweis
title 94 Titel
to 14 *(Uhrzeit:)* vor
together 35 zusammen, gemeinsam
togs 78 *(NewZE:)* Badeanzug
toilet 71 Toilette
toll free 23 *(AE:)* gebührenfrei
toothpaste 133 Zahncreme
top 44 Oberteil
top (of the page) 60 Kopf (der Seite)
top man 30 Spitzenmann
topic 113 Thema
total 91 Gesamtanzahl
tour 100 Rundgang, Tour
tourism 120 Turismus
tower 70 Turm
toy 141 Spielzeug
track worker 139 Gleisarbeiter
tractor 98 Traktor
tradition 135 Tradition
traditional 134 traditionell
traffic 55 Verkehr
traffic lights 57 Ampel
to train 22 eine Ausbildung machen
to train sb 60 jdn ausbilden
traineeship 120 Ausbildung(splatz)
trainers 16 Turnschuhe
training 121 Ausbildung
training centre 121 Ausbildungszentrum
training session 36 Übungsstunde
tram 86 Straßenbahn, Tram
to transport 52 transportieren, befördern
to travel 98 fahren
travel agent 120 Reisekaufmann/-frau; Reisebüro
trick 15 Trick, Kniff
trilogy 114 Trilogie
trolley 109 Einkaufswagen
trouble 138 Schwierigkeiten, Probleme
truck 30 *(AE:)* Lkw
truth 125 Wahrheit
to try 16 *(Kleidung:)* anprobieren
Turkey 121 Türkei
Turkish 120 türkisch, Türkisch
twice 88 zweimal
twins 9 Zwillinge
typical 25 typisch, normal

U

unattended 53 unbeaufsichtigt
underground 72 U-Bahn
unemployed 60 arbeitslos
unit 32 Lektion
university 142 Universität
unsuccessful 60 erfolglos
until 38 bis
up there 100 da oben
upright 125 aufrecht, gerade
USA 6 Vereinigte Staaten von Amerika
useful 71 nützlich

V

vacation 67 *(AE:)* Ferien
vegetables 16 Gemüse
vehicle 28 Fahrzeug
videophone 115 Bildtelefon
village 44 Dorf
virtual reality 108 virtuelle Realität
visit 96 Besuch
visitor 46 Besucher/in
visual aids 134 visuelle Hilfen
vocational college 15 Berufsbildende Schule
volt 53 Volt
to vote for sth 94 für etw stimmen

W

wages 69 Lohn
waiter 16 Kellner
walking 10 Wandern, Spazierengehen
war 76 Krieg
warden 10 Herbergsvater/-mutter
wardrobe 70 Garderobe
warehouse 100 Lager
warm 108 warm
to warm 111 erwärmen, sich erwärmen
washbasin 71 Waschbecken
washing machine 10 Waschmaschine
Watch out! 31 Achtung! Vorsicht!
to watch TV 17 fernsehen
web page 43 Webseite
west coast 139 Westküste
western 31 westlich, West-
wet 53 nass, feucht
What about you? 6 Und du?
What time is it? 14 Wie spät ist es?
whether 23 ob
Wi-Fi 90 drahtlos, wireless
work experience 120 Berufserfahrung
to work out 15 trainieren
workaholic 105 Arbeitssüchtige/r
worker 8 Arbeiter/in
workshop 28 Werkstatt
worst 39 der/die/das schlechteste

Y

yeah 16 ja
… years from now 108 in … Jahren
yoghurt 109 Joghurt
You're welcome. 10 Bitte. Gern geschehen.
Yours, … 25 *(Brief:)* Dein/e …, Ihr …
yourself 65 dir/dich/euch (selbst)
youth 16 Jugend
youth hostel 16 Jugendherberge
youth worker 138 Sozialarbeiter für Jugendliche

Z

zone 51 Zone, Bereich

Factfile: The English-speaking world

	United Kingdom (UK)	The United States of America (USA)
Size (sq. km.)	242,514	9.8 million
Highest mountain	Ben Nevis (Scotland) 1,343m	Mount McKinley (Alaska) 6,194m
Capital/largest city	London/London	Washington DC/New York
Population	60 million (English 84%, Scottish 8%, Welsh 5%, Northern Irish 3%)	300 million (white 67%, black 13%, Hispanic 14%, Asian 4%, Native American 1%)
Top people and parliament	Queen, Prime Minister, *House of Commons, House of Lords*	President, *House of Representatives, Senate*
Important exports	banking, insurance, manufactured goods, chemicals, food	computers, electrical goods, vehicles, food, military equipment, planes
Average income (year)	€26,000	€30,000
Money	pound sterling (£)	US dollar ($)
Popular sports	football, cricket, rugby	American football, baseball
Internet domain	.uk	.us
International dialling code	+44	+1
Famous people	William Shakespeare, the Queen, David Beckham, Robbie Williams, J.K. Rowling (author of *Harry Potter*)	George Washington (first president), Henry Ford (first mass-produced cars), Neil Armstrong (first man on the moon), lots of film stars!

▶ population *Bevölkerung*   ▶ Governor General *Vertreter der britischen Königin*   ▶ insurance *Versicherung*